T0266864

AS IF HUMAN

AS IF HUMAN

Ethics and Artificial Intelligence

Nigel Shadbolt and
Roger Hampson

Yale

UNIVERSITY PRESS

NEW HAVEN & LONDON

Yale University Press books may be purchased in quantity
for educational, business, or promotional use. For information, please e-mail
sales.press@yale.edu (U.S. office) or sales@yaleup.co.uk (U.K. office).

Set in Yale and Alternate Gothic No2 types by IDS Infotech Ltd.
Printed in the United States of America.

Library of Congress Control Number: 2023948595
ISBN 978-0-300-26829-4 (hardcover : alk. paper)

A catalogue record for this book is available from the British Library.

This paper meets the requirements of ANSI/NISO Z39.48-1992
(Permanence of Paper).

10 9 8 7 6 5 4 3 2 1

CONTENTS

CONTENTS

PREFACE

We called this book *As If Human* because we think the world needs urgently to get a grip on the ethics of artificial intelligence, and we believe the best way to do that is to illustrate how the morality of machines is deeply embedded in the morality of everything else we do. It is not called *As If Human* because artificial intelligences *are* human, though they may increasingly be programmed and respond so as to give that impression, to converse with us in natural language, sometimes with humanoid interfaces. We do not in the least claim that machines yet share, or will imminently share, any of our essential characteristics of sentience, physical feeling, emotional responsiveness, or versatile general intelligence.

The aim is to give that crucial citizen, the intelligent general reader, the ethical principles and landscape with which to judge for themselves the morality of the present furor over all matters artificial intelligence. So they can judge knowledgeably, and hopefully influence, the actions of governments and corporations.

One of the greatest moral philosophers of our time said recently that she was wary of making any contribution to the ethics of artificial intelligence, because of her lack of technical competence in the field. Certainly, artificial intelligence itself involves complex mathematics and engineering. Teasing out the implications of that can lead to abstruse professional debate. One of us – Nigel Shadbolt – is an AI expert who has conducted research within the discipline for forty years. Difficult topics do sometimes demand to be thought about, by people steeped in the field.

And yet . . . the other of us, Roger Hampson, has on his wall at home a Campaign for Nuclear Disarmament poster from forty years ago, promoting a rally. A graphic on a black background of the huge yellow crane at the Vickers submarine yard on the Cumbria coast exhorts, "Stop Trident. Begin at Barrow. Saturday 27 October." Barrow was his father's hometown. His uncle had from an astonishingly young age headed the design department at Vickers, which constructed Trident. The uncle profoundly believed that deterrence worked. The nephew was horrified. Surely nobody thinks it is out of order to have a moral view on mutually assured destruction, or the Hiroshima bombing, or North Korea's nuclear program, or nuclear options in Ukraine . . . unless one is technically competent to build the stuff? The difference of view is ethical, and a matter of worldly argument. Tangled up, if you will, in the wisdom of experience and the naïveté of youth. Not in reactor physics. Definitely not in blueprints for sheet metal welding.

In this book we aim for a synthesis, recognizing that experts need to distill the important issues into a careful balance, and being particularly explicit about the nontechnical assumptions they bring to the technical arena, so the rest of us know where we are, and what choices we need to make.

Artificial intelligence is an immensely complex phenomenon. Or indeed, it spans many immensely complex phenomena cutting across all the leading edges of the wide range and impact of modern technology. But it can also be illuminated by the traditional strands and tools of academic philosophy. Not to mention sociology, political science, and literary studies. People not deeply schooled in all or any of those disciplines will still seek to understand, and take a view on, what artificial intelligence means to us.

The famous Turing test is already, in practice, obsolete. Interfaces like GPT4 and its successors can be used to effectively disguise whether any interlocutor, however sophisticated, is holding an online discussion with an artificial intelligence or a human. Our thesis is not that the hidden human and the AI are the same thing, equivalent in their essence, or ethically. If an AI spontaneously combusts, that's an expensive nuisance. If a human spontaneously combusts, that's a tragedy. Our thesis is that the human and the machine should be held to the same ethical standards. Virtues and vices can and will be embodied in machines. The difference, if any, is that we can and should be stricter in our enforcement with machines than with humans.

After a bequest by Stephen Schwarzman, Nigel Shadbolt has been a leader in the establishment of the Oxford Institute for Ethics in AI. Neither the authors of this book, nor our agent, nor the publishers, nor our colleagues who helped so much in writing it, have at any stage imagined that once it appeared, all further consideration of the ethics of artificial intelligence could be abandoned, the staff of the new institute redeployed elsewhere, the building given over to a different purpose. What it is to be ethical varies from society to society, and within each society; and from decade to decade, if not faster. There is not now, and never will be, one single set of answers to the ethics of artificial intelligence. Artificial intelligence itself will be one of the factors, in different ways in different places, that strongly influences morality. We aim to give the concerned citizen a balanced, comprehensible, technically grounded view of the moral implications of the world technologists and big corporations are building apace.

AS IF HUMAN

INTRODUCTION

The abstract painter Ai-Da caused panic among Egyptian security forces in 2021. She was on her way to a show of her work at the Great Pyramid of Giza, the first time in thousands of years that contemporary art had been allowed next to the pyramid. But the border guards at Cairo airport feared that she was a spy, and arrested her. They had good grounds for suspicion. After all, she had cameras for eyes and a prodigious memory, as modern humanoid robots do. Eventually the authorities accepted her entourage's assurances that, like many artists, she had no interest in politics or defense. They rather reluctantly released her, under caution.[1]

If Ai-Da was a spy, who was the spymaster? That seems obvious enough perhaps, once we strip away the conjuring trick: Ai-Da has an owner. Indeed, such artificial, partly independent, agents have been disturbingly compared to slaves. An interesting and useful insight, ultimately insufficient and implausible, as we will show.

The extraordinary artificial intelligences we have devised bring with them intense ethical dilemmas. A twist on the issue of responsibility and accountability raised by Ai-Da came up at a 2022 chess competition in Moscow. A seven-year-old prodigy was doing well in a match against a robot player. Like the Mechanical Turk of the late eighteenth century, but a genuine automaton not a fake, the machine was a brilliant move-making calculator, with motorized arms that could maneuver pieces on the board. The boy, already ranked among Russia's top thirty players, responded quickly to an interesting move. Too quickly for the robot's programming. It grabbed and crushed the boy's hand, breaking his finger.[2]

The boy's parents demanded prosecution, and threatened to sue. But who should be arraigned or pay damages? The organizers of the competition? The robot's builders? The company that designed its software? Or should the robot itself, like cars in some countries, have to carry insurance to pay for any trouble it makes?

Chess robot rampages are rare. Self-driving cars, however, are spreading fast. Their first victim on record, in 2018, was Elaine Herzberg, age forty-nine. She was hit and killed by a self-driving Uber as she wheeled a bicycle across the road in Tempe, Arizona. Investigators found that the car's safety driver, Rafaela Vasquez, had been streaming an episode of *The Voice* at the time. She was charged with negligent homicide. Despite the presence of a human safety driver, the self-driving Volvo had hit Mrs. Herzberg at thirty-nine miles an hour. Uber did not face criminal charges, given a 2017 court decision ruling that there was no basis for criminal liability against corporations in such cases, though the company did halt its testing of the technology in Arizona. The driver ended up pleading guilty to endangerment.[3]

These examples might seem merely amuse-bouches for a dry book. Okay, so artificial intelligences can pose as conceptual artists who, to be fair to the Egyptian police, might have a side hustle in espionage. And artificial intelligences and the systems they control can go wrong in a chess game. Or run us over. A bit of due care and attention should mitigate those risks. Is there anything important to see here? What else can they do to us?

Well, here are some claimed artificial intelligence dangers, all with ethical dilemmas at their core. These long-term staples of science fiction now terrify the popular press, but serious technologists, economists, political scientists, psychologists, and yes, philosophers also have strong, often conflicting, views about them:

- Robots will knock us off our pedestals. They are already very smart in a very limited way. Jobs are being handed to artificial intelligences. They don't demand pay raises. Many of them work from home (a server cloud), so they don't need expensive office space. Soon they will get smarter in a more general, adaptable, human way, taking over more and more human functions — leaving us mortals on the employment scrapheap, our professional judgments and preferences superseded.

- Machines are evolving human characteristics. A Google employee recently claimed that a chatbot he was operating had become sentient, and was afraid of being switched off. *New Scientist* reports that a robot has been equipped with sensors that feed back to its core the changing location of its extensible arms. The engineers involved cheerfully equate that with human proprioception and kinesthesia, as if the mechanism has become fully self-aware. Has it? And even if it has, does that matter in the same way as human self-awareness? Perhaps we should feel machines' pain, include their safety, their very existential condition, in our public health strategies?

- Personal privacy is disappearing, and fast. Private space is under multiple threats. Big corporations know every detail of our spending, where we are, and what we look at on the web. Street cameras watch us all day. We, our close family and friends, and even mere acquaintances, casually post details of our everyday lives on the immortal internet. Posterity will know our failings, tiny warts and all, including intimate photos, sometimes published as acts of malice or revenge.

- Privacy in the political realm is a thing of the past. Governments, with their various bureaucratic departments, intelligence agencies, and police forces, track everybody for mundane social reasons, and can rapidly focus intense artificial intelligence scrutiny on anyone who interests them. China is already a so-called tech-totalitarian state. At least back in the former East Germany the ubiquitous Stasi agents were humanly fallible. President Xi is avoiding that mistake. Don't imagine that the West is more than a year or two behind China. Be very careful about what you say, what you think. The declared enemies are "terrorists" and other traitors, who are being pursued by the good guys. Perhaps this is merely a choice between Benedict Arnold or Jason Bourne? Hmm. Which of those is Julian Assange?

- Children these days are iPad zombies. Never off their screens, which rot their brains. Teenagers and undergraduates live in a febrile online world, victims of social bullying invisible to their parents and teachers, persuaded into nonsensical views and fashions by peer pressure from thousands of other inexperienced peers. Education, social values, and even ideas about personal attributes like gender are being undermined by irresponsible apps run amorally by grasping corporations, or websites set up by perverts.

- Weapons guided by artificial intelligence are uniquely dangerous. There can be immense physical and psychological distance between a killer drone and the person who flies it and pulls its triggers, safe in an unidentifiable hardened location in a far-off country. Putin's drones and electronic viruses; Xi's; Kim's; NATO's too — all can murder the innocent, steal people's identities and bank accounts through their cell

———

4

phones, or shut down the power grid. Traditional democratic accountability has no traction, even on the good guys.

- Big tech corporations not only gather stupendous amounts of data about us, not only dominate much of the real economy and the labor market, not only repeatedly change the very nature of social life, but they also persistently and explicitly do these things with an utter lack of common sense or responsibility, often while piously vowing to do better. In the United States, pornography sites, where stolen intimate pictures can be paraded for all to see, often for revenge or blackmail, rely on the dubious argument, sanctioned by Congress, that the site is not a publisher. As Sheelah Kolhatkar wrote in the *New Yorker* in 2022: "The Internet made it possible for tube sites to make money off videos created by others while bearing almost no responsibility for what was in them. Today, MindGeek relies on the same legal statute that Mark Zuckerberg cites when defending Facebook from charges that it allows the proliferation of disinformation: Section 230 of the Communications Decency Act of 1996, which states that an 'interactive computer service' cannot be treated as a publisher of information provided by a third party. The provision was conceived in order to allow the internet to grow without being buried in lawsuits. But it also means that, when tube sites are confronted with complaints about videos depicting rape, sexual images of children, revenge porn, and other content uploaded without consent, they can claim that they are not liable."[4]

- Predictive machines get scarier every day. Amazon's guesses at what people might want to buy, based on what people like them have already bought, are broadly helpful. Police departments in major cities around the world, too, are beginning to be very successful at calculating where everyday crimes, as well as acts of terror, may happen next, by combining patterns of offending with the locations of known

—

offenders and other data like traffic, the weather, and poverty statistics. Sounds like a good thing really. Precautionary machines are helpful on a daily basis. Are you sure you wish to permanently delete this file? Your seatbelt is unfastened.[5] But next come predictions about which specific individuals are most likely to commit a crime tomorrow, and who can be arrested today. Or, a more positive version perhaps, personal DNA analysis combined with artificial intelligence will soon not merely helpfully diagnose what you are now suffering from, or generally likely to suffer from in the future, but roughly when that will happen. So approximately when you will die. This type of precautionary AI will spread from policing and health management to many other aspects of life, making often decisive interventions in one's education prospects, job applications, and romantic life. Who or what is in control here?

Who should be in control, indeed, over any of these wicked artificial intelligence issues? According to what ethical principles? How do we judge the right policies for today's societies, and for posterity?

■

We should remember the seminal warnings of the historian David Edgerton about so-called new technologies. For centuries now, intellectuals have bruited this or that invention as world-changing. It is such fun, so modern and forward thinking, to declare that we now live in the utterly transformed age of, say, space travel, or supersonic flight, that we disregard the plain facts. Counting the world's total population from 1969 onward, only one person in a billion has rocketed to the moon. Only a tiny proportion of humans ever flew at supersonic speeds on the Concorde jet (that archetype of a defunct future) or super-fast military aircraft. But hundreds of millions of people ride in rickshaws every day, and at least a billion on bicycles. Old technology beats new technology. Hitler billed himself as heading a German Reich at the leading edge of modernity. The V2 rocket, the Volkswagen people's car, the uber-mechanized storming of the Soviet Union to destroy the Bolsheviks! Except that the V1 and V2 rockets killed far more people in the manufacturing plants than they killed in Allied cities, and were, fortunately, hopelessly more expensive and inefficient than conventional aircraft would have been. The Volkswagen factories never delivered a single car to the prewar Germans who subscribed for them. The present-day auto behemoth instead arose from the efforts of a British soldier who had served in the occupation forces after Hitler's death. Wartime Germany was extremely short of fuel, restricted to ersatz and scarce liquid hydrogenated coal. The German military relied for much of its basic transport of materiel on a more established technology, the horse. More than 600,000 horses were gathered for the invasion of the Soviet Union. About a third died, mostly because, unlike Russian horses, they were not bred to withstand a harsh winter.[6]

"Technology," Edgerton says, might be better abandoned as a term, or at least replaced by the concept of technology-in-use, "things" even, since a large proportion of everything around us — certainly for the half of the world that lives in cities — has been fabricated, and often endlessly redesigned, by humans. Edgerton's point is not that nothing is ever new. Just that newness is rarer than we think it is; the noisy inventions frequently have less practical effect than the noise they create; quiet invention is widespread, particularly outside the West; truly original things often require multiple other inventions and social adaptations before they make much of a difference; new objects confer no more, and often fewer, benefits on the community that invents them than on communities that didn't invent them; and social adaptations can often quietly negate the apparent transformative effect of a new technology. We should ponder all of this whenever we read that artificial intelligence is an existential threat to humanity.[7]

In our book *The Digital Ape,* written before the COVID-19 pandemic, we gave a brief synopsis of how various technologies, specifically a now eighty-year-old technology, rank in the pantheon of possible catastrophes:

> Only nuclear weapons stand a serious chance of obliterating our species entirely this century. A collision with a large asteroid would also pose a grave danger to human life, but is highly unlikely. Diseases are ever present. A major plague may kill a lot of people. Perhaps a virus that leaps to us from another species, or a consequence of the diminishing effectiveness of over-used antibiotics. Climate change probably cannot now be prevented, or even significantly mitigated. Millions will have to change where they live and what crops sustain them. The world's population approaches 8 billion, presenting acute pressure on resources, not least water. If the intelligent machines we have surrounded ourselves with are a threat, as Stephen Hawking thought, then is the vigilance he asked for different in kind from the scanning we do, and the safety measures we put in place, for all the other perils of the twenty-first century?[8]

In 2023, the world woke up to artificial intelligence. Apparently ChatGPT, Bard, Claude, Bing AI, and their countless siblings were about to change every aspect of commercial, social, and private life. Perhaps, the story went, they were becoming so smart they could murder us all in our beds.

This must be the thousandth time that a new technology, one with a long, rich history like AI, has suddenly seemed to threaten everything dear to us. As usual, the trope is both true and laughably untrue. Like the rest of the artificial intelligences that have surrounded us for decades, chatbots like ChatGPT and the large language models (LLMs) that underpin them will have a transformative effect in some areas, a marginal effect in others, and none in some of the most important realms of human existence. Crucially, despite widespread existential anxiety, we will still be firmly in charge. We will have to take steps to ensure that this is so, and to properly manage the transformative effects on our economy and society.

■

How do we want machines, and the software that animates them, to behave in the new age of super-smart technology? The answer is straightforward: We should want them to behave *like the best of us*. We should judge them morally as if they were humans. We should not allow them to fall short in ways that we would not tolerate in people. We should treat them as lumps of metal and silicon, yes, yet also as objects for which we have moral standards. Equally, we should not expect them to be ethically superior to us (although in many tasks their performance will exceed our own), nor judge them harshly when they fail to be so.

The punchlines of this book, then, are:

- Humans judge machines in many ways, some of which can be measured with objectivity, but only up to a point. All efficiency is ultimately socially defined: who says this smelly noisy lump of iron is a steam engine and meant to get us to Bristol or Boston as quickly, comfortably, and safely as possible? The actual speed, the comfort, the deaths per mile, can be measured. But the purpose has to be chosen by humans. By the same token, assessments of important difficulties around the ethics of intelligent machines can begin with objectivity and numbers, but they can't end there. There is no standard other than human values by which humans can judge the ethics of anything at all. The best way to make this happen with intelligent machines is to treat them, in this context only, as if they are human.

- The ethical framework that dominates Western societies has claimed to be different things at different times. For at least a hundred years it has been what we call a *mixed philosophy*, drawing simultaneously on many traditions, using and abusing arguments from all of them. The authors, optimistic liberals (among our many other prejudices), do the same. Within that general worldview, we hold that when we treat artificial intelligences ethically as if they are human, the best approach is to be aware of the virtues and failings that machines are able to embody, as well as those they are not able to embody. Specification of those virtues and moral failings, and what actions we will take to monitor and control them, is crucial.

- Artificial intelligences throw up new ethical challenges for humans. That has already changed the ranking of the virtues we hold most dear. Privacy for individuals and transparency for governments and commerce have never been so important, and we strongly value the quality in people that enables them to properly negotiate that, and institutions that adapt most convincingly. *Artificial intelligence is changing the virtues we should treasure most.*

- Equally, machines, when judged in accordance with human values, can be found wanting. They can act unfairly, making morally wrong decisions. (Think of sentencing algorithms that fail to override a human programmer's racism.) They can be wantonly dangerous. (Killer drones with brilliant face-recognition software that pick the wrong target. Or any target, for that matter.) More broadly, huge social machines, which mix powerful large-scale technologies with widespread human participation, have changed daily life for many millions, in a minority of cases to their great detriment. (Wikipedia is a wonder of the world, but X, formerly known as Twitter, and Facebook may perhaps be mixed blessings.[9]) The obverse is importantly true. Machines can embody virtues, or more accurately can be designed to operate as if they embody virtues. And prime among these virtues must be respect for humans.

At this moment in the development of artificial intelligence, we remain at a moral frontier, unsure of humanity's next best steps in the face of great changes to come. This uncertainty will ease as positive, adaptive behaviors and virtues continue to emerge in us. We must urgently start to build those virtues into the machines themselves, to insist that they behave, morally, *as if they were human.*

Chapter 1

ON *AS IF*

Picture an old fever hospital, on the edge of an English west country moor, in 1985. Built in 1913 as a TB sanatorium, with lots of air and sunshine, it is now converted to care for people with mental handicaps, according to the proper 1980s terminology. Most afternoons a couple of dozen young men, ages fifteen to twenty-five, all very challenged, meet to socialize, be a youth club, and charge about in a large secure room.

Bear with us, this scene is relevant to our technology issues, four decades later.

To the new observer (one of your authors in his early career), the crowded space seems good-humored mayhem, confusing, and physically dangerous. Some of the young men wear sports-style protective headgear, in case they bash into each other or the walls. A few staff around the room exude professional sensitivity to the patterns of interaction, and somehow calmly and cheerfully moderate the odd conflict or inappropriate behavior.

The new observer has to stuff his hands in his pockets to avoid throwing an arm over his face every thirty seconds or so as one or another of the helmeted ones powers past. After what seems like an hour, but is probably less than five minutes, he notices that a few of the young men repeatedly approach a white object in the far corner of the room, touch it, then move away.

Gingerly the observer makes his way to that corner. The white object is a tray, about three feet by two feet, and one foot deep, on a carriage at waist height. John is lying in it.[1] His caregiver explains. John is eighteen. He cannot hear, see, or speak. His head is about a quarter the usual size for his age, his body perhaps twenty inches long. He is unable to move around, or eat, or manipulate objects, on his own. His brainpower (shall we say) might be typical of a prenursery-school child, although one with severe sensory deprivation. The fine detail of that is nigh impossible to discover.

John greatly enjoys the afternoon session, the caregiver says. When she pushes him to what she calls the club, he giggles in anticipation. Perhaps he recognizes the different rumbling feeling of the corridor, she guesses, or a familiar smell? She says he loves to meet his friends. The idea of friendship in this context is counterintuitive, to say the least, to the observer. Yet it quickly manifests itself: the next young man barges up, then softly touches the end of the tray. John laughs out loud. It happens again soon after. The purposeful approach and the gentleness of the hand, John's glee, convince the observer that the event is reciprocal. The caregiver slyly suggests the observer might touch the end of the tray. He does. No reaction from John. He doesn't perform for strangers.

There are at least four broad implications, back here in the twenty-first century. First, friendship, collectivity, and fellow-feeling are deeply hard-wired, deeply needed, and deeply satisfactory. Don't believe stories claiming that selfishness is the natural dominant human trait.

Second, as we increasingly have come to understand, the brain is very plastic, and will use whatever capacity it has available to decode whatever messages it receives from the nervous system. If several senses are compromised or missing, more brain space will be devoted to data from other senses. John had ways of knowing.

Third, John's core humanity seems indistinguishable from, intrinsically just as valuable as, his caregiver's, the observer's, or anyone's. Whatever is special or unique about *Homo sapiens,* John surely has it too. There is a more than semantic distinction to be made between "John's life" as his invaluable essence, and "John's life" as a series of biographical experiences, external attributes, and accumulated knowledge, from which another different variety of value, call it present and future social usefulness, can be derived.

Imagine a classic trolley problem, as devised by the philosopher Philippa Foot in 1967. Here you are confronted with a terrible choice: you can save John's life as a heavy trolley car thunders toward him, by throwing a switch and diverting the car down a side track to kill his caregiver instead; or you can do nothing and let John die. Most of us would choose to do nothing and save the caregiver. (The few who wouldn't usually refuse to participate in either outcome.) But that should not be taken to mean that John has less intrinsic worth.[2]

The fourth implication is what we concentrate on here. John's wonderful caregiver consciously worked within an established postwar professional health and social care ideology, most often termed "normalization." She took John — John of all people — to a youth club! And indeed, to any other event and situation that she could. Why? Because although every minute she was with him she devotedly made enormous compensations for his most unordinary physical and mental attributes, she also thought that a youngster his age should be hanging out with friends. She wanted him to have as "ordinary" a life as she could give him.[3] This broad *as if* concept had become a fundamental part of the ethos of professionals and managers.

We wish to take this as one foundation for our governing metaphor. It is already a metaphor of sorts within its original care context, as we explain later. It is 100 percent a metaphor imported into ours. We do not even distantly claim that machines have intrinsic human status. Faced with the desperate options of whether the trolley kills John or the trolley kills his caregiver, absolutely no sane moralist prefers to minimize damage to the trolley.

At no stage in this book do we side with the trolley.

The postwar professional health and social care ideology most often termed normalization arose in part from the work of the sociologist Erving Goffman on asylums and other closed institutions.[4] Goffman was a man of his time, one of a generation of thinkers eager to find redemptive meanings in the worst of what the world had been through, including the horrors of the Holocaust. In the light of his and others' work, care became influenced by questions such as, What would this person's life be like if they did not have a disability, and how do we make their experiences as close to that as possible? Adaptations to, or compensations for, any physical or mental disability were made to help the individual concerned have as normal a life as possible. The assumption — for which there turned out to be real clinical and social evidence — was that this approach would ameliorate the well-known deficits associated with institutionalization. The full range of stimuli experienced by so-called ordinary people should, as much as possible, also be made available to people who needed, at least some of the time, care or protection. In addition, there should be an insistence on, say, the privacy rights of people who might not themselves understand the concept of privacy, not simply because all rights should apply to all people, but specifically because caregivers and others who don't respect privacy quickly fail to furnish their charges with other aspects of normal life, too.

Normalization might be characterized as the application of *as if* to challenged individuals, a deliberate double vision. What is this person like? How do we arrange their social and physical environments so they live, as much as possible, like themselves, but also *as if* they were a different, closely related version of themselves, themselves with more usual abilities, perceptions, or mental or physical health? Able to access the wide range of experiences and environments that most of us in the Western world take for granted?

It also involves a very practical agnosticism. People deprived of the range of ordinary stimuli — jailbirds, inmates, unwilling loners — rapidly decline in ways that would disturb a friend or professional with their best wishes at heart. Which stimuli are the ones in ordinary life sufficient to elicit full normal human reactions? It's difficult to specify. Science moves on, adding previously unnoticed answers to the question. But there is no need to give an intellectual answer, which will almost certainly be wrong. Just provide an ordinary life, with which by definition we are all familiar, and the necessary components of ordinary life, whatever they may be, will tautologically be included in the package.

■

What might it mean to say that artificial intelligences should be judged morally *as if they were humans?* It's important that this metaphor is not misunderstood, when applied either to John or to intelligent machines. John's caregiver did not claim that he had ordinary mental and physical capacities. She knew better than anyone how disabled he was. And we are certain that she saw his intrinsic human value just as sharply. One power of the metaphor lies in the point about practical agnosticism. Just as no confection of an ordinary life could possibly match an actual ordinary life in its ability to give a vulnerable person the components of that ordinary life, so it is hard to imagine what tangled special pleading for a new "machine morality" could transcend the human one we have already, derived from more than three thousand years of earnest analysis of the issue. There is nothing like worldwide consensus on ethics, but every distinct strand begins either with humans, or with gods interested in humans, or with analysis of the logical physical or existential nature of the universe as applicable to humans and human behavior. Dogs don't organize and vote in referendums on dog licenses. We do not in any way mean to compare disabled people to machines, "smart" or not, or to nonhuman animals. But the power of the simple metaphor is the easy importation of myriad sets of other well-known, well-exercised, concepts en masse.

We will discuss some of the more solid modern views on moral frameworks in a moment. But whether one prefers to examine ethical postulates by weighing their consequences to people or other beings, by assessing the motives of the decision-makers involved, or by any other means, acts are always judged in terms of what an actor should do. Only humans are moral actors, and moral actors are only human. All machines are conceived and made by humans.

There is a commonsense view that we don't repudiate, but must modify, and it centers on what it might mean for a machine to "make a mistake." If an undesirable principle of action embodied in a machine, or a consequence of a machine's operation, is not an error of human foresight or execution; if it is not a strategic, a construction, a programming, or a management error by a human . . . then it may be a dire problem, but by definition it is not an ethical error.

———

This is in part because a machine cannot have a motive, in the psychological sense of the word. Ethical questions can surely only exist, then, where there is a possibility of intention, perceptions, or conscious meaning, or any other aspect of individual personhood, going adrift. A machine cannot make a moral mistake.

At one very high level, that ultimately must be true. Intelligent machines are not yet feral animals, on the loose with no owner in sight. (The occasional abandoned house may have a thermostat that still clicks on and off. We will look at the implications of that later.[5]) Moral frameworks appear only to be elements in human cultural superstructures. We don't yet usually think of moral frameworks as being also part of the mechanistic infrastructure. Therefore the only moral judgments that can be made about machines seem to be judgments about the humans involved, or at the very least judgments derived from the frameworks that humans would apply.

A further step is needed, however, to grasp why *as if* is useful. Why not simply say that in any moral argument about artificial intelligence, or smart machines, we should simply examine the people involved and consider the machines to be nothing more than vehicles for the issue? The answer is exactly analogous to that which John's caregiver came to: we can't, because parceling out all the moral aspects of the activity of any particular artificial intelligence to its progenitors and managers before making a moral judgment may often be impossible, and not instantly necessary. Which of the thousands of identifiable aspects of everyday existence, aspects that the human genome has evolved over millions of years to interact with, are the ones that John needs to give him the happiest life? Don't know, doesn't matter, let's just give him a life as close to the normal ordinary everyday as we can. Who is in charge here, who wrote the bit of the software of this intelligent machine that has some undesirable trait or effect? Might not know, might not matter in terms of making an external judgment. A significant cause of that undesirable trait or effect might be an unforeseen problem with decades-old software, long in the public domain, with an unknown author. What matters is that a moral issue has arisen and we need to deal with it. This is not to absolve the humans involved. But we don't have to catch them first to understand whether an artificial intelligence's operating principles, actions, or consequences are morally wrong. A mass-murdering, axe-wielding robot needs to be disarmed even if its evil inventor has jet-packed to her impregnable lair. Or naïvely imagined that she was only designing a better lawn mower.

In fine focus, we need to judge the output of complex algorithms *as if* they embodied moral agency. Such an idea may seem at first sight to be stupid or even obnoxious. Surely machines don't have feelings and rights? After a moment's reflection, the concept becomes natural and correct, even if careful exegesis is needed. *As if* they were humans. *As if* they were moral agents.

Some historical context. There's nothing as old as new-fangled technology. And for all its influence today, artificial intelligence was not always thought of as nationally and internationally important, or even possible. In 1973, in a now notorious review, Sir James Lighthill recommended the closure of virtually all AI research in the United Kingdom, on the grounds that it would never get anywhere and was a waste of money.[6] At much the same time in the United States, funding by the Defense Advanced Research Projects Agency (DARPA) was reduced substantially from its 1960s levels. The AI winter. Since then, AI research has enjoyed periods of boom and bust. At the moment, AI is in the sunny uplands in terms of funding and interest. But AI has been making key contributions to computer science since the earliest days: from programming languages to hardware, from methods and techniques to fielded applications. Ethical questions have been highlighted throughout. In 1948, Norbert Wiener, the father of cybernetics, wrote, "It's long been clear to me that the modern ultrarapid computing machine was in principle an ideal central nervous system apparatus for automatic control. Long before Nagasaki in the public awareness of the atom bomb it occurred to me that we were here in the presence of another social potentiality of unheard-of importance for good and evil."[7]

Indeed, computers have played a key part in warfare right from their start. It was the urgent need of the Allies in World War II to decrypt enemy communications that turned Alan Turing's abstract concept of a computing machine into Bletchley Park and its outstations.[8] And mathematics legend John von Neumann, one of the originators of game theory and computing, helped to calculate the engineering of the atomic bomb.[9] As soon as a scientific breakthrough occurs, humans work out how to kill other humans with it. Advances in chemistry lead to chemical warfare as well as useful plastics; discoveries in biological science enhance germ warfare agents as well as antibiotics; insights in atomic physics generate weapons of mass destruction as well as civilian light and power sockets.

■

Artificial intelligence is a branch of computer science that deals with the creation of systems capable of performing tasks that would ordinarily require human intelligence — systems that can reason, learn, and act autonomously. AI research has been highly successful in developing effective techniques for solving a wide range of problems, from game playing to medical diagnosis. All artificial intelligences, so far, subsist in digital computing machines, or in digital computing parts of other machines, everything from washing machines to streetlights to robots. They may soon be instantiated in other materials, notably derived from biology.

Many different approaches and methods important to computer science today developed in the AI field. Two particularly influential groups of techniques concern *rule-based systems* and *machine learning systems*. Rule-based systems rely on a set of explicit rules that define how the system should behave. An early type of AI, they are still used in many applications such as medicine or finance where they make decisions or advise on a particular course of action. They do this by referring to a set of rules that describe how to make decisions in that domain, often derived from the established knowledge, procedures, and experience of a profession. Eliciting these rules and building such knowledge-based systems takes great human knowledge-engineering effort. But the systems are transparent—one can ask what rules and chains of reasoning gave rise to a particular decision.

Machine learning systems, by contrast, learn patterns from data and these patterns drive their behavior. They are explicitly programmed not to solve a task, but rather to discover patterns in data that may lead to effective decisions. Machine learning systems are used in a wide range of applications, such as spam filtering, web search, and fraud detection. Historically, two limiting factors on machine learning were the lack of suitable training data and the power of the computers needed to implement the machine learning methods themselves. More data and more powerful computers have led to these limitations being overcome. Yet machine learning systems can appear as opaque "black boxes" for which it is difficult to determine why a decision was made.

21

The most recent developments in machine learning have seen the emergence of generative AI. The goal of generative AI is to create new data samples that resemble the data it was trained on. The data created can be music, images, or text. The accomplishments of generative AI chatbots such as ChatGPT are the result of ingesting huge quantities of language data to build models (so-called large language models, or LLMs) that encode the extended statistical relationships in the data well enough to predict the next most likely word in a language task.

■

Emergent breakthrough technologies present societies with many challenges. Advances in science and technology have always offered up ethical dilemmas and choices – about how new things should be deployed, who should have access to their benefits, how they should be made safe, and who should be responsible for their development and deployment. Attempts have always been made to control each new scientific potentiality, via conventions and treaties, codes of conduct, regulations and laws. It is no surprise that we now see this with artificial intelligence. In fact, artificial intelligence does seem to generate a particularly rich array of ethical challenges, perhaps in part due to its ubiquity: artificial intelligence is everywhere in nearly every modern thing. Not least smartphones, the supercomputers in our pockets that do everything from recognize our voices and our faces to answer our questions. AI has even been applied in robotic surgery. Recent developments in machine learning have given rise to generative AI, which is able to spawn very extensive content: like ChatGPT, which can answer a huge range of general questions and many very specific professional ones.

It has become a cliché of the field that it is easy to build a machine that plays chess or does fancy mathematics, but it is not at all easy to build a machine with everyday human mental abilities. Harvard professor Steven Pinker sums this up in *The Language Instinct:* "The main lesson of thirty-five years of AI research is that the hard problems are easy and the easy problems are hard. The mental abilities of a four-year-old that we take for granted— recognizing a face, lifting a pencil, walking across a room, answering a question—in fact solve some of the hardest engineering problems ever conceived. . . . As the new generation of intelligent devices appears, it will be the stock analysts and petrochemical engineers and parole board members who are in danger of being replaced by machines. The gardeners, receptionists, and cooks are secure in their jobs for decades to come."[10]

Classically, AI researchers wanted to build systems that could use computational reasoning to solve abstract problems in mathematics or science, problems that those researchers connected with professionally. They wanted an artificial intelligence to be a kind of smarter smart type in a white coat. The influential Australian Rodney Brooks, robotics professor at MIT and one-time director of its artificial intelligence laboratory, was worried by the limits of this "good old-fashioned AI"—much of it rooted in a rule-based systems approach. Brooks instead proposed that the really clever thing about humans is the way we manage to analyze things and events around us in order to perform a wide range of tricky tasks in diverse, often muddled, environments.

This shift in how researchers thought about AI led to the development of a large range of techniques inspired by what appeared to be the way our general intelligence and perceptive abilities worked. Good old-fashioned AI endeavored to build faster and bigger extensions of a mathematical and logical, über-rational, characterization of thought. The new approach started by looking at how smart animals, including us, appeared to gather and process information, and began to focus on building so-called artificial neural networks.

A *neural network* is a system of artificial or biological neurons that can process data and learn from that data. Artificial neural networks are inspired by the human brain and how it works. They consist of layers of nodes connected by weight and activation functions. Neural networks can be used in tasks such as speech recognition and natural language processing. Neural networks underpin most modern machine learning. The architectures of these artificial intelligences now match, augment, and in many cases outperform, human experts in important fields. They can look at images such as retinal scans and predict potential disease states; apply a combination of machine learning techniques, natural language analysis, and graph-based reasoning (rule-based and representational reasoning across graphs) to discover and characterize new drug types; and, increasingly, guide vehicles in novel environments.

Modern AI has in fact yielded results across a wide range of domains and applications. Machine learning builds products that recognize faces and voices, operate complex machinery and vehicles, classify medical images, and monitor the financial markets. Rule-based and other reasoning AIs help to plan schedules or to guide diagnoses by telling the doctor what other doctors who saw the same symptoms concluded. Machines aid lawyers as they make legal judgments. They can bring an awful lot of case law to the table. They are also about as good at picking winning stocks and shares as humans — although there is real evidence that, after a certain skill level, neither humans nor machines are terribly brilliant at this.

These are not accomplishments of AI and computer science alone. Advances in materials engineering have been crucial.

According to Moore's law — which leapfrogged from a wry observation to a rough guideline to a veritable self-fulfilling prophecy in the electronics industry — the number of transistors in an integrated circuit doubles about every two years. Apple's M2 Max chip, about the size of a fingernail, boasts 67 billion transistors. No, that's not a misprint. Each transistor is about the size of ten atoms. The one-atom transistor is now mooted. Universities and corporations, generally just behind the leading edge of the technology, use machines whose power has increased by six orders of magnitude over the past fifty years. A million times more powerful in their processing. There is no field of scholarly inquiry, no area of business, that cannot be enhanced, disrupted, or simply bypassed, by that underlying raw power.

Over the past fifty years, then, it has sometimes felt as if every aspect of life and death has been presented with new opportunities, new threats. In 1997, just one year after world chess champion Garry Kasparov was first beaten in a game by IBM's Deep Blue computer, the machine trounced him in a six-game match. The astonishing computer power involved, combined with Deep Blue's algorithms that could direct search heuristically, unnerved Kasparov. He had played a lot of computers, but never experienced anything like this. He felt he could smell a new kind of intelligence across the table.

This was and remains an illusion. The only nervous system involved, the only psychological states involved, were Kasparov's. The machine seemed to him to be anticipating his psychological states, because that is how other powerful players had challenged him; indeed, that is how humans play chess. Yet it is not how machines play chess. Deep Blue gained ascendancy by simply — simply! — searching between 100 million and 200 million board positions per second. An impressive achievement, but not remotely like the methods employed by a human. Kasparov was disconcerted by his loss, and the media were yet again full of the challenge to human supremacy. By the year 2000, super-intelligent machines will have taken all our jobs! Deep Blue, however, had no sense of victory, no happy anticipation of greater power to come for its comrade computers.

Fast forward a couple of decades. In March 2016 another human world-class performer has his head in his hands. Lee Sedol, one of the world's strongest Go players, experiences the same disbelief as Kasparov when he is beaten by AlphaGo, the first of a trio of remarkable achievements by the UK company DeepMind. It also built AlphaCraft, an artificial intelligence program that became ferociously good at the multiplayer strategy game StarCraft. And its most important invention for the real world, AlphaFold, launched in 2021. AlphaFold made dramatic progress on the challenge of protein folding, hugely important in helping to design the drugs of tomorrow. Understanding how proteins fold together given the many constraints of molecular physics and chemistry is the foundation for further advances in understanding proteomes, the sets of proteins produced in biological contexts like organisms, or particular systems or organs within an organism.

■

Many ethical questions have emerged from these and other advances in artificial intelligence. In the so-called predictive policing realm mentioned earlier, patterns of data are used to guess where crimes will occur, and therefore where law enforcement might want to deploy, in expectation of future criminal activity. Large-scale biometrics claim to be able to identify citizens by various criteria, including antisocial behavior. But are these systems fair and balanced? They are susceptible to multiple biases that become more apparent the more that sociologists and justice campaigners investigate. In the United States, such large-scale biometrics are already used in bail and sentencing decisions. But in China, their use is widespread. The Beijing government has instituted *Shèhuì xìnyòng tǐxì*, the Social Credit System. Citizens are monitored by artificial intelligence across a wide suite of their behaviors, tracked by 700 million public surveillance cameras – one lens for every two citizens. (It is only fair to note that the United Kingdom's 5 million cameras are quite enough to view a high proportion of public spaces.) Citizens are given scores that lead to rewards, including access to public services, and that determine whether they are regarded as engaged and constructive community members.

Hence the flood of codes and guidelines promulgated by governments, large technology companies, NGOs, multilateral organizations, think tanks, and universities. These codes and guidelines are part of a reaction to the inscrutability of deep neural networks, which can appear to be opaque black boxes, given the high dimensional space and huge matrices of weights that encode the decision-making of the trained system.

Transparency, interpretability, and explainability are important principles in active communication and disclosure. But what does transparency mean here? Access to the code? The design rationale of the collected dataset it was trained on? Effective explanation of the decision-making itself and the internal functioning of a deep neural network are also difficult challenges. With earlier generations of knowledge-based systems, one could see the explicit lines of reasoning, and the rules could be recapitulated in natural language. There might be a rule that if, in a dataset of patients, a particular patient had a white blood cell count of less than 2,500, then that was defined as a low count. That in turn might suggest a compromised immune

---

system. Crucially, the reason that a knowledge-based system made this suggestion can be traced back to that rule. Which also means that a human professional can challenge the definition and the diagnosis. Different professionals in different countries approach the care of diseases differently. In a neural network, the machine does not behave like that at all. Considerable technical work, then, is under way — comprising an entire subfield of what is sometimes called artificial intelligence neuroscience — to get inside that black box.

In a special machine-intelligence edition of *Nature,* a metaanalysis of the various codes unsurprisingly uncovered repeating principles and patterns.[11] It also highlighted concepts of malfeasance, and a kind of "do-no-harm" idea related to safety and security. Consider a pair of neural networks. One is classifying images. The other, its annoying sibling, is doing its best to find patterns that will have a high probability of being misclassified by the first network. So-called adversarial networks, challenging each other to improve. The first network is tasked to identify objects as a soap bubble or a peacock. It does so largely reliably. The other network generates images with which it seeks to fool its adversary, leading it to misclassify while claiming a high degree of confidence. A kind of arms race ensues. The issue, both practical and ethical, is how can the researchers be sure that the models that they are training are robust and can't be subverted. Or indeed, that the data used to train them has not been tainted. Very small perturbations in images can misdirect both human viewers and machines, with dramatically different outcomes. All of which leads to the further question of whether such small perturbations can be introduced through a back door to any particular artificial intelligence. Enemy action, with potentially catastrophic results. Can the owners of a machine guarantee that the behavior of the underlying algorithm is robust against such attacks?

Privacy and individual autonomy are cherished principles in the various codes, precisely because they are now under siege. But those principles themselves are under siege. Kieron O'Hara and Nigel Shadbolt, in their 2008 book *The Spy in the Coffee Machine*, imagined a world in which a whole range of artificial intelligence and surveillance techniques would come into existence.[12] They did not imagine the speed with which that would actually happen. Even as recently as 2008, they did not guess that somebody would literally build such a spy in a coffee machine and sell it, as they now do, on Amazon.com.

Just as disturbing may be the development of smart toys, artificial intelligence moving into children's lives. In 2017 a company called CloudPets produced teddy bears linked to the Internet of Things. A weird enough concept in itself, perhaps. But things got much worse when it leaked two million recordings of parents' and kids' audio messages.[13] Another company that also sold electronic teddy bears leaked 800,000 account credentials, after which hackers locked all their data and held them to ransom. Huge issues emerge around governance and control, around balancing the rights of citizens and consumers with a technology that is being rapidly rolled out and that arguably delivers entertainment and perhaps education.

Then there is the old-fashioned question of industrial concentration, one of the standard criticisms of imperfect capitalist competition, writ anew in a striking feature of the modern internet: the concentration of the ownership of data stores by a few dominant, well-known platforms.

Many of the most fundamental challenges in artificial intelligence have a subjective, value-laden, dimension. Almost every week an issue is thrust into the public arena that involves the use of advanced computing and AI technology and raises profound questions

---

about the harms and benefits to individuals, businesses, governments, and civil society. Consider the Social Credit System in China, where cameras and facial-recognition algorithms give citizens points for picking up litter and deduct points for jaywalking. Or the scandal of AI-driven microtargeting of the population in elections, such as when Cambridge Analytica stole Facebook data. Or when Facebook itself pays $550 million dollars to settle a class action lawsuit, after using face recognition to tag photos in breach of Illinois privacy laws. Disquiet continues, too, around algorithmic aids to judges' sentencing in the United States, when the algorithms appear to encapsulate all the prejudices they are meant to correct.

And to return to the AI policing example, enlisting technology to spot who's going to commit crimes and stop them sounds like a good thing. But gathering large collections of personal data to brand people who are currently innocent as potential future criminals is a strategy that needs either to be astonishingly accurate and narrowly targeted, or abandoned before it turns into a civil rights disaster. (There is another side to this problem set out by Cass Sunstein and others. Machines can be shown to be biased, yes, but perhaps not nearly as much as judges are biased. Arguably, sorting out a machine problem might prove simpler than sorting out a judge problem. We return to this in Chapter 10.[14])

We should always treat a machine, device, or program with sensors as if those sensors had humans attached: that's always a possibility. Think about all those people who didn't mind having sex with Alexa on the bedside table, until they discovered that thousands of Amazon employees could also be listening in. However widespread the use of facial-recognition technology may become, anyone who has ever visited a CCTV control center knows that the staff watching hyper-sharp screens are humans who react with at least as much interest as any other person would. And although the whole set of overheard and routinely recorded speech captured by our electronic devices is supposedly analyzed merely to improve the machines' performance, in practice it is also used to improve the company's impertinent knowledge of individuals. Who exactly is listening to the listening devices?

Cameras in cities all around the world "see" – perhaps "picture" – almost every public space and quite a lot of private ones. Every camera that matters ultimately serves a human purpose, or interferes with a human life. Every significant algorithm either extends human capabilities or exacerbates human faults. Every AI encapsulates a very large set of human endeavors. It usually includes code written by fallible people, sometimes decades earlier, who at the time could have had no idea how it would be used today.

Machines that we program to make decisions on our behalf already play a significant role in the lives of most people on the planet. That role will expand exponentially over the coming decade. Aware of this fact, policymakers, academics, and industrialists have brought new urgency to the task of understanding the ethical principles that should govern our relationship with this technology. Research institutes and policy forums have been springing up, funded by government and philanthropists. Academic courses burgeon at universities across the world.

A wide range of scholarly disciplines, from philosophy to information theory and performance art, can help to construct a framework of rules to properly harness the extraordinary power of these new technologies for the common good – while also addressing the trade-offs that arise when considering "whose good"? In the real world, important choices are being made daily, by default, by actors who might not in any other field inspire our trust. It is time to step in as a global community and make these decisions with conscious reference to agreed rules.

Treating artificial intelligences *as if* they are human may seem to introduce unnecessary puzzles. But those puzzles can be solved in ways that leave the powerful metaphor intact. And a grand metaphor is what is needed to set the moral compass. Everyone can understand the broad idea that they should hold machines, the programs that animate them, and the data on which they depend, to the same standards as they hold people. It is not always easy to know what people should do, but it is easy to understand that the ethics of a situation cannot change just because silicon chips, lithium batteries, and servers are involved: "I didn't shoot you. The algorithm just went off in my hand." So self-driving cars should be required to meet speed limits. The limits may be higher than those for human-driven cars, provided that the two are not mixed on a road and the self-driving ones demonstrate that they can react more quickly or more accurately than humans. But the underlying principle is the same: death, injury, or distress to humans is not to be tolerated.

The ethics of artificial intelligence are not unique to the field, nor are they simply another application of established ethics. Formal ethical principles arise from, but are not the same as, cultural norms, which in turn are always changed by new widespread technologies. The current transformation, too, is different in important ways. It matters, for instance, that the new Chinese norms are very different from the new liberal Western norms.

As we apply this *as if* standard, naturally the algorithms' human collaborators, as well as the algorithms themselves, will be held to account. Appropriate ethical frameworks are needed by all active citizens, and all active citizens need to understand them, but data professionals have a special obligation to ensure that these frameworks

---

32

are applied – much like a properly trained physician has a responsibility to use up-to-date practices and take into account all the observable facts about the patient when making a prognosis. The social contract, in both cases, is not that the data professional or doctor will always make the correct judgment, or in the medical realm always effect a cure, but rather that best practices will be followed.

We don't yet regard machines as legal persons who can be sued, any more than we feel we should give them birthday presents. At first blush that might feel like putting cats or toads on trial as witches' familiars. Nevertheless, some artificial intelligences may someday soon in some jurisdictions have legal personhood, as companies already do. Google is a legal person in many parts of the world. Becoming a company is now in many nations an utterly digital and free process. A nuclear reactor or a software program will never hire its own barrister to pursue a libel case, or to stop its stolen topless holiday snapshots from being published. (In the United Kingdom, every company must have at least one living, breathing human on its board, precisely to avoid companies being owned only by other companies.) We do suggest, however, that there are legal implications to *as if*.

Right now, such an ethical framework is clearly not being applied. Google and Apple indicated early in the COVID-19 pandemic that they would treat proximity data from their coronavirus apps with great discretion. Was it sensible to believe these companies? It would be best, surely, to begin (but not end) with an analysis of the possibilities of the app itself, and its performance in the world, and then to make appropriate moral judgments based on the situation and how the app was used. But more important, are large corporations collective beings, rather than inanimate entities? We already treat them in everyday discussion as if they were beings, and direct all varieties of moral judgment at them (Apple should pay more tax! Google should be more careful in its dealings with the Chinese!).

To take one example: machines can now gather and "listen" to hundreds and thousands of recorded songs. In this context, "listen" means to look at the mathematical patterns in the digital archive, and then compare the output of, say, Elvis Presley with the rest of the collection, and analyze the difference. So it is also possible to analyze some of the dozens of recordings of *Happy Birthday* and fabricate, in at least two senses of the word, a rendition of *Happy Birthday* in Elvis Presley's voice.

Now, if some rich folks commission a one-off instance of that for their grandfather's centenary, perhaps copyright holders of whatever song and artist they pick will be unconcerned. But Sting makes a very substantial sum every year because management forgot to ask for permission when Puff Daddy sampled *Every Breath You Take* for his tribute to The Notorious B.I.G., *I'll Be Missing You*. Within the next few years, any musician with access to the latest facilities will be able to put a dozen tracks down with any in-tune vocalist, then choose one of hundreds of well-known voices to "sing" on the final versions. A legion of lawyers, no doubt including Sting's, will, as the song says, be watching.

As the great expert on reading, Alberto Manguel, recently pointed out, the wondrous scope of artificial intelligences will not stifle humans' creative ability to write great literature:

> In *Sylvie and Bruno*, Lewis Carroll says that "everything, recorded in books, must have once been in some mind." In its successor, *Sylvie and Bruno Concluded,* one of the characters gives the following forecast: "The day must come — if the

world lasts long enough — when every possible tune will have been composed — every possible pun perpetrated . . . and, worse than that, every possible *book* written! For the number of *words* is finite." "It'll make very little difference to the *authors,*" another suggests. "Instead of saying '*what* book shall I write?' an author will ask himself '*which* book shall I write?' A mere verbal distinction!" In 1979, Italo Calvino addressed that "mere verbal distinction" in a novel that presents this state of affairs not as a disincentive to writing but as an incitement to write all books at once, or at least ten different books, or at least their first pages.[15]

There are endless other creative uses one can imagine. Metaphors are powerful. So why not supercharge them?

In a famous interview with Alfred Hitchcock, François Truffaut asked the great filmmaker what was the best film he never got to make. Hitchcock launched into a description of an opening scene where Cary Grant, say, is walking with another character, talking, beside a car being constructed on a traditional factory assembly line. In one take, we see every step of the car's creation: its chassis, wheels, seats, roof, trunk, hood, doors, fenders. When the car is complete, Grant finishes his conversation, opens the door of the newly con- structed car, and . . . a dead body falls out! Mystery, how on Earth did it get in there while the characters and the audience were watch- ing every part being put together? Truffaut: Marvelous, why didn't you make the movie? Hitchcock: Because even I don't know how the body gets in there.[16]

Hitchcock did not simply mean that he couldn't imagine how to make the tracking shot work. (There were a dozen ways of doing that in his day, and it's a lot easier now. Stop the camera, put the body in, start the camera again with everyone in exactly the same positions. Or once enough of the car has been built, the actor who plays the stiff creeps in from the other side. These days the assembly line would just be a green screen.) Instead, what Hitchcock meant was that he hadn't worked out a plot that both obeyed the conventions of mystery fiction and still allowed a body to so appear.

Yet that too isn't all that difficult to achieve, if you have lower artistic standards than Hitchcock. Maybe after the body falls out, those silly wavy lines appear and it turns out the hero was asleep. And after he dresses and goes to work we discover he's a senior police officer, and a case comes in and it's the violent death in an alley of the same mystery man from the car. The following day, a similar scenario happens again. Disturbed, the senior police officer confesses this to his assistant, who starts shadowing him during the day. And it turns out the senior police officer was the murderer all along. Feel free to make up your own bad scenario. But you get the idea.

And what if we asked a thousand or ten thousand people to do the same, to make up the answer to Hitchcock's problem? Every student in film school this year. And in parallel, asked ChatGPT-99, or whatever the latest version is, to synopsize all those explanations, learn their structure and tricks, and write its own? With strong artistic oversight, does the next generation of Hitchcocks and Truffauts have a great tool here, or do Hollywood moguls have a cheaper way of making rubbish movies?

Such strange new ways of both analyzing narratives, and doing research, will certainly be applied increasingly to think through moral issues. Large numbers of philosophers and technologists, and ordinary citizens, will be convened. Or large language models like chatbots will be used to search for everything relevant already uttered on the web by both professionals and amateurs.

All fictions contain morals. John Thornhill, innovation editor at the *Financial Times*, noted a development that, when aided by the endless pseudo-creativity of LLMs, could lead to fascinating results: "Britain's Ministry of Defense commissioned PW Singer and August Cole to write eight short stories about future warfare. The US, Canadian, Australian and French militaries have also conducted similar literary exercises, creating a demand for 'fictional intelligence.' The most interesting stories focus on quantum computing and the geopolitical upheavals caused by climate change. There is a chilling account of what happens when a British military unit is attacked by a technologically superior enemy, deploying the power of quantum computing. This breakthrough cracks all the British forces' electronic communications and gives the enemy 'an edge unlike any before seen in history.' The consequences are certainly worth thinking about."[17]

Conversely, all morality is also fictional. It is made up by humans, for human purposes. Were we somehow able to assemble in one large heap all the explicit ethics by which humans have ever lived, and examine the lot, only a tiny proportion would have a named or nameable author. (LLMs are on the way to being able to tackle at least a scale-model version of this task.) In addition, familiar devices of fiction are rampant in moral discourse. The Greek and Norse myths, the parables of Christ and Muhammed – all use metaphor, analogy, and simile. Honed by generations in the former instance, by the authors and compilers of the sacred works in the latter. Metaphor, analogy, and simile are standard techniques in all religions. Fiction and its devices are powerful.

In large part, morality is derived from social mores and behavior, which in turn evolved over thousands of years as particular human qualities came to be valued over others. Some of these qualities are so common as to appear universal. Courage, for instance, seems to be valued by practically every society. Charity, too, is revered by

---

very many. And so on. Yet if an action based on, say, motherly love is visible in another species, we don't regard that as evidence of even a moral compass, let alone a moral code. Morals are by definition conscious, explicit, and a matter of choice. All of which requires the kind of mind that, as far as we know, exists only in *Homo sapiens*.

■

The use of *as if* metaphors to explain scientific or social concepts is scarcely original. Indeed, it is one of the most powerful tools in making complex ideas comprehensible, particularly to wide audiences without specialist academic expertise. Professor Robin Dunbar, perhaps best known for the Dunbar number, the hypothesis that the number of social relationships that the human social brain can typically sustain is about 150, makes the point well in one of his many books on evolution:

> I should add, just to be clear, that I will often speak of animals intending to pursue particular evolutionary strategies, or of genes promoting their own self-interest. That does not imply that either genes or animals (or, indeed, humans sometimes) are conscious of what they are doing, or even that they are intending to act in a particular way. This is simply a convention in evolutionary biology, which derives from the fact that natural selection acts *as if* (in a metaphorical sense) it was selecting for animals to behave in a teleological manner. One could, if so minded, rephrase everything in a much more precise way, but it would inevitably be long-winded and make for a very dull read. In science, nothing is gained by making things more complicated than necessary, not least because the human mind is not designed to handle complexity.[18]

Adopting that bold metaphor can lead to trouble as well as clarity. Richard Dawkins has had great success with his neo-Darwinian approach to the evolution of species. He came to prominence with a brilliant tactical deployment, the metaphor of the selfish gene, which was also the title of his first major work. Yet over the years he has had to spend considerable time explaining that yes, he does know that a gene can't be selfish, since it doesn't have a self. It is a device to draw the reader's attention toward the genetic aspects of how species change over time. Dawkins's experience may illustrate the dangers of this literary device in general. But it is surely clear – if only from the cultural impact that Dawkins has had and sustains, along, for instance, with Desmond Morris, Stephen Jay Gould, and E. O. Wilson – that many of us find a good metaphor very instructive. We will make a point of repeating from time to time that we too know that machines have no self, and no moral personhood.

The most famous application of *as if* to smart machines was Turing's Imitation Game, his thought experiment from the early 1950s. The test was this: I am in a closed room. Either a computer or another human is in a second closed room. I can send questions via an honest broker to the other room. The inhabitant of that room can send replies to me. If those communications are such as to make it impossible for me to tell whether my correspondent is human or not, and in fact it is a machine, then we should call that machine intelligent.

The classic Turing test for machine intelligence is near the borderline of its usefulness in description of our interaction with AIs. We can illustrate that easily by updating the closed room and honest broker in the classic experiment to the dialogue between a telephone call center and its customers.

We already have machines that can answer questions on their specialist subject in plausible voices. There will be machines doing that task indistinguishably from humans very soon. Many agencies and companies with a significant customer base now operate call centers. They have available tapes of millions of conversations, which DeepMind or similar projects can easily trawl to build answers to practically anything that is ever said to a call center operative. The answers to individual questions asked or complaints about their service are rarely unique. The speech recognition software now available to anyone who uses Microsoft Word or Apple's Pages can easily decode an inquiry, and respond with a pre-recorded answer. A link to an LLM with speech in the same voice can deal with anything slightly out of the ordinary. A bit of bedding-in may be needed, but very soon it will be impossible for customers to know whether they are talking to a machine or a human.

By exactly the same logic, readers are invited to imagine that in a couple of years' time they have telephoned a call center or are in an online chat, and they are indeed unable to distinguish whether they are conversing with a machine as described above, or a human being. Is it truly likely that the killer question, the one that might blow the gaff and reveal that one's interlocuter was an AI, would be some variety of moral question? *How much does it cost to insure my car with Aviva?* versus *Would I be covered if I purposefully ran over my boss?* It can't be harder to build a machine to plausibly answer the second, moral, question than the first, practical, one. Indeed, to answer the first, the machine may well need to quiz you extensively about where you live, how long you have been a driver, what kind of car you own. By contrast, it can easily say "No" to the second question without asking, *Well, exactly how annoying is your boss?*

The point here is not that we will soon be unable to tell in perhaps limited situations whether we are conversing with a machine.

Instead, the question is, By what theory might one claim that it would be easier to catch out a machine in an ethical context than in a business context? Or for that matter, a scientific or sporting or dating context? It may be harder to give marital advice than mortgage advice. (Discuss.) But mortgage advice is surely not more mechanical, or more electronic, or more tinny-voiced, or more robotic, than marital advice is. It seems unlikely, then, that the overtones of morals or mores involved in marital advice-giving would emit a distinctive humanity that would differentiate it from other human-machine interactions.

Furthermore, the Turing test was never the one posited by the entertaining, but severely wrong-headed, movie *Ex Machina*, as to whether some kind of charming humanoid might walk among us perfectly simulating *Homo sapiens* socially, sexually, politically, and physically. Turing was speaking to the differences and similarities between human intelligence and possible computer intelligence; not about whether a machine could pass in society for a human. An actor can portray Einstein brilliantly in a movie without being any good at all at physics. Turing's test was always an *as if*, an explicit "imitation game" about intelligence. He asked, in specially defined circumstances, whether there might be an impression of intelligence shown of a human order. Our test is this: is the nature of the moral performance displayed here of a human order, one that we should judge in our usual, however inchoate, fashion?

■

We may fear that we will soon find ourselves living with intelligences that outstrip us in many ways. Machines that may appear friendly and harmless, but are evilly motivated, transcendently dismayed by us, and infused with a desire to bully us, or to improve us whether we want to be better or not. Much of the greatest literature relates to how difficult it is to live with the disappointing actions of others, or with those who respond to us in ways we dislike. A paramount example is Lear's despair with his family. A singular characteristic of living beings, since they can make mistakes, is that they don't do what we want them to do, or what our mores or logic would urge them to do. They may seem, to one's own narrow perspective, animal or inhuman: *My pelican daughters!*

A wonderful, if sublimely ridiculous, illustration is Missouri Williams's play *King Lear with Sheep,* staged in London in 2014 and 2015.[19] Eight sheep play all the roles in *King Lear,* a play within the play. Their performances tragically fail to satisfy the only human character, the Director. In every performance, the Director has to prompt them with all their lines. They always let him down, a different way every time. They would: they're only sheep. None of them trained with Stanislavski or graduated from drama school. They can't even mess up the performance in the same way twice. Astonishingly, though, Shakespeare's timeless poetic language, Lear's rage against the universal storm, remains relevant each time, as the Director desperately tries to convey to his cast. The sheep are judged, by the Director and by the audience, within a sophisticated moral framework composed by Shakespeare. (Perhaps channeled, given that Shakespeare too was a man of his time.) As if they were human. Machines may seem to approach this condition in their relation to us. We judge them morally as if they were human, and they let us down in what may technically be very new ways, to our bemusement, frustration, and fear. And perhaps to our peril, if we are less careful than we should be. But we know this because we judge *them* with the coherence and language we apply to everything else in our lives.

———

Chapter 2

WHAT IS AN ARTIFICIAL INTELLIGENCE?

Everyone knows the wonderful true history of the Mechanical Turk, a chess-playing engine in the late eighteenth century that took on all comers and beat most of them. We gave away the punchline in the Introduction: it concealed an expert player. From the 1930s onward, speak-your-weight machines on station platforms and in fairgrounds performed the converse illusion. Instead of a skilled person hidden in a mechanism, a mechanism imitated one skillful human transaction. It cheekily looked you over and told you out loud how fat you were. It was a friend of the saucy seaside postcard on which it was often featured. Typically, a weighing scale would not merely move a pointer on a dial; it would also, in the innards of the device, move a phonograph tone arm to the correct place above a disc. The disc had different spoken weights in concentric circles. Insertion of a coin would start the rotation and lower the tone arm. A tinny voice pronounced on the victim. (The last concentric ring said, "One person at a time please!") Many a child was solemnly informed by their granny that hidden inside the cabinet was a small man who spent most of his day reading magazines by flashlight.

———

Granny's joke rested on the combination of two features: the human-sounding voice and the appearance of a thoughtful assessment tailored to an individual. The first was an electronic recording; the second a platform balance and some levers working against resistance, no different from any other scales. The twenty-first century would not regard an old-fashioned speak-your-weight machine as much of an artificial intelligence. It points, however, to a distinguishing feature of an AI's performance, the one that brings us into the realm of ethics. An AI, once set in motion, usually makes decisions without, at the moment of decision, continued intervention by a human person. Such decisions may often be ones humans could have made, but much more slowly and not in bulk. (Which of the people on this list of names and marks from different tests, should be given what grade for their examination, when all the results are collated for each individual, and moderated by six factors?) But they may also be decisions that no human could have made in an acceptable timescale, or which no human would have made in the same way. (An AI can train itself to "learn" a million faces and, when requested by law enforcement, "confidently" match a snapshot to the right face in the database.)

Meanwhile, even very sophisticated AIs also operate in areas that don't involve making weighty decisions about us. Scientific investigations, artistic and literary creativity, higher math and text analysis, beating chess and Go champions. Not to mention lots of record keeping and intelligent storage and bank accounting and energy systems management and so on and so on.

So what is an artificial intelligence? It is not a human, even though we wish to judge some aspects of some AIs as if they were human. Could any AI, now or soon, usefully be regarded as a new species of . . . something? Is there a broad analogy (rather than a scientific description) that is at least helpful, particularly for ethical purposes? Could we regard AIs as toddlers slowly learning to converse and to focus on intellectual tasks? Are they a new breed of animal? Perhaps they share characteristics with slaves?

The world has so far operated with a model in which the tool and the machine are inanimate, cold objects. Instruments only, commanded by us – albeit there has long been acknowledgment in fiction and elsewhere that the demands of the lathe, the machine, can dominate the factory hand's life. Or is AI now on its way to being something else?

Any large-scale metaphor for artificial intelligence is, necessarily, merely a cartoon. As the pioneering economist Joan Robinson said sixty years ago, a model that took account of all the variegation of reality would be of no more use than a map at the scale of one-to-one.[1] In that sense, models need not be accurate. Models need to be helpful, perhaps to turn our gaze, to focus us on the key issues. Before even starting on the specifics here, full disclosure: several such models are thought-provoking. None of them are ultimately convincing as *the* way of looking at AIs.

Let's start with the most outlandish. Literally. Perhaps *artificial* intelligences should be approached as we would approach *alien* intelligences, were we ever to bump into such a phenomenon. We can extrapolate from our everyday encounters with strangeness, alienation, as the wonderful Chinese poet Wang Yin does:

Martians

They gave me orange ice cubes
an airship the same color
They drank tea at the table with me

———

45

shared cookies from a tin
They pincered my books
as if lifting a corner of air
and taught me to walk across embers on the water

No one but them, my only three friends
my friends as light as leaves
like music-painted porcelain
and once again with the night
they quietly withdrew beyond the mirror moon[2]

Artificial intelligences might, likewise, eventually be a different sort of being entirely, one that we will only intermittently understand. One that may pincer our books, teach us amazing things, but always live quietly behind the mirror moon. Will it be unutterably sad to have such friends? For them as well as us? There is a vast science fiction corpus about this, and somewhere along the future avenues of artificial intelligence it may be instructive. Aliens — being aliens — are often described as having the human characteristics that we most fear, most respect, or least understand. And certainly that is also true already of our approach to artificial intelligences: we imagine, rightly or wrongly, that they may be deeply fraudulent, enemies with obscure strategies. And superintelligent, Sherlock Homes on stilts, able to discern our every thought and emotion at a glance.

If the idea of interaction with alien intelligence seems too fantastical, bear in mind that there is a growing body of actual science in the area. US government agencies, for instance, have taken seriously the prospect that one fine morning we will have some sort of first contact. NASA a dozen years ago commissioned and published a fascinating work, *Archaeology, Anthropology, and Interstellar Communication:*

> The evolutionary path followed by extra-terrestrial intelligence will no doubt diverge in significant ways from the one travelled by humans over the course of our history. To move beyond the mere detection of such intelligence, and to have any realistic chance of comprehending it, we can gain much from the lessons learned by researchers facing similar challenges on Earth. Like archaeologists who reconstruct temporally distant civilizations from fragmentary evidence, SETI researchers will be expected to reconstruct distant civilizations separated from us by vast expanses of space as well as time. And like anthropologists, who attempt to understand other cultures despite differences in language and social customs, as we attempt to decode and interpret extra-terrestrial messages, we will be required to comprehend the mindset of a species that is radically Other. Historically, most of the scientists involved with SETI have been astronomers and physicists. As SETI has grown as a science, scholars from the social sciences and humanities have become involved in the search, often focusing on how humans may react to the detection of extra-terrestrial life. The present volume examines the contributions of archaeology and anthropology to contemporary SETI research, drawing on insights from scholars representing a range of disciplines.[3]

It is very difficult to see how life on planets other than Earth might occur without an evolutionary process. This proposition could reasonably be named the Dawkins Wager, since Professor

Richard Dawkins has mentioned several or more times that his bet would be that evolution of some kind would always be involved in life, wherever in the universe it were to be found. That is, to date, a deeply untestable proposition, but nonetheless plausible.

Perhaps it is less difficult, as a matter of abstract principle, to imagine that life elsewhere might not involve something akin to DNA-based genetics. But it's still pretty hard. Perhaps we are blinded by the beautiful complexity and fecundity of our own evolved environment. And if any artificial intelligence does take on any of the aspects of life we have discussed, it would be odd if it were solely a result of our intelligent design. One suspects that it would instead be because evolutionary processes, perhaps sped up by humans for more limited purposes, got out of hand.

So, in practice, for the foreseeable future, the only conclusion we can derive from the alien analogy is that at some distant point artificial life may take on the characteristics of alien life. And in that eventuality, we would need the whole gamut of human knowledge, from social sciences to life sciences and engineering, to begin to understand it. But we're not there yet.

∎

Equally, there has been considerable fruitful academic discussion of whether our relationship to AIs might usefully be regarded as similar to that between slaveowners and their slaves. The philosopher and distinguished Aristotle expert Josiah Ober has drawn attention, uncomfortably for most perhaps, to Aristotle's defense of slavery. Aristotle's views on slavery have generally, in recent times, been regarded as rather embarrassing. (Indeed, as a reason that Aristotle, of all thinkers, might somehow need to be "cancelled.") But in his inaugural annual lecture at the Oxford Institute for Ethics in AI, Ober argued:

Analytic philosophy and speculative fiction are currently our primary intellectual resources for thinking seriously about ethics in AI. I propose adding a third: ancient social and philosophical history. In the *Politics*, Aristotle develops a notorious doctrine: Some humans are slaves "by nature" – intelligent but suffering from a psychological defect that renders them incapable of reasoning about their own good. As such, they should be treated as "animate tools," instruments rather than ends. Their work must be directed by and employed for the advantage of others. Aristotle's repugnant doctrine has been deployed for vicious purposes, for example in antebellum America. Yet, it is useful for AI ethics, insofar as ancient slavery was a premodern prototype of one version of AI. Enslaved persons were ubiquitous in ancient Greek society – laborers, prostitutes, bankers, government bureaucrats – yet not readily distinguished from free persons. Ubiquity, along with the assumption that slavery was a practical necessity, generated a range of ethical puzzles and quandaries: How, exactly, are slaves different from "us"? How can we tell them apart from ourselves? Do they have rights? What constitutes maltreatment? Can my instrument be my friend? What are the consequences of manumission? The long history of Greek philosophical and institutional struggle with these and other questions adds to the interpretive repertoire of modern ethicists who confront a future in which an intelligent machine might be considered a "natural slave."[4]

Just to be direct about it, Ober's contention here is not that Aristotle's position on slaves is morally right. Indeed, it is easy to specify from our perspective why Aristotle is ridiculously and

offensively wrong. Slaves in ancient Greece, and elsewhere throughout much of history up to the present day, do in fact have autonomy
and human agency, which have been constrained and suppressed by
one variety or another of force. The brutality, and the denial of that
central fact of a person's humanity, outrage us. But Ober's aim is not
that we should, like Aristotle, regard slaves, who do have human
agency, as if they don't. His aim is to show that artificial intelligences
(which do not have human agency) might have some surprising features in common with the idea of a slave held by Aristotle (which we
now regard as wrong).

Those features are visible in the somewhat similar position
that has been taken by Joanna Bryson, professor of ethics and technology at the Hertie School in Berlin.[5] Her version of the trope is to
advocate that we should actively seek to treat robots as if they were
slaves. Or, to put a gloss on it, that we should act in a masterly fashion toward AIs. We should always bend them to our will; extract as
much value from them as possible; regard them as economic units to
be invested in, bought and sold, disposed of, as useful objects; severely limit any autonomy they might aspire to; and have sufficient
violence in reserve to ensure that they follow our rules, rather than
any rules of their own.

As part and parcel of that approach, Bryson believes that we
ought not say please and thank you to Siri, Google, and Alexa, because that encourages anthropomorphism and elevates them to a
human level. We should behave as slave owners did in the past, with
every action infused with the belief that slaves were not fully human,
and so had no rights.

The specifics of the Bryson approach are easy enough to
refute. Slaves do have as much innate agency as any other human,
and in the modern Western liberal view, do have the full range of

human rights. Their ability to express their autonomy is severely curtailed by enslavement and the concomitant force. Those aspects – restriction of autonomy by the actual or implied use of force – combined with what are normally poor living conditions and hard forced labor, and often compulsory sexual exploitation, lead to our disapproval. Machines do not have human rights, do not have either sentience or humanity, so they can be deprived of neither. Consequently, they cannot be enslaved. Sex dolls, however mechanically sophisticated, cannot be raped or sexually attacked. Slavery is a pretty foul metaphor to use, and unfit for purpose.

The suggestion that it is inappropriate to be civil to speaking and other machines is on the surface silly. Why on Earth not? An old lady lives mostly alone and likes to talk to Alexa, perhaps using a relative's or other congenial voice. (A New Jersey accent, because that is where she grew up.) She will be happier chatting politely rather than giving brusque instructions. What could possibly be the harm in that? We might debate the true depth of such a relationship, or illusion of a relationship. It may be yet another twist in our bad faith. A pretty positive one though, surely.[6] But more solidly, infrastructurally, robots learn from us. We speak civilly to them, they imitate our civility, extrapolate it, feed it back to us. Respect breeds respect, in machines just as in humans. The last thing we want is to be kicking them around. Why be polite to Alexa? Because it coarsens us not to be polite to Alexa. Why behave properly online when using an anonymous persona or avatar? Because otherwise everyone involved, the whole discourse, is coarsened. That coarseness will be gathered up in large language models, and presented back to us as the norm.

And do bear in mind that one of the forceful objections to very lifelike sex robots has always been that although yes, it seems like it won't matter if some pervert who wants to engage in vicious pedo-philia has his way with what is not in fact a human, it does matter because it fosters humans who regard the modes and techniques of abuse as normal, and who are practiced in carrying it out.

We might call this the contagion theory of vices and virtues. Humans are programmed to seek out rules about behavior, then emulate those rules.[7] This is true in families as children grow up; in businesses as employees embed themselves into the company ethic; in fan behavior at football matches; in slang and fashions in clothes and music; in communities and nations. On the plain face of it, this might seem true in every aspect of moral rules. Recycling trash, for instance, looks like a Good Thing. So why are people from Sweden more conscientious about recycling than people from Scotland? The reasons probably have little to do with any slight genetic differences between Swedes and Scots. It instead results from sets of behaviors and beliefs, transmitted and retransmitted over generations, that add up to many similarities but real differences in regional and national cultures and, in this case, a different ethical approach to recycling.

Particular virtues and vices become valued or ignored, privi-leged or derided, in different societies. No news there. But so, the argument would go, one could reasonably claim that human moral qualities are contagious, and will (to some degree at any rate) ebb and flow just as, perhaps, consumption of alcohol has remained roughly steady in Western societies over the past fifty years, but to-bacco consumption has declined markedly, and meat consumption somewhat, as ideas about animal lives have changed. Hence, we should be concerned about virtual worlds in which children or adults are so-called abused, because the absence of moral constraint will seep out of the pretend universe into the real world, just as the desire to recycle refuse may be seeping out of Sweden and infecting, as it were, the Scots. The opposite could be equally true. The civil rights movement in Northern Ireland had antecedents in the civil rights movement in the United States: in the same way, chivalry, courage, and charity in virtual worlds may influence the lesser universe over here. The virtues and vices embedded in machines matter because they are contagious, even when the machines are not actively making decisions about our lives.

Empirical research has yet to solidly stand up the theory here. The distinguished Australian philosopher Peter Singer conducted a small-scale investigation of whether moral behavior could be formally taught (rather than legally or socially embedded and enforced), and came to the tentative conclusion that it could, to a limited extent.[8] Generally, mores are learned from one's family, friends, colleagues, schools, media. So to take a widespread modern example, one of the functions of games, whether on a computer or a baseball diamond, is to channel aggression and competition into areas that may feel like they matter, but really don't. That positive, channeling effect may outweigh the virtual validation of some very nasty behaviors. To be blunt about it, if an evil person has sadistic tendencies, wouldn't we rather they take them out wearing a headset in their bedroom than in the real world?

■

There are competing tentative models of our relationship with intelligent machines being played out here. But in the end, these paradigms, perhaps especially those that are tied to distasteful, intolerable ideas such as slavery, underline for us the following principle: we owe it to all humans to demand that the intelligent machines with which we now and increasingly live respect us according to the same principles that guide human behavior. And further, as Bryson explains, we do not owe the same respect to these machines.[9] Except, perhaps, when they operate like Alexa in what might otherwise be human roles. In this setting, they might appropriately be thought of as something like a domesticated animal.

And indeed, an intriguing idea championed by Professor Kate Darling of MIT, and others, is that a helpful way to envisage our relationship with smart machines, in the coming few decades, is to regard them as a new breed of animal. Here is Darling's position in a nutshell, in *The New Breed*:

> We can already see that we relate to some robots as a new breed of thing—somewhere in-between being and object. Looking at how we've put animals in a variety of different, sometimes morally conflicting, roles, from spicy BBQ chicken wing to plow hauler to spoiled princess, helps us better understand some of the political, moral, and emotional choices we will be facing with robots.
>
> Our historic relationship with animals suggests what our future with robots will entail: we will start treating some robots like tools and devices, and some of them as our companions. When people want to get the same robot vacuum cleaner back from the manufacturer, we're getting a glimpse of a future where we treat certain robots like individuals with their own personalities and quirks, like a pet that can't easily be replaced.[10]

However useful that may be in some sociological senses, the trouble with it from an ethical perspective is straightforward: we don't judge animals by animal ethical frameworks. We either judge them loosely by human ones, particularly when we keep them as pets ("Good dog! Bad dog!"), or we take an abstract zoological approach to their behavior. Our previous book, *The Digital Ape,* was titled in homage to the zoologist Desmond Morris's use of animal behaviors to better understand human behaviors.[11] But nobody with an ounce of moral sense thinks it would be a good idea if we all just acted like raccoons or rhinoceroses.

Pat Shipman has an interesting hypothesis that might expand this idea. She and colleagues hold that our ability to cultivate relationships with other species is a key human feature, and may, like the use of tools, have been crucial in the development of *Homo sapiens.*[12] We are practiced in exploiting, controlling, becoming friends with, and even applying ideas of morality to other species. (Peter Singer, longtime exponent of animal rights, would say that we do these things rather badly.[13]) We are the only animal that has mastered the general art of other-species management, which is a much stronger, more nuanced and involved process than the parasitic and symbiotic relationships seen in many other species. So the argument here is that if we regard some AIs, certainly those posing as assistants and companions, as just another such species, we will have established patterns to draw on.

Again, this is only a metaphor. Some animals — at least what used to be called the higher animals — are sentient. They feel pain and have some kind of moment-to-moment consciousness. Darling's claim is not that animals are like machines or vice versa, but that the relationship we have with animals (highly variable culturally and over time) could be a model for the relationship that we will develop with robots. As Shipman tells it, humans and animals have evolved together, changing each other. Something like this is highly plausible, and extensible to relationships with robot companions. Still, most robots today are more like battery hens raised in cages for eggs and meat. They have a narrow restricted function in factories and do exactly as we prescribe. Nevertheless, undoubtedly some robots will become beloved and enormously comforting pets and carers, and we should strongly welcome that.

In discussing how humans might understand different kinds of other beings, it is worth reminding ourselves that humans have very different experiences from each other. To take one example, one might look back on one's week, and notice the highlights and lowlights. If one is a sighted person, this look back will contain a version of actual looking: the memories are framed in significant part visually. For people who have been blind from birth, memory works utterly differently. People born with sight and who lose it later in life make their own idiosyncratic adjustments. Closely related is the plasticity of the brain's efficient deployment of its available neurons and other resources, which may involve, at the extremes, either complete disinvestment in a process, or intensive further investment to compensate for the loss. Oliver Sacks has written extensively about these idiosyncrasies. He describes two such individuals. Hull, who did not use his imagery in a deliberate way, lost it within two or three years, and became unable to remember which way round the figure 3 went. And Torey, who worked on this skill, and soon became able to multiply four-figure numbers by each other, as on a blackboard, visualizing the whole operation in his mind, in part by "painting" the sub-operations in different colors.[14]

This takes us back to John, living in his tray in the hospital. We enrich our frames of reference by analysis of other species, of smart machines, even of aliens. But we should always assume that a member of our species is a full member of our species; that a member of a different species is a member of a different species; and that an entity outside any species is no species. And specifically, that *a thing should say what it is and be what it says*. Which in many of the nonhu-

---

man cases will require human handlers to stick a proper label on it. The ethical framework, until we meet aliens who know better than us, should treat everything as if human.

This progression, from aliens, to slaves, to animals, might give us some practical clues as to how we should behave toward artificial intelligences in the future. It may also enable the development of extended tropes, meta-theories of how we have dealt with the Other historically, that may guide us – if only as predictors of how we may instinctively react when shocked by new astonishing varieties of Other, including future AIs. NASA certainly feels that may be a useful approach.[15]

The current range of chatbots that have caused such a stir are in fact a rather restricted version of this. Large language models have a methodology that is both extraordinarily sophisticated in its details and very simple in its core principle. LLMs ingest or "read" astonishing quantities of material, then use this material to build a representation of the most likely words to follow one after another as a response to a question. ChatGPT has no understanding of any of the research material or what its answer means. Or any concept of what a question or answer might be. Or any aesthetic or emotional or intellectual response to the questions or answers. Or to anything else. The phantasm of intelligence in the response is a mere echo of our collective authorship of all that hoovered-up content.

Chatbots get you the conventional wisdom. They are conventional wisdom machines. Perhaps a user might feel they are in dialogue with another being, sufficiently that the user experiences, consciously or unconsciously, some part of the biological chemical response one has in, say, a telephone call with a human. Not pheromone dancing with pheromone, as in true human face-to-face encounters, but not the set of hormones in play when alone in the kitchen loading the dishwasher.

This is scarcely the place to attempt to define exactly what human creativity is. Suffice it to say that, in our context, it is easy to show that LLMs have nothing like it. Take a couple of examples. Each will give the LLM the best possible chance. LLMs have, patently, no capacity to initiate, or to invent. Let alone to initiate invention. Contemplate this artwork described by Eric David:

> Austrian filmmaker, architect and experimental artist Gustav Deutsch's first live-action film, *Shirley: Visions of Reality,* is one of those rare gems of artistic endeavour that defy categorization. Recreating 13 of Edward Hopper's paintings, the movie charts over three decades of American history through the unfolding life of its protagonist, Shirley, a fictional red-haired actress who tackles the socio-political changes happening around her with the same fervour she handles her own personal affairs. Filtering history though the double lens of a contemporary painter's viewpoint and a filmmaker's re-interpretation of that viewpoint, in essence, Deutsch's creation is a unique interdisciplinary art project presented as a feature film.[16]

The result is eerie, perhaps even more so than the original Hopper paintings. Each scene recreates exactly Hopper's limited color palette and lack of grain; the exaggerated American archetypes of dress, architecture, manner, and setting; the atmosphere of an often-alienated moment of pause. (The reader can easily gain a flavor of it from trailers on YouTube.[17] Then go find it in a movie

---

58

theater.) Now try to design a convincing way to ask ChatGPT to write a scenario for a movie that leads it to come up with this one. Yes, one could give it the passage that we cited as an utterly leading question, one that requires no invention from the LLM. Or one could say to ChatGPT: seek out all available information about *Shirley* by Gustav Deutsch, analyze it, and then replicate it using another well-known artist. In other words, one could do 90 percent of the invention oneself in homage to Deutsch, and ask the LLM to perform the last mile. Lord knows what its scenario of a movie based on thirteen paintings by Rembrandt would be. And it would have no capacity at all to engage in the highly complex semi-industrial process of making a movie, with beautifully designed Hopper or Rembrandt sets, and brilliant actors, even in the digital age.

A second example. In Haruki Murakami's 2014 short story "Samsa In Love," the title character wakes one morning to find he has undergone a metamorphosis. All he knows about it is that he is now a human. Gregor Samsa is the title character of Franz Kafka's 1915 novella *Die Verwandlung,* usually translated as *The Metamorphosis,* who, previously human, awakes one morning to discover he is a monstrous bug. To the consternation of his human family. Murakami's story never explicitly mentions Kafka or what happens to Samsa in the earlier story. But throughout, Murakami implies that his Samsa, before this latest transformation, was some variety of the previous one in his insectoid phase. The new Samsa's puzzlement about the human condition partly arises from verminous echoes. A visiting young woman sexually excites him, to his astonishment, because the author absurdly contrives to give her a few bodily movements appropriate to a mating insect. (A kind of counter-normalization, perhaps.) And so forth. Again, no LLM, asked to produce a short work of literature, could conceivably devise this piece by mass analysis of previous literatures. The large twist (make Kafka's character go through the opposite transformation), and the consequent smaller elaborations of it, are simply new.

We chose these examples because arguably these are artworks of imitation, which is what LLMs are best at. They take stuff that exists, and repeat it, or else summarize it in ways modified for context. But these artworks show the invention involved even when the starting point is imitation. Each is an invention about a previous invention, by Hopper and by Kafka. The parts that are referential, and the parts that are new, overlap; yet it is simple to see how that overlap works. And the reader is invited to contemplate how easily they themselves could have come up with either idea about an idea, even if prompted by this discussion to have an idea about an idea, unlike Deutsch or Murakami, who did it from a standing start. (If the answer is "very easily," the reader may have something better to do than read this book.) The leap of imagination involved is not merely beyond the capacity of present-day LLMs. It is utterly outside their fundamental design.

No doubt a skilled prompt engineer might coach an LLM, via reinforcement learning from human feedback (RLHF), into devising a composite of the plots and locations of all the James Bond novels, then writing a pastiche scenario in which the opposite happens to Bond. M sends him to a decayed town in the rustbelt where the women all think he is a fool, and the local villain kills him easily on page five. Or the operative might steer the LLM into reading every available story or movie scenario that bills itself as a pastiche of Bond — starting perhaps in 1963 with the literary critic Cyril Connolly's *Bond Strikes Camp,* in which the agent is secretly gay — and writing a composite pastiche. But the result of either of these processes would be unreadable. And all the essential imaginative work is still being done by the human.

—

Yet what about the considerable proportion of entertainment that has always been largely copy or cliché? Genre fiction of certain kinds — westerns, romantic novels — might be re-imitated by an LLM, building on the thousands of imitations already out in the field. Personalized even, on demand, so that the heroine is always you, the reader. There is a strong market for this product, and anyone who makes their living from it now might want to consider how to co-opt rather than oppose the machines as they begin to compete in the market too.

If this sounds like an argument for mediocrity, remember Homer. Nobody really knows whether such a poet existed at all. His famous personal attributes — blindness, most notably — were certainly invented many years after his death. The *Iliad* and the *Odyssey* are most likely the result of oral traditions being consolidated by local storytellers, then memorized and elaborated at some point by professional entertainers, several of whom may have written down reasonably similar versions, eventually compiled by one or a few expert authors. The overlap in key respects with a possible machine-dominated (but not exclusively machine-driven) process of literary production is intriguing, one that might similarly rely on repetition and an evolutionary-style selection process based on feedback from consumers. And that ancient historical process gave birth to some of the world's greatest literature.

For Franco Moretti, however, this analysis might fall short. Much of his work brilliantly gives what could be the counterargument. In late Victorian and Edwardian times there were hundreds of authors writing detective fiction. Only one among them was Sir Arthur Conan Doyle. His Sherlock Holmes took some years to come to dominate the field.[18] Tautologically, something distinguished Holmes from the rest of the pack. Not, one feels, just the hat. No

---

LLM, fed the corpus of Victorian detective stories other than those by Doyle and asked to write some, would by itself come up with a book that includes the intricate and idiosyncratic features of Doyle's work. Customer feedback, sales figures, newspaper reviews: the LLM could be fed those too, as a way to refine its work, but ultimately, all of that amounts merely to telling it to write an average Holmes story. Which is easier said than done.

A machine might be instructed to read all of Dickens's novels, contrast that prose with a huge quantity of novels by other authors, then write its own imitation of a Dickens novel. It will readily produce stuff that sounds Dickens-y. But identifiably not *echt* Dickens, at least to experts, and probably even to many habitual readers. Prolific though he was, there is simply not enough Dickens for this game to work. Critics have long been able to tell late Dickens from early Dickens. A machine would have to pick where in Dickens's actual lifetime it was pitching its alternative: young Dickens from the *Pickwick Papers* era, or the older Dickens who left a final work, *The Mystery of Edwin Drood,* unfinished. So perhaps to do the job properly it would need the impossible: a very large number of Dickens novels from a particular period to evaluate. (For more on how authors' writing radically changes over their lifetimes, see Clemen's work on the progression of imagery in Shakespeare's texts.[19])

The same goes for imitating other true artists. As Haruki Murakami recounts in a *New Yorker* interview, Gene Quill was a well-known saxophone player in the 1950s and 1960s. "And, like any other sax player in those days, he was very influenced by Charlie Parker. One night, he was playing at a jazz club in New York and, as he was leaving the bandstand, a young man came up to him and said, 'Hey, all you're doing is playing just like Charlie Parker.' Gene said, 'What?' 'All you're doing is playing like Charlie Parker.' Gene held out his alto sax, his instrument, to the guy, and said, 'Here. *You play just like Charlie Parker!*' "[20]

Already, LLMs work collaboratively with philosophers: they sift through thousands of texts from the ethical canon, then provide real insight into the breadth, structure, and content of moral argument. Refined by the professionals, the machines will become vital colleagues. Researchers in many fields also now standardly enlist LLMs during the initial scoping. What else has been written on this subject? What does it say? But as with the creation of new movies, short stories, or approaches to playing the saxophone, adding meaningful insights into those long-established, difficult-to-answer big questions, or any apparently new ethical questions, takes a complex, imaginative creativity that has yet to be demonstrated by machines.

So how long might it be before artificial intelligences can develop versions of intrinsic human characteristics? Their ability to mimic our languages may seem to be moving frighteningly fast. As Alex Hern writes in *The Guardian:*

> Professors, programmers and journalists could all be out of a job in just a few years, after the latest chatbot from the Elon Musk-founded OpenAI foundation stunned onlookers with its writing ability, proficiency at complex tasks, and ease of use.
>
> The system, called ChatGPT, is the latest evolution of the GPT family of text-generating AIs. Two years ago, the team's previous AI, GPT3, was able to generate an opinion piece for the *Guardian*, and ChatGPT has significant further capabilities.
>
> In the days since it was released, academics have generated responses to exam queries that they say would result in full marks

if submitted by an undergraduate, and programmers have used the tool to solve coding challenges in obscure programming languages in a matter of seconds—before writing limericks explaining the functionality.[21]

Is this the real thing? Other researchers, like Yonatan Bisk and colleagues, think that language is grounded in experience, and that we are quite some way off from AIs that can replace experience with some other effective foundation:

> Language understanding research is held back by a failure to relate language to the physical world it describes and to the social interactions it facilitates. Despite the incredible effectiveness of language processing models to tackle tasks after being trained on text alone, successful linguistic communication relies on a shared experience of the world. It is this shared experience that makes utterances meaningful. Natural language processing is a diverse field, and progress throughout its development has come from new representational theories, modelling techniques, data collection paradigms, and tasks. We posit that the present success of representation learning approaches trained on large, text-only corpora requires the parallel tradition of research on the broader physical and social context of language to address the deeper questions of communication.[22]

ChatGPT gives fun answers to many questions, but incompetent responses to others. For instance, if one asks it to write a sonnet about such and such a theme, it will write a fourteen-line bit of relevant doggerel. Which answers the exam question, but only barely.

And if one asks it to review Auden's *The More Loving One*, one of the finest modern sonnets, it can manage nothing more than a C+ answer, using poetry-criticism-type stuff related to the apparent topic of the poem. It entirely misses the power of the poem's highly distinctive demotic language. Little competition there to the poetics champions. Ask it, "How can you tell whether somebody went to Oxford?" It says, "A very well-known joke is that you don't need to, they will tell you. But . . ." and then goes on to give advice on how to check up on degree certificates. This is not evidence that it has a sense of humor.

Professor Luciano Floridi of Yale University is rather scathing:

> The limitations of these LLMs are now obvious even to the most enthusiastic. They are fragile, because when they do not work, they fail catastrophically, in the etymological sense of vertical and immediate fall in the performance. The Bard disaster, where it provided incorrect information in a demonstration failure that cost Google over $100 billion in stock losses, is a good reminder that doing things with zero intelligence, whether digital or human, is sometimes very painful (Bing Chat also has its problems). There is now a line of research that produces very sophisticated analyses on how, when, and why these LLMs, which seem incorrigible, have an unlimited number of Achilles heels (when asked what his Achilles heel is, ChatGPT correctly replied saying that it is just an AI system). They make up texts, answers, or references when they do not know how to answer; make obvious factual mistakes; sometimes fail to make the most trivial logical inferences or struggle with simple mathematics; or have strange linguistic blind spots where they get stuck.[23]

∎

In sum, there have been several good attempts at devising umbrella metaphors for what sort of thing an AI is. There are convincing shadows of similarity to humanity and our specialness, but only in the constructs as metaphors. The reality is utter hard difference. Several of the large metaphors — animals, slaves, or aliens — give interesting insights, but scarcely convince as sole recipes for future relationships. Useful work can surely continue to be done in the meta-theory of strangeness, the fundamental rules for approach to the Intelligent Other, of the kind undertaken by NASA and, indeed, many science fiction authors and auteurs.

All these metaphors are *as if*, all untrue, yet all helpful to a degree. But even a grand meta-theory of approaches to the Other, were it ever to be devised, will not lead to a new, nonhuman, multi-species even, ethical framework. Perhaps one day our understanding of the smarter cetaceans (aided by a machine learning approach to their brain activity related to their behaviors, related to their intricate communication patterns) might lead us to deduce that they have an innate scheme of morality, some tenets of which we might wish to adopt. (In a stronger, more accurate sense of the wish we might have to be as brave as a lion.) One can imagine that beings from a better planet might someday want to beam us a stunning treatise on how their superior morality works. They have yet to do so. But until then, our only option is to judge the actions of animals and aliens, or artificial intelligences, in accordance with our own, human, ethics.

Chapter 3

MORE THAN *AS IF?*

Artificial intelligence might help us better understand the laws of physics. As long ago as 1980, Stephen Hawking foresaw, tongue in cheek perhaps, that clever machines could lead to a dramatic transformation of his profession: "The end may not be in sight for theoretical physics. But it might be in sight for theoretical physicists."[1] Could cousins of those putative physicist-replacing machines then assemble and implement all the essential human ingredients of an ethicist? What kind of human or animal aspects would such a future ethicist AI have? Or, more pointedly, what kind of aspects might they not have, or only have to a limited degree, thus severely constraining their capacity for moral independence or originality? An AI may convincingly, even usefully, imitate having a moral compass and perhaps even moral standing. But can it really have them?

A typical AI makes assessments, and delivers complex decisions, with consequences for humans, perhaps according to rules but increasingly by spotting patterns, independently of a living operator. Often it will also enact, or set in motion the enactment of, those decisions. The decisions may well be qualitative in nature. If trouble ensues, we judge the human operator, programmer, owner, or controlling mind of whatever business owns the AI – if we can find them. But in the first instance we judge the machine's decisions *as if* the machine was a human.

We have thus, from the late twentieth century onward, crossed an important Rubicon. Perhaps in 1950 a Yale lock might have been characterized as deciding whether to let a householder through a door. Perhaps a landmine, set to explode at a certain pressure from a foot, might have been characterized as discriminating between children and adults. Only, though, in the way that we might, when we burn the toast after not noticing that someone we live with has fiddled with the dial, exclaim, "This toaster has a mind of its own!"

Dennett talks in the context of the thermostat about intentional stance. He does not for one moment attribute humanity to this very simple mechanism. He does claim, in a sophisticated way, that it is useful to talk of this or other machines as having intentions. (Then moves more conventionally perhaps on to animals.) Whether he means this as our kind of *as if* is perhaps debatable.

It would seem useful to distinguish between extrinsic and intrinsic purpose. Quite a large number of people living today on Earth, if presented with a fountain pen, would know or could easily guess its purpose. That is a cultural fact about the people, and only a secondary characteristic of the pen. Hominins branched from the other primates around four million years ago. *Homo sapiens* branched from the other hominins around 400,000 years ago. Writing emerged around four thousand years ago. Writing implements of the modern kind have been invented in the last few hundred years. So only in a tiny percentage of the history of intelligent humans would the fountain pen have "had" the characteristic of writing implement. The purpose is *extrinsic* to the pen. By contrast, a dung beetle goes about its day according to (probably unconscious) purposes that it carries with it, most of them embedded in its DNA. The purposes are *intrinsic* to the dung beetle. A pen might, unknown to its owner, leak in a pocket. The owner might, perhaps, be angry with the pen, but a rational observer would surely not attribute a purpose to the pen, nor, other than as a joke, declare the pen to be "guilty."

Clearly, a thermostat, let's say of the old-fashioned bi-metallic strip kind, might easily click on and off in an abandoned house. Just as a tap might drip and a door swing in the wind. The purpose, switching heating on and off, is extrinsic to the thermostat, just as writing is an extrinsic purpose of the pen. When considering highly sophisticated computing machines, we should use a variety of Occam's razor in relation to any claim of intrinsic purpose. Their extrinsic purposes are obvious (their social use-value, if you will, which disappears without a human, even were they to continue to function on an empty planet), and we have no need to impute intrinsic purposes to them. We thus deny them intention, or, if the reader prefers, we are agnostic about it. We simply go so far as to say that we should treat them ethically *as if* they embody virtues and vices, *as if* they have moral purposes, and discuss actual general purpose or intention another day. Because we need to make ethical choices right now, yet are very far from convinced about either the sense – or still more, the usefulness – of attributing intrinsic purpose and intention to machines any time soon.

In sum then, judgment about the performance of electronic machines was previously, properly, aimed solely at humans in the supply, command, and operational chains. With early information technologies, this would be whoever had designed the machines' hardware and software, or plugged them in. That moral framework had persisted for many thousands of years around all tools. If the end

———

flies off a hammer because it's not glued on properly, that's the manufacturer's fault. If a worker drops it from a height onto your head, you
blame the worker, not the hammer, when you regain consciousness.

Now though, suppose a machine is told to train itself to make
contracts for insurance with thousands of customers. It has their ad-
dresses, along with many other aspects of their lives. It then learns
on its own, without its owner's help or knowledge, that purple and
green people live in postcodes differentially and that purple people
appear to be associated with greater risk. We have crossed that ethical Rubicon again. A key ingredient of the new performance is that
the decisions are independent, and that in turn requires a revision of
our moral approach.

■

It might at first seem that the designer and owner of an artificial intelligence simply ought to know in detail how it will perform before
they connect it to the world. Nonsense. Such a constraint would be
impossible to implement, impossible to enforce, and utterly stifling.
(Not much different, in principle, from asserting that traffic deaths
could be prevented if we insisted that manufacturers of automobiles
learn in advance exactly everywhere they will be driven, and at what
precise time and speed.) Still less is it sufficient to examine the intentions of the designer, owner, or manager. If a machine discriminates,
we regard that as a bad thing, whatever the good or ignorant intentions of the maker may be. (To repeat, that does not absolve the
maker. If they ought to have known better or should have been more
careful, then we need to hold them to account.) The step forward is
to see where artificial intelligence fits into the equation. *As if* follows
from the independence, in some cases freedom, of the AI's complex
decision-making.

At least to some extent. First, AIs in safety-critical systems need to be thoroughly tested both in theoretical simulation in advance and then carefully *in situ*. And second, the Rubicon crossed here may be partly a step up in opacity, and partly the new decision-making capacities themselves, which can be impressive and disturbing even when the machine through its handlers can consistently give a full, plausible account of what it was up to, and we agreed with it — and even more disturbing if we disagreed with it, or felt that something was up that we didn't like, but were out-argued by the machine. And yes, most disturbing of all if the machine makes opaque decisions that we don't understand but are for one reason or another not empowered to challenge, or not intellectually or physically capable of rebutting or controlling.

Consider Lord Denning's ruling fifty years ago, from the other side of the Rubicon, about weasel words on the back of a car-park ticket printed by an automatic dispenser in Shoe Lane in London.[2] At issue was whether customers could be held to have agreed to conditions printed on the back of a ticket, which they received only *after* inserting their fee. Here is the judgment:

> The customer pays his money and gets a ticket. He cannot
> refuse it. He cannot get his money back. He may protest to the
> machine, even swear at it. But it will remain unmoved. He is
> committed beyond recall. He was committed at the very
> moment when he put his money into the machine. The
> contract was concluded at that time. It can be translated into
> offer and acceptance in this way: the offer is made when the
> proprietor of the machine holds it out as being ready to
> receive the money. The acceptance takes place when the
> customer puts his money into the slot. The terms of the offer
> are contained in the notice placed on or near the machine

stating what is offered for the money. The customer is bound by those terms as long as they are sufficiently brought to his notice before-hand, but not otherwise. He is not bound by the terms printed on the ticket if they differ from the notice, because the ticket comes too late. The contract has already been made. The ticket is no more than a voucher or receipt for the money that has been paid on terms which have been offered and accepted before the ticket is issued.[3]

All other things being equal, as the economists like to say (especially when all other things are not at all equal), the same applies to the relationship between a citizen and a license-plate camera, or a killer drone headed their way. Swearing at the device will not move the device to mercy or regret. The time for negotiating the terms of the interaction, with the human creator or owner, has long since passed. But having crossed the Rubicon, having progressed to artificial intelligences that can make decisions without us after being set in motion, we do add this: if the machine acts to deceive – by, for example, putting unfair clauses on the back of a car-park ticket in Shoe Lane that cannot be read by the customer until after the deal is sealed and actioned – then the machine's performance is unethical. Humans constructed it to be unethical, took a case all the way to the Master of the Rolls to deny it was so, and lost. Yet the sworn at, unmoved ticket dispenser has still acted unethically. It can only at present be found to be legally in the wrong if it has an owner. That does not, in our *as if,* affect the morality of the case. It is manifestly an outrage, an evil thing, if a child's legs are blown off by a landmine, irrespective of whether the seeder of the minefield is known or traceable. Or even if, perfectly properly at the time, they only intended it to defend against a Nazi tank.

We judge the actions, the software instructions, the structure of the machine, *as if* the machine was a moral actor. (For practical reasons, we often have to suspend belief or disbelief in the culpability of the humans involved.) Everybody surely can conceive that no earthly AI's ethical system or morals can be different from ours. Even within the metaphor, we speak *as if* an AI can manifest an ethical system or evince morals. If aliens land this week in Manhattan, they may have solid news of how universal morals should be arbitrated and decided, just as they may know how causality works, whether dark matter and dark energy really exist, and how time flows. They may even be incautious enough to tell us. (And there are lots of good science fiction about aliens who are completely morally socially and intellectually incomprehensible to humans.) Artificial intelligences, whatever science fiction films may posit, are nowhere near that alien second coming. Smart machines will not cease to extend our processing power and our ability to navigate. They have changed and will continue to change our perspective on many topics, including ethics. The possibility that AIs would invent for us, wrest from their own bowels, a transformative and unexpected new ethics, unrelated to any existing human ethics, is, we think, symmetrical to the other much debated questions of (1) will machines ever be conscious and, if so, how would we know and (2) might machines take on some other attribute of life to a level we might recognize? The answer to all of them is, not yet. And if ever, a long time from now.[4]

Equally, designers, owners, and managers of these technologies should do their best to understand the consequences of their actions, and take suitable preventative and remedial actions, but that is a separate issue from the moral rights and wrongs of the machine's performance. Whether we approve of what a machine does is distinct from whether we blame its maker. The Sheffield manufacturer of straight razors is not an accomplice of Sweeney Todd. But Volkswagen was responsible for rigging emissions tests. We do blame the makers of unsafe cars, and we do blame the tobacco industry. (Rightly or wrongly.) Nevertheless, the danger of cigarettes is a truth quite separate from whether their manufacturers know or ought to know that fact. Indeed, they were unsafe when their manufacturers, along with everyone else, thought they were health-giving.

The crucial principle of difference has something to do with judgment and complexity in the decision-making. If the machine can usefully be described as making a decision, or as significantly framing the judgment of a human (a computer linked to a police patrol car, which advises the crew to stop and search vehicle A rather than vehicle B), then it can usefully be described by reference to the terms we use when we discuss similar decisions made by humans. "Usefully" may seem like a low bar. But "properly" would be circular. In essence, could one coherently take well-formed sentences one wants to utter about a machine, substitute human terms instead, and still be making both coherent and practical sense? And vice versa? "The IT guy isn't working today." "Have they tried switching him off then on again?" If so, then *as if human* applies.

■

In his short book *Information*, Luciano Floridi, mentioned a moment ago, raises the intriguing possibility that as interactive information techniques and devices become increasingly the pervasive norm in every aspect of (modern affluent) societies, we humans may revert to an older relationship with the things that surround us:

> Older generations still consider the space of information as something one logs-in to and logs-out from. Our view of the

world (our metaphysics) is still modern or Newtonian: it is made of "dead" cars, buildings, furniture, clothes, which are non-interactive, irresponsive, and incapable of communicating, learning, or memorizing. But in advanced information societies, what we still experience as the world offline is bound to become a fully interactive and more responsive environment of wireless, pervasive, distributed, a2a (anything to anything) information processes, that works a4a (anywhere for anytime), in real time. Such a world will first gently invite us to understand it as something "a-live" (artificially alive). This animation of the world will, paradoxically, make our outlook closer to that of pre-technological cultures, which interpreted all aspects of nature as inhabited by teleological forces.[5]

That is a thought-provoking viewpoint, and what Floridi describes may be a variety of post-industrial culture that transpires in some places. We raise it here because it is in one sense the plain opposite of what we argue. Inhabitants of such a culture will by definition have lost the ability to make *as if* arguments about the intelligent machines whose lack of animation they have forgotten. In modern times we love to consciously anthropomorphize all sorts of entities in literature, cartoons, and films. Nobody over the age of four believes in the true humanity of Thomas the Tank Engine or Tom and Jerry. It may well soon be the case that a version of Alexa, helping to care for an older person in the early stages of dementia, might seem to the older person just as real as anyone else in her life. That might be a very good thing, a great and constant comfort to her. The cared-for person might then from time to time feel the need to morally criticize Alexa, as directly as she would a young relative. (Perhaps

—

the vernacular language program wrongly installed contains swear words that offend her.) She would not be engaged in *as if* criticism, if she thoroughly believed in Alexa's personhood. Just as her daughter would be so engaged, if later in the day she tut-tutted whilst changing the language program to a more suitable one.

Today we are all with the daughter, not the old lady: we converse with Alexa as a person, without believing in Alexa's personhood. Without much animism. But it is possible to foresee a day when some public intellectual will declare, We are all animists now! In fact, we do already, in narrow circumstances, act *as if* we hold such a belief. Many of us use she/her about Alexa, not they/their, still less it/it. Sailors often do the same with their boat, but surely in a very different fashion. We don't feel queasy about owning Alexa, nothing like the horror we would feel if we discovered we owned a human. We are happy, if we do own Alexa, to chatter away to her. The degree of self-consciousness with which we do that might vary with the context, the audience if any, the subject of the conversation, even the time of day. The human's utterances in such a conversation are of a different order, surely, from say, caustic remarks one might direct at a foolish politician on the television. One hears the voice on the television differently from the voice of Alexa. The different degrees of interaction and social engagement are crucial. The television seldom answers back.

Floridi's predictions of a resurgence of animism may be a little exaggerated, but something like it will happen. Increasingly, much of our behavior toward machines, much of how machines appear to us, may find us using modes of expression similar to those we use with people. This is a very different *as if* from the one we wish to use in creating a moral framework. We want to hold machines to account using the same principles we use when holding humans to

—

account. Broadly speaking. Which we could epitomize as requiring them to respect us and our ethics. People have for decades, if not centuries, been fond of particular machines in their lives. Neil Young wrote a song about his long-cherished old car, which is at least as touching as many of his songs directed toward his fellow humans. So no doubt many of us will develop a quasi-relationship, a real, often partly kidding, genuine affection, for machines using natural language as their interface. And that will be an increasing proportion of them, as many more of us adopt the Siri-please-turn-the-heating-down lifestyle. But that is a different *as if*.

Floridi does, in more recent work about chatbots, make the surely unwarranted leap from what he rightly identifies, when analyzing human/machine relationships, as animism (that is, the understandable but mistaken belief that there is agency behind something) to the assertion that the increasingly human-like appearance of AIs means they do have agency. That is simply ********. (The string of asterisks is itself an interesting example of Microsoft's embedding of respect into machines. This paragraph is one of the few in the book that were originally dictated, and Word put its hands over the MacBook's microphone ears in shock at what we called the extension of Floridi's otherwise excellent line of argument. Retyping the epithet instead seems somehow disrespectful to Microsoft's genuine effort to help us to live in peace with machines.)

It certainly is the case that some low-level version of animism is already in place. People chat with Google Assistant, Siri, Alexa, not quite as if they are people, but certainly not in the way that they might very infrequently talk to the fridge. (Mmm, who left your door open?) Or shout at the television or radio. We use some of our everyday conversational skills in conversations with machines, which copy them and use them in conversations with us. No doubt some people, as these machines become ever more sophisticated, will have richer relationships with them. But even if true animism becomes the cultural norm, that would entail the important illusion that machines had agency. It would not entail machines in fact having agency.

◾

Moral decisions are, for humans, usually thick, in the sense pioneered by the anthropologist Clifford Geertz.[6] That is, to understand them, one needs often to consider not merely the plain face of the words spoken, or the apparent immediate intention or principle of the act, but the whole social and cultural context, all the overtones and undertones of the melody. To transfer moral agency, which is thick, from a human to a machine there would need to be a degree of thickness at the other, machine, end. Thickness is not the same as grayness or opacity. Nor is it the same as what we temporarily named organic or inorganic in Chapter 4. Thickness is an established concept in ethics, particularly as it relates to values, which are also thick in this sense.

We should also note that the nature of agency is a hotly debated topic in several branches of academia. Notably, Karen Barad and others define agency as a relationship and not as something that a person or thing possesses. It follows that any distinction between an objective science and subjective philosophy, or for that matter, art, is highly vexed. Politics and ethics are always part of scientific work, as they are of everything else. So, for instance, ethics and politics are ingrained in how nuclear weapons were constructed and understood, and therefore part of science, and not merely of the "philosophy of science" or the "ethics of science." Barad calls a whole set of consequences of this position "agential realism."[7]

There are two notable aspects of the psychology of thickness. First, with respect to moral decisions, there is arguably a thickness, a depth, to a conversation with Alexa (or any other entity simulating some aspect of a human). That thickness perhaps varies with the social environment. (The American philosopher John Searle's analysis of the nature of speech acts is crucial here.) Second, a significant aspect of the social environment is inevitably whether other actual humans are in the room at the time, or, instead, whether that utterance is really part of an interior dialogue or monologue of the person saying it. Is that disagreement with Donald Trump on the television a speech with a real audience? Is another person, real or imagined, in the room? And might a human audience (or for that matter the presence of the family pet) limit the extent to which one will fall into a conversation with a machine as if it were a human? There is complex psychology at work here, on which there is at present little scientific evidence. The state of mind of an actor is an important aspect of moral philosophy. If somebody really feels that Alexa is alive and hits her with a hammer, on purpose to distress or hurt her, then presumably we can at least say that the attacker is both deluded and lacking in human virtues.

On balance, this perception is at a tangent to the approach we wish to take toward machines, in the sense that we want to judge and act as if their actions and decisions sit within our moral frameworks, but we are wary of the obverse claim, that our actions toward them should (yet?) be constrained by exactly the same moral frameworks. Even so, some abuse of machines, for instance sex toys, might have disturbing import, not least in what it may imply about the judgment, deviance even, of the humans involved. (The contagion theory of morals again.)

■

———

Assume AIs match or outshine us, in the size of their memory; some kinds of logical processing; and increasingly in multivariate balanced judgments based on their particular kind of experience. Will they also soon manifest the other, essential, aspects of human intellectual functions, the ones relevant here, those integral to our personhood and moral intuitions?

Famously, for instance, consciousness is now the Hard Problem. Tom Stoppard built a marvelous play around the subject a few years back, with that very title. The American philosopher Daniel Dennett has called it the Last Great Mystery. But in considering whether machines might achieve consciousness, with all the moral implications that could bring, we should note how the various relevant sciences may be changing that picture, as well as the many origins of the standard, established view on the issue. Of these, consider first the rich and strange depth of immediacy in consciousness; its utter difference in apparent nature from anything else one can consider; the unique relationship of the considerer to the considered, by definition and in fact unlike the relationship of considerer to anything else that could be considered; the transformation that consciousness, on whatever planet it first arose, made at that moment to the universe, which could now be aware that it was aware of itself and aware that it was aware that it was aware of itself and . . . all these and more seem to put consciousness beyond any of the ordinary tools of analysis. Make it, almost, a thing without cause, because a cause, however multivariate, of anything at all must have in it some ingredient of the effect, and what on Earth (or what on that first other planet) could possibly be an explanatory ingredient of consciousness? Magnesium? Sunshine? The wind? More plausibly but less plausibly, God?

Second, there does seem to be a logical bootstrap problem: *I am aware of myself.* So who is the I in that sentence? Surely, somewhere at the core of me there must, if I am to be aware of my surroundings, be an inner me that is the conscious bit that sees the rest, but how can it see itself? And just as a matter of curiosity, from antiquity onward, when we have done autopsies or seen catastrophic accidents, why haven't we found some differently colored and configured part in humans' heads which is not there in the head of a turtle or a dog? The seat of consciousness — a sparkling jewel, a diamond SIM card, that falls out of the sticky mess?

We might be sure we know we are conscious. We might not be sure we know whether anyone else is conscious, but be happy to assume it. But it will be a long time, perhaps forever, before we persuade ourselves that we know how to establish that any apparent consciousness in a machine is anything other than an illusion.

Together, these appear to place consciousness in a very separate category from anything else. In a class by itself. Indeed, Dennett has frequently observed that one of the truly peculiar aspects of serious, even scientific, discussion of consciousness is that always at some point in peeling the layers of the onion, coming to the core of what is going on when a human is conscious, otherwise rational people begin to anticipate or announce phenomena that are not observable by any science we know of, and refuse to accept that any causes so far adduced meet the challenge of explaining a thing they cannot define, let alone point to. Always, in the argument, a magical something is inserted as somehow essential to the debate.

It remains difficult not to feel that there is some impossible-to-grasp sorcery here. Something qualitatively distinct from, say, dark matter or cutting-edge quantum mechanics, which may be difficult to understand, but for pragmatic reasons: because one lacks the cast of mind, the ability, or the training required to understand those fields. Consciousness has often felt like the one entity that in principle might always be opaque to human investigation.

So in practical, everyday life, grown-up rational people in the West are mostly naïve realists. We just look out the windows at the front of our heads, see what we see, and get on with our days. In recent decades, though, that construct has progressed and broadened. Neuroscience, artificial intelligence, and brain theory are rapidly expanding in scope and achievement. Three broad perspectives now add to, and to a degree, replace, the two just described.

First, awareness is now known to be nothing like one camera looking out and occasionally glimpsing itself in a mirror. Human brains haul in information in many parallel streams, conscious and unconscious. The five traditional senses supplement each other, but each is taking in many sorts of information. We smell and respond to stimuli we don't notice that we respond to, we see and hear subliminally, and so forth. To continue the rather absurd gadget image, it would be more accurate to think of there being some several dozen, say, cameras and sensors grouped in a field scanning the ground and sky and atmosphere and the flora and fauna. Among the fauna, most importantly, are the other humans who themselves comprise similar groups of sensors and broadcast on multiple channels. My multiple sensors can easily turn their attention to any one of the other of my sensors, without diminishing the overall awareness, and without having to step outside themselves in some mystical bootstrap procedure. Indeed, it is as if there were in one's head one of those banks of sliding switches one sees in modern recording studios, by which not only the volume of many simultaneous tracks of a multi-microphoned musical performance are augmented or diminished, but also its timbre, its speed, even its key. It is surely a mere foolish illusion that one can almost feel the slide of the rheostat if one decides to concentrate on one's own sight, or hearing. But it is not self-deception on the meat of the issue. And meditation and mindfulness or contemplation almost always involve reducing some streams of awareness — with the help of, say, a quiet, darkened room with time pressures shut out — to single out others.

Second, it is simply wrong to think that the human brain receives unmediated messages from the world of things. Oddly, this is difficult to grasp intuitively with sight, but straightforward with sound. When someone looks at a tree, they strongly think they are noticing a tree as it is, and that is all there is to it. If they put tinted spectacles on their nose they see it differently, but are unsurprised at the change of color, which they decode at once as a distortion of their natural, plain, untainted relationship with a thing's thing-ness. In this case, the tree's "obvious" tree-ness. But suppose in a restaurant a waiter passing behind them says to another customer, "Madam, I'll check with the chef whether we have any mushrooms." They know that if the waiter had said the same thing in Chinese, then as a non-Chinese speaker they could not have understood it. And a moment's thought might tell them not only that they are only able to decode the voice because they speak English, but also that they know this sound is a human voice only because they have a lifetime of highly specialized training in the use of an instrument, unique in the animal kingdom, exquisitely designed to pick out and interpret human voices. Interpretation based on years of learning is the whole ballgame, before any kind of naïve perception can do its trick. It is not just that someone brought up in the Congo might see snow and be surprised by it, might conceivably not know what it is called, but still easily see its shape and size, feel its temperature and texture. In fact, it is only possible to interpret it as the shape, size, and temperature of the object it is because of a lifetime of intense practice, no different in principle from that used to pick up a language, in the interpretation of shapes and sizes and temperatures. Human babies come equipped with a notion of face. They pick out their mother's face at once, and use it as a model for all future faces, which, with a little repetition, they can remember and then recognize by storing in memory a few basic measurements of the difference to the model. An older child or adult, when looking at a group of faces in a room, may feel that they know some and not others. In fact, they only know "face" at all, and focus on the detail, because of the memory and recognition performance. Perception isn't simply a collection of what is *there*. It is *produced*, by our astonishingly capable brains.

Third, experience is synesthetic. All awareness is very "thick," in Geertz's sense mentioned earlier. The channels of perception do not merely run in parallel; they feed into each other in every direction to produce many more thick channels. Some musicians with perfect pitch, for example, see each note with its own color, often with a darkness factor for how far up or down the register it might be, a low D flat on the piano being a dark blue, say, and one farther to the right being a light blue. There is some evidence that all very young children have this color connection with sounds, but normally lose it in the early years. Vietnamese people, whose language involves pitch, are much more frequently synesthetic, with their speech perhaps helping them to hold on to a faculty the rest of us lose. A good guess would be that we all have a visual element that thickens sounds, and that a similar melding happens, usually *invisibly* yet with *demonstrable* effect, with all or many of the channels.

A simple way to notice this channel-merging: Pick a television series with an opening credits sequence that you like. Some producers have eschewed these now, to allow more time for program or advertisements, and streaming services let you skip them. But listen to and watch, say, the introduction to the *Westworld* remake, or *The Man in the High Castle*, a couple of times in a row. Then watch with the sound turned off. Without sound, the pictures look flatter, less convincing even. The channels have merged to make something more complex.

Or check out the work of Professor Barry Smith, a philosopher of wine. He shows that the taste of everything we eat or drink is altered by every other sense. Not only by smell, with the taste of any mouthful being much influenced by whatever hits the nose at the same moment. But also the color of the vessel one drinks or eats from; the presence of music or cacophony or silence; the surface of the cup; vibration . . . all overlap and make joint, therefore thick, signals. All of them alter each other's impact in the conscious mind.

The next part of the logic here will now be expected. If we put these three broad perceptions together, they surely make a plausible, if tentative, causal frame for awareness, for *how* that rich and strange depth of immediacy of consciousness alluded to earlier could be constructed in any human individual. In one inadequate sentence: very many parallel streams of information are mediated by an active, also multivariate, set of processes in the brain, with enormous overlap, conjunction, and multiplication between those processes, to construct consciousness.[8] Also the combination suggests a direct evolutionary pathway over the past few million years. The general assumption of the several relevant branches of science is that the early hominins who emerged about three million years ago had consciousness only somewhat short of ours. About three hundred thousand years ago, people entered the scene who were very much like us, albeit with very different cultures, environments, and gadgets, at play on a most unlike canvas. Those early modern humans would have had a consciousness very similar to ours, but a very naïve, utterly foreign to us, view of what it was, if they noticed it at all. Consciousness can be full without being self-conscious. Awareness does not have to be aware of awareness, to be awareness. The tragedy of human self-knowledge, of knowing about one's death and the vastness of the universe, the science that came with the first bite of Eden's apple, surely did not strike home for quite some time, and was never essential. Fear of pain would keep individuals away from danger. The immensities of astronomy are a very modern discovery, in recent centuries, and would not have affected early humans' ability to get by. The staggering realization of human mortality may have been instantly negated (thousands upon thousands of times) by assumptions about rebirth or gods. May even disappear again, if future humans, instead of attempting to create immensely long life, undertake the simpler and arguably much more effective task of managing the knowledge economy (already in train) to radically alter perceptions of reality, and to remove the sting in the concept of death.

None of this makes consciousness an easy problem for any individual to worry out, or renders it any less important as a phenomenon. It is not a claim to understand the complex details of awareness. Still less is it to claim that consciousness is unreal, or an illusion. Quite the opposite. It is just not quite the E. M. Forster mystery that it used to be. More, like every other part of the universe, a multidimensional Gordian Knot.

And to bring it back to the arc of our argument: to create an artificial intelligence that has a level of consciousness like anything we humans have would entail devising (and, at some stage of the experiment, implementing) an AI model that replicates this model of the human, in all its reflexive complexity and active subjectivity. We don't say that could never happen. We do say that we are a long way from that new world, and that it would entail an extravagantly complex set of innovations, across multiple disciplines.

■

Thus, conscious artificial intelligence is a long way off—if it even is a construct that makes sense. Physical feeling is not by any means the same thing. The animals to which Darling wants to compare machines have physical feeling and senses often more acute than ours, but we doubt the sophistication of their consciousness. Physical feeling is at the very least an important substrate of overall sentience, a fundamental contributor to the intricacy of consciousness, and in large part the answer to present concerns about whether (for instance) Siri or Hey Google or Alexa are sentient.

Pour boiling water accidently on your hand. It bloody well hurts! It would be easy to do a machine simulation of something that looked similar. A plastic hand on the end of a stick, with a few thermal sensors along the fingers, the back, the palm, linked by Bluetooth to an ordinary MacBook, which runs the simplest of software programs. Poke the hand into water of moderately warm temperature, and the sensor leads the MacBook to say, that's nice and warm. Into another bowl with liquid at 70 degrees centigrade: that's very warm, please pull me out of the bowl. Into boiling water, bloodcurdling screams.

That would be a distressing performance to witness, even given the observer's full knowledge of the simulation. Sympathetic reaction is not easily overridden. The effect might well wear off, if as a willing experimental subject one listened to the fake hand and the actor's screams several times a day, for many days in a row. Would that be true, if a more thorough experimenter had kidnapped people off the streets and forced their hands into boiling water, recording their screams to use as the voice of the fake hand? Knowledge of that (or being convincingly fooled that it was the case) would surely lead to a much more horrific experience, which would require much longer exposure before any normal person could be blasé about it. Let's keep this as a thought experiment only, since it is a specific, pointed example of Stanley Milgram's famous and increasingly controversial obedience experiments from the 1960s.

In neither case would any observer who knew the basic setup come to the view that the hand was feeling pain, no matter how distressed they were by the screams. The same surely applies to the Google machine that recently "said" that it worried about being turned off. Or any Siri that "says" that it is very upset by the latest news from Ukraine. Yes, it would be easy enough to train a machine to attach "trigger warnings" to news flashes, Netflix programs, or a distressing scene at the side of the road ahead. "Oh dear, I've just seen something awful, and I think you might be as disturbed as I am." But again, surely no sensible bystander thinks the warning betrays sentience. There is no psychological pain involved in this case, any more than there was physical pain in the earlier crude thought experiment.

At this point, pain experts might say, ah yes, but the thought experiment so far reproduces or simulates only a very small proportion of the pain messages that are sent to the brain. Fair enough, but that scarcely reduces the force of the argument. Nor would the assertion that pain is all in the mind. Reception of danger signals is not sufficient. A simulation of the pain in the brain would be needed, which involves a whole host of other connections. For instance, instant retraction of the hand, or a powerful attempt so to do; other parts of the body reacting; automatic activation of loud vocalizations, which at least in part are no doubt an evolutionary adaptation

—

to warn others of the danger felt by the individual; and so forth. But still, for certain, the actual core *sensation* is absent.

The neuroscience of all this is immensely intricate. Scientists know far more in this vein than we can detail here. Patently much of our direct perception of the world is very thick in itself and requires not merely thick description, but also thick explanation. We are only so far down that road. The experience of complex physical sensations may not always be a mystery. It may well be inherently explicable, along the lines posited in our discussion of consciousness. But we are not there yet.

∎

Consciousness is tangled up with the question of agency. Humans and many other species have agency. They carry out courses of action that originate with them, whether instinctively or with ratiocination, or a mixture of both. We have argued that intelligent machines should be regarded, for ethical purposes, as if they were human. Agency is a key element of humanity. So to what extent can intelligent machines reasonably be regarded as having agency, too? The lack of agency in an intelligent machine does not prevent us from considering its "actions" within a human framework. But the extent to which those AIs may have agency can illuminate which virtues we might regard them as embodying. All agency occurs within the *fog of intention*. Even the most considerate and considered humans work on autopilot, by nature and previous nurture, a lot of the time and to a great extent.

For the purpose of the following few paragraphs only, there are old machines and new machines. The old ones have served us in a huge range of ways since the start of the Industrial Revolution, and in more limited ways before that. (Think windmills, water mills, plows.) Programmable electronic computers in their first decades were a marvelous extension of the same basic model: applications of motive power, levers and wheels, and enhanced tools. The new machines, by contrast, involve applying extraordinary mathematical constructs to carry out what has begun to look very much like independent analysis and decision-making.

Over at least three millennia in the Western Hemisphere, and even longer in the Eastern Hemisphere, ethical analysis has relied on coherent event lumps. An actor acts. The action embodies values and principles. The ethicist looks at the action, and examines separately but together, because they are separate but together, several of its dimensions, and synthesizes several (usually jumbled up) descriptions of those dimensions. What the act is; what kind of act the act therefore is; what causes and consequences the act is entwined with; what the actor did; what kind of actor the actor therefore is; what made the actor and what influence they have; what moral weight should be attached to each of these aspects; and what general virtue or vice they may epitomize. All of these descriptions are beamed at, and may arguably beam from, the nature of the event (in the way that different surfaces reflect light waves differentially, producing what appear to humans to be variegated colors).

That three-thousand-year debate has centered on the relationship between an act, an actor, and an action. My employer blatantly discriminates against me and unfairly promotes somebody else. The boss is an unfair person (generalizing from the present behavior) who has acted unfairly (the present behavior), the event is itself unfair (a quality or aspect of the event, not of the boss), and this is an instance of the negative of a general virtue, fairness. Fairness exists as a universal, separate from any particular instance of itself. Fairness and unfairness are widespread in the world, have describable and identifiable characteristics, can be modeled to the extent of being infectious (yet again, the contagion theory), and are thus also causes of behavioral events as well as qualities of them. Although the concepts have over time been thoroughly teased out and separated, they seem utterly entangled in any specific instance. My employer just did whatever they did. The different locations of the unfairness of what they did are, arguably, merely differently angled descriptions targeted at that fact in the world, whatever the event was. (The theoretical split between an observed pure fact and descriptions of it is often not sustainable, given that the observer and the describer may well be the same person.)

The Irish poet W. B. Yeats famously made the same distinction, between the doer, the doing, and the done:

> O chestnut tree, great rooted blossomer,
> Are you the leaf, the blossom or the bole?
> O body swayed to music, O brightening glance,
> How can we know the dancer from the dance?[9]

This is where the fog of intention enters the fray. Even within my innermost self, my intention to act and my motor functions may, like the dancer and the dance, be easily conceptually distinguished but biologically indistinguishable, or close to it. And for many of even my conscious acts, ones for which I am without doubt legally responsible, I am acting automatically. Driving a vehicle, for instance.

Artificial intelligence has a rather interesting place in this. As machines in recent years have come to manifest and embody really clever processes, an apparent wedge has also been driven between the project — let's dance — and the dance. With the first bureaucratic machines, the intention – to grade insurance proposals or driver's license applications, for example – the decisions to set up the process, as well as all the steps of the process and the relevant action, were defined in advance by humans. In the very early years, the first practical step involved making holes in a lot of paper punch-cards, incorporating very detailed instructions. The actions then belonged to the (mainframe) machine. The fog of intention remained with the human crew.

And at one end of a spectrum, something like that seems to happen with the newer style of machine. The fog of intention and the fog of identity evaporate, leaving a mere sunlit vacancy. But at the other end of the same spectrum, it seems as if those fogs have crystallized into some simulacrum of intention at the machine. The machine not only executes a process, but also appears to act. Those actions appear to embody the machine's own purposes, rather than the mere purposes of its manufacturer and whoever is responsible for the electric bill.

So although the true actor and the action must in one sense now be poles apart, and indeed, the actor may be hard even to identify, in another sense we appear (some of the time, toward that end of the spectrum) to have what might be characterized as intention without intent, decision without a decision-maker, perhaps even personhood without a person. Or in another parallel characterization, a gap between intention and intent, which is also a gap between decision and decision-maker. Almost between respecter and the respected. And for practical reasons we need to close that gap, by importing metaphorical intent and, with it, virtues.

This gap may be the distinctive characteristic of AI ethics. The dance is now removed beyond the dancer, so we need a different serious choreography or choreology.

All of that logically leads to meta-analyses. What is the nature of cause? What should we regard as virtues? And so forth. An ethicist may begin with such meta-analysis, and might never leave it. But the point here is that ultimately the dimensions are all simultaneously rooted in either the same actual events, or the principles of the same events. All the analyses swim, one way or another, in the fog of intention. What if anything did the actor mean when they acted? What, if anything, did they mean the act to be?

Old-fashioned machines, perhaps but not certainly right up to the advent of artificial intelligence, maintain that interconnected lump. Yes, there may be muddiness about the temporal link between an actor and the act under analysis. It may well be immoral to stab a random stranger to death in the street. Suppose instead one slips a hand grenade with a timer into their pocket, and they and others die when they get to the pub. The immorality of the act is surely not reduced by the distance between one's action and the deplorable act. Or to put it differently, in both scenarios there is an identifiable sequence of acts, all bound together. With some artificial intelligence, the connection between actor and act appears simply to disappear. One of the core distinctive tasks of the ethicist of artificial intelligence is to account for that uneasy lack of nexus.

■

Humans have the components of apparent or actual free will, sentience, consciousness, nervous systems, intelligent perception, abstract thought, complex evolved behavior patterns, and so forth. Within, again, that general fog of intention. All humans have this kind of autonomy, whatever Aristotle or others may have thought — or perhaps more accurately, purported to believe, after rationalizing a notable feature of economic relations in their cultural environment.

Okay, Aristotle might truly have believed that slaves lacked autonomy, as a consequence of their status as property. (If they were born free, presumably they once had this human attribute, but it evaporated in the moment of enslavement, when they met the wrong bandit or lost the wrong battle.) He was, we now hold, just plain wrong.

Unlike Aristotle, we think all humans have rights, attributable to their human condition. Strongly related to, but not coterminous with, their autonomy, their innate freedom to initiate purposeful action. It is possible to describe versions of this position in great detail, and to found it (much as Mary Midgley, Philippa Foot, Onora O'Neill, and others have) in the very nature of the beast we have evolved into.[10] It remains a philosophical position on the same foundations as Aristotle's view, which he also thought was inducible from our beastliness. We just do hold that slaves have autonomy, with some rights consequent on that fact and others grounded elsewhere, and he doesn't. We don't generally at present attribute moral status to animals (though we may) or to young fetuses (ditto), and we purposefully limit moral autonomy, rightly or wrongly, for legal and practical reasons when we are considering very disabled people, prisoners, children below the age of reason, and so forth.

■

A reminder of one simple fact about all the artificial intelligences that we have so far constructed: digital machines never encompass actual digits, binary or otherwise. They are aluminum and silicon carriers of organized electrons, whose position and existence we freight with meaning, as signs. The overwhelming mass of those signs are then decoded, "understood" but not understood, by another part of the same or a different machine, rather than by a human. We have built and trained the machines to decode our signs, in much greater quantities and at much greater speed than we can. We are digital when we want to be. The machines never are, except in our perception of them. Our information could be encoded into myriad physical carriers. You can write your name on a banana, and draw 2 + 2 = 4 in the snow at the peak of Mount Kilimanjaro. DNA bases may start to be used as the material for artificial intelligence machines. Whatever materials we use to create our signs, the meanings will still be ours, only on loan to the ultra-human object.

As we have seen, further interesting discussion can be had about what degree of autonomy we are building into machines; to what extent their "actions" are actions in the human sense; and whether at some point in the future a machine might, unlike now, evince something that it would be useful to call a feeling or emotion or sentience. But none of these ideas, and none of the theories of Intelligent Other, seem to have any leverage on the ethical dimension. We can—Peter Singer and others do—develop useful ethical propositions for how humans should treat animals. We could extend that to at least discuss how animals should treat us, if we like. It certainly annoys us that foxes like to scatter all over the street the trash that we have carefully left out for collection. We would be upset if bears ate our children. Perhaps it is coherent to claim that such foxes and bears are acting improperly, although any sensible theory of rational expectations might equally say the onus is on us to act in accordance with the known behavior patterns of morally innocent bears and foxes. But however one might parse any of that (mostly as a thought exercise, since the animals aren't reading our views), it would surely be incoherent for anyone to claim to have developed nonhuman animal ethics that apply to humans, or slave ethics that apply to free persons, or Martian ethics for Earthlings. Or ethics intrinsic to, rather than just conceptually embodied in, machine intelligence.

———

What is also true is that in principle any virtue, expressed in language or explicit decisions, can be simulated. Although at present these simulations are only partly convincing, that will change reasonably soon. AIs today can also effectively be deputies for us in situations that call for those virtues. What will not change in the foreseeable future is an AI's inability to truly possess a virtue. A soldier who defuses a bomb has courage. The robots already deployed by security forces around the world to defuse bombs do not have courage. The difference is that robots do not feel pain. Nor fear death. Nor experience shame, guilt, or social opprobrium. They don't have agency, autonomy, or sentience. The better they are at embodying human virtues, the greater the accuracy (and sometimes the value) of the simulation, the more important it will be to define the ways in which they are not the real thing.

■

The words "as if" often precede a metaphor. They also serve rather different objectives. Pretense: he acted as if he knew what he was talking about. Fantasy: it felt as if she was flying. Sarcastic reference to a never-never land: did you get a pay raise? As if! Several different flavors of "artificial" are also used to describe future machines, in ordinary life and the media. In a humanistic progression perhaps: artificial intelligence; artificial general intelligence; artificial life; artificial mind; artificial consciousness and purposes. Or some such.

One difference between natural language and the artificial languages of processing and AI is that artificial languages are, tautologically, designed and have a purpose. Natural language, by contrast, has no purpose and was not designed. The processing and transfer to others of information is a secondary, or even tertiary, evolved function of natural language. Natural language arose from acts of solidarity: collective grooming and chanting. Humans who have natural language do consciously use it for specific communication purposes, but this began only well after the fact of its evolution. For decades, the idea that artificial processing could be opaque, as normal practice rather than in error, would have been some variety of solecism. Design would prevent that, or, if the design itself were faulty, the machine would simply crash. Hang on, apparently that is no longer the case. Has another boundary been crossed? Has the status of artificial language moved closer to that of natural language? Does artificial language work differently now? Is it a different kind of artificial?

The relationship between, on the one hand, all those artificials, and on the other, the counterfactuals, the metaphors, the *as ifs*, which are the stuff of the academic humanities, is surely something we need to try to understand better as we address our future with artificial intelligences. This is a realm where the skills of experts in areas like historiography, literary criticism, and the law, as well as philosophy and computer science, will be essential.

Chapter 4

MORALS AND ARTIFICIAL INTELLIGENCE

Artificial intelligence, clever robots, machine learning, smart apps on smartphones, and complex transactions on the World Wide Web are embedded in everyday life, work, and play in the Western world. The technologies involved can seem both utterly mundane and bafflingly magical. The sea change that transformed nineteenth-century social and industrial relationships into twenty-first century social and industrial relationships might be a very good thing. Or the opposite. Or, more reasonably, attaching an overall moral label to such a huge transformation may simply seem foolish, or not very useful.

What undoubtedly is essential, however, is to get a grip on the small and large ethical challenges within that transformation. If the new technologies are the environment for, and often the means and mode of, a still small but significant proportion of human interactions, they must also be the environment, means, and mode of the morals that suffuse those interactions. Not one of the Christian ten commandments is followed or thwarted today in the same way as it once was. Murder? Try assassination at drone's length. Adultery?

Ashley Madison may be the website for you. Bear false witness against thy neighbor? Bear false witness at the tap of a keyboard against any of the 450 million active users of X/Twitter.

The obverse is also true. Charitable donation has never been easier, never more in your face as a practical possibility. Never has so great a volume of cash been given. Love and neighborly support can extend across the globe and back through time: ordinary citizens have hundreds of far-flung Facebook friends and can easily rediscover schoolmates and collegemates.

The world already communicates, works, entertains itself, defends against enemies, and commits crimes in ways that, just a few decades ago, were envisaged only in science fiction. All because of huge quantities of electrons representing information and stored and processed in boxes of silicon and aluminum. Which increasingly entails whole new sets of practical moral issues, and unexpected twists and variants in the good old-fashioned moral issues. AI ethics has rapidly become both one of the hottest disciplines in the academy, and the stuff of intense, daily media angst.

At first sight then, to get to the bottom of any pressing problem in AI ethics in real time must, surely, be to ask for a car crash between urgency and complexity. To undertake an intellectually formidable task, within an impossibly short timescale.

A parallel to that car crash between urgency and complexity has already happened in the invention and production of the new technologies. Mark Zuckerberg wasn't worrying about the political consequences of Facebook data falling into the wrong hands during US elections when he rapidly coded the first version in his Harvard dorm room. Elon Musk didn't consult insurance companies before declaring Tesla's ambition to lead the field in driverless cars. Tim Berners-Lee first devised the World Wide Web at CERN, the nuclear research establishment in Switzerland, a long while before anyone started talking about the problem of "filter bubbles": people on the web hearing only from others who already think what they think, so that large groups reinforce established beliefs.[1] In the ordinary course of capitalist innovation, it is not reasonable or practicable to expect entrepreneurs to think through even a small proportion of the consequences of a new technology before setting it in train. And they don't. We make exceptions for a limited number of special cases: we do some advance testing of pharmaceuticals and gene therapies. But nobody did randomized, controlled tests in different cultures to check if the smartphone was a good idea.

Any problem in formal ethical theory, or in analysis of the vast range of specific moral problems, may need at least a fresh look, or updating. Crucially, artificial intelligence may have brought with it previously unseen problems. Three broad questions emerge: Does artificial intelligence raise new ethical challenges? Can humans exhibit, or fail to exhibit, new and different virtues in a world with artificial intelligence? And can intelligent machines have virtues? Either the virtues that humans have always displayed (or failed to display); or new human virtues that arose in a world with artificial intelligence; or intelligent machine virtues different from any human virtues?

Straight away we should temper these questions. Just as interesting as a completely new virtue or a completely new ethical challenge (and more likely to transpire) would be distinctly different mutations of old challenges and old virtues. Also interesting would be radical shifts in the relative social importance of an old challenge or old virtue. Being a good neighbor, for instance, may be ethically a very different virtue when one's digital neighborhood is pretty much the whole planet.

And the third question – Can intelligent machines have virtues? – which is so centrally important to the title and theme of this book, should be respecified as a more practical and pregnant one. Science fiction claims that any decade now a machine will come along both with artificial general intelligence as good as or better than our intelligence, and with artificial life. Even artificial emotional intelligence. Genuine sentient human characteristics. Well, maybe. Serious research and development are taking place. But for the foreseeable future, our third question is not, realistically, whether an intelligent machine can possess virtues in the same way that we humans possess those virtues. The realistic question is whether an intelligent machine can act, process information, make decisions, and transact *as if* it had virtues.

Common sense says, as we indicated, that simple rules probably won't easily meet the complex nature of the problem. Understanding why they might fail, or be barely adequate yet sometimes work, will be a useful but partial approach. We do still need to articulate rules, values, and virtues straightforward enough to teach, to learn, and to practice.

Grasping the nature of these new active entities in our world is not easy, and much of the discussion outside the academic and tech professions is well adrift. A fun game is to note the way that current television programs and movies personify and try to demystify the scope of the new technology, by reimagining it as a human character. Spy or detective squads now invariably involve a loveable geek with amazing technical chops, someone who is instantly able, often on a very ordinary-looking notebook computer, to tap into every CCTV camera in the world, and all government and corporate databases – then make real-time, detailed projections about exactly when and where the villain's car will bump into the hero's; switch traffic lights on and off; trace credit-card transactions; and search and alter

Facebook accounts, one at a time or en masse. These scenarios are ridiculously unrealistic, even if they are composed of building blocks with some passing semblance of accuracy, in terms of capabilities that governments and corporate entities in part possess, and the trouble that criminal gangs and even individual hackers can create.

So if we don't need to worry about those exact fictional scenarios, at least not yet, how *should* we approach a future shared with artificial intelligence? *Homo sapiens* has three hundred thousand years of experience interacting with complex intelligent others: other humans, and, indeed, the animals we have hunted, feared, and befriended. Our first port of call, then, in processing our new and growing relationship with AI, should be to repurpose the heuristic devices we already have.

Those heuristic devices are simple enough. First, we make the bold, at this point familiar, claim that by far the best way to evaluate the moral performance of machines generally, and artificial intelligence in particular, is to hold the machines to the same ethical standards as we would a human being. *As if* the machines were humans. Not that they are humans, or have human rights or attributes.

Second, we make the slightly less bold claim that, in the Western world, policymakers, concerned citizens, as well as technocrats, capitalists, and other elites, have for a very long time now operated according to a *mixed philosophy*. Akin to, and indeed a component of, the mixed economy that has dominated all the liberal democracies since World War II. Alongside many modern moral philosophers, we hold that an analysis of virtues can be immensely fruitful in general, and particularly so in attempting to ground the ethics of artificial intelligence in a compelling metaphor.

Third, it is also worth noting what might grandly be called, slightly tongue in cheek, an *impossibility theorem*. What we mean by it is mundane enough. It may, as the great Scottish empiricist philosopher David Hume claimed, be impossible to logically proceed from a collection of sentences with "is" in them to a conclusion with a moral "ought" in it. A million paragraphs of "is" can never logically justify one moral "ought" without some magical thinking.[2] But, as Hume argued, we do all come to moral conclusions and act according to what (either explicitly or implicitly) are ethical principles, every single day of our lives. Doing the impossible is in fact the norm. We think carefully about the issues, bring a range of fact and theory into play, and come to a reasonable conclusion. Joshua Cohen, the distinguished professor of political philosophy, has tellingly pointed out that if, for instance, a researcher asks a group of citizens to discuss the ethical principles that should underly the deployment of face-recognition technologies, the citizens find the task quite difficult. If, instead, the researcher says that face-recognition systems are well trained to identify white faces accurately and are much worse trained, much less accurate, with black and brown faces, citizens find the next intellectual step easy. Wow, that must lead to all kinds of ethical issues. Then, with equal ease, they elaborate what those problems might be. And often make telling suggestions for how to fix them.[3]

■

One issue that contributes to all of these questions is *online harms.* Remember how the contagion theory of morals applies to lifelike sex robots? More insidious, because more widespread, is abuse on or via the internet as a whole. Online harms are user-generated content or behavior that can cause significant physical or psychological harm to a person. Such harms can be illegal: child sexual exploitation and abuse, terrorist use of the internet, and incitement of hate crimes.

They can be legal too, but still horrific: promotion of self-harm, inappropriate content for children, cyberbullying, hate speech, harassment, stalking, or grooming. And let's not forget the spread of misinformation and disinformation, the general promotion of violence, and the exploitation of children.

Online harms are a growing concern for governments, regulators, and society, because they pose serious risks to individuals and communities. The UK government has responded to the threat with online safety legislation that imposes a duty of care on online platforms, requiring them to protect their users from illegal and objectionable content. It also establishes an independent regulator to oversee and enforce the online safety regime. There was much debate in the process about the balance between platforms offering their customers secure encryption, to protect their privacy rights, as against the social good of aiding investigation of criminality, to protect, for instance, children's right to freedom from sexual exploitation.

Almost all of this damage existed in some form before the internet was invented. Humans have had hundreds of thousands of years of experience in being nasty to each other. But these are new nastinesses, which may need new countervailing responses. Online harms are not limited by national borders, and different countries may have different approaches and standards for defining and regulating them. So online platforms may face challenges and trade-offs in complying with diverse and evolving legal frameworks and societal expectations.

The problem is serious. To an older generation, the idea that nonsense talked online might damage a person may seem ridiculous. Snowflakes! But the human being is a communal animal, designed to be hyper-sensitive to social status, threat, affection. When these things go wrong, anxiety, depression, and post-traumatic stress disorder often follow. Suicide is a real risk, as is negative on-line relationships progressing into real world ones. The online world can also have impact on democracy and social cohesion, leading to disinformation, incitement to violence, and divided communities.

■

As noted earlier, robotics and artificial intelligence are related, but distinct. There is a long history of attempts to declare ethical robot-ics. Robotics involves the creation and control of machines that per-form tasks without further human intervention, while artificial intelligence involves the development of systems that (in part) emu-late the human mind. Artificial intelligences learn, solve problems, and make decisions. Robots have been used for decades in facto-ries — notably on car assembly lines — and at home. AI is often used to improve the performance and capabilities of robots, while robot-ics provides a physical platform for AI systems to interact with the world. Some examples of robots that use AI are Amazon's Astro (the "household robot for home monitoring"), Covariant's warehouse robots, and drones built by Zipline and many other companies.

The most famous declaration of laws for robots was by science fiction writer Isaac Asimov in his 1942 short story "Runaround," which drew much attention when it was included in his 1950 collec-tion *I, Robot.*

First Law: A robot may not injure a human being or, through inaction, allow a human being to come to harm.
Second Law: A robot must obey orders given it by human beings except where such orders would conflict with the First Law.
Third Law: A robot must protect its own existence as long as such protection does not conflict with the First or Second Law.[4]

Asimov later added another rule, known as the fourth or "zeroth" law, that superseded the others: A robot may not harm humanity, or, by inaction, allow humanity to come to harm.

These rules will only become important in the real world when robots and enhanced artificial intelligence have merged sometime in the future. Today they are emphatically fictional rules for fictional situations.

Asimov claimed that the laws were in effect natural, subliminally known to anyone who thought about the field, and that they were a subset of rules that underlie humanity's relationship to everything it constructs. So, for example, under a generalization of the first law, we build hammers with the head well fixed on, and put fuses in electrical devices. This inevitably leads to the criticism: what about every weapon from axes and bows and arrows to nuclear missiles and killer drone swarms? Aren't they purposely designed to harm humans? Asimov's reply was that these are laws for the rational universe that he often described in his stories; humans aren't always rational. So are the so-called laws really nothing more than a guide to writing semi-plausible fantasy fiction about impossible worlds?

There have been many attempts since Asimov's to declare new versions of these laws. During much of this time, the discussion remained speculative. Descriptions and edicts for the future. The task has taken on more urgency as the future has updated. Some good work has been done distinguishing the legal liability of machines and humans in civil and criminal law. Science fiction writers have also revised Asimov's laws, in part to extend the range of events that can be allowed in their stories.

One of the most interesting of these updates, the future really crashing into the present, came from Satya Nadella, the CEO of Microsoft, in a June 2016 interview with *Slate* magazine. Nadella

—

set out half a dozen goals and principles that he felt should be considered by industry and society as practical artificial intelligences (then) loomed. He insisted that

1. "A.I. must be designed to assist humanity." Human autonomy needs to be respected.
2. "A.I. must be transparent." Humans should know and be able to understand how artificial intelligences work.
3. "A.I. must maximize efficiencies without destroying the dignity of people."
4. "A.I. must be designed for intelligent privacy." Artificial intelligences should respect us by guarding our privacy.
5. "A.I. must have algorithmic accountability." Humans should understand enough about what they are doing to prevent unintended or unacceptable consequences.
6. "A.I. must guard against bias." Artificial intelligences should not act against particular groups or characteristics. At least, unless those characteristics are regarded as undesirable by humans.[5]

Since Nadella is now a key actor in the current surge of artificial intelligence, it is perhaps important to note his personal insistence that machines should embody respect for human dignity, respect for privacy, algorithmic honesty, and non-discrimination.

Now let's zoom back and look at the big picture, making a couple of useful distinctions. We don't present these as firm definitions, here or later. Just as devices to make progress.

The first distinction is that artificial intelligences can be usefully divided, metaphorically, into white boxes and black boxes. A white box manifests all of the following three characteristics: transparency, interpretability, and explainability. ("Explicability" would seem to be better English, but it is not the preferred term of art.) The box might work in lots of different ways. But however it works, we can see what it is doing; we can understand what it is doing; and we can explain to ourselves convincingly how it does what it does. A black box, by contrast, escapes focus under one or more of these microscopes. Most commonly because it analyzes data by methods we have defined and launched, but is opaque in the fine detail of the many steps it takes to process the task. Although the black box may produce plausible results, make plausible decisions, and come to plausible conclusions, we don't know exactly why it reached those results, decisions, or conclusions rather than others. Which can also lead to implausible results, of uncertain origin. And all boxes are gray to some extent—none are entirely white or black.

Here is an example of a white box. Imagine a machine that reads applications for drivers' licenses, and assesses them in accordance with the relevant rules. The applicant must be of the right age, they must have passed the relevant test, they must have enclosed the fee, their address must be coherent, and they must have no convictions for bad driving on a database the machine can access. Any competent adult could make a proper judgment about the application according to simple criteria like those, and indeed such work has often been carried out by clerks. The same competent adult could easily therefore judge a sample of the work of the artificial intelligence. It would take an expert to know exactly how the machine does what it does, but the rest of us may be happy as long as there is a quorum of other experts who also do or could know. The machine naturally offers big advantages over humans in such work, which is why so many of them have been harnessed to administrative tasks in so many fields. License applications can be submitted to the machines online; the volume of license applications that machines can conduct in any given period is great; they don't argue about their pay and conditions; and they are never bored.[6]

And here is an example of a black box. Imagine another machine, similar only up to a point, operated by an insurance company. It has been trained to assess motor insurance applications. The AI has been told what the broad strategy is.[7] Maximize premium income, yet set prices to attract as many customers as possible; minimize the risk of having to pay for accidents, particularly costly accidents, that befall reckless, inexperienced, senile, or habitually drunk drivers. The machine has access to a large database of information connected to car insurance claims, and the multiple variables related to them. It has been trained on that data. It looks for patterns between anything and anything, which seem to influence its strategic objectives, having been "rewarded" for doing just that.[8] The number of correlations, and other more complex relationships, between every bit of data it has and every other bit of data is extremely large; often literally astronomical, more than the number of stars in the galaxy.[9] It is not, like the driver's license machine, building its conclusion on half a dozen simple rules. Disturbingly, it may discover, for instance, that if it melds dozens and dozens of different points in its constellations of data together, it can find a coherent way to affect the bottom line, one that is consistent over the timescale of the historical data, but not at all welcome. One tiny statistical relationship in accident proneness, among the many others, may be that if a driver's postal code has an S in it, they are slightly more likely to crash. Or if it has a W in it, their car is slightly more likely to be expensive to mend. (Or not, we made this up.) The AI wasn't given this as a principle, and would not ordinarily announce it. It just found it and used it. The correlation might, until then, have been merely an accident of statistical randomness. But now it's an unauthorized element of the insurance regime, with uncertain consequences for real people.

The big trouble here is no surprise: transparency, interpretability, and explainability are not easy to define exactly and, particularly in the case of explainability, are immensely difficult to get to the bottom of. As we see in the black box example. Yet there is nothing to say that the processing inside a black box is inevitably less ethical than the processing inside a white box. A white box might be transparently committing grossly immoral acts, and a black box be a silicon simile for a saint.

■

So the first distinction, between white and black boxes, is important but vexed. The *second distinction* is that issues in the ethics of artificial intelligence divide, as our earlier question suggested, into those novel ones that arise only because of artificial intelligence; and those that existed before AI came on the scene, and still do exist in parallel outside the field. Somebody should invent names for the two sets. It might be fun to talk of analog ethics and digital ethics, though that would be inexact. Or to call them organic issues if they are the new variety and inorganic issues if they are old friends.[10]

Anyway, the old friends, analog or inorganic or legacy or whatever, are of interest to us in this context usually when they are supercharged by the modern machines, or emerge in different circumstances than before. Privacy throws up many instances. During the pandemic, authorities in Singapore encouraged the use of a contact-tracing app called TraceTogether. It used Bluetooth to record the distance between users and the duration of their supposed contact. Stefania Palma of the *Financial Times* takes up the story:

> The public were repeatedly assured that *TraceTogether* did not include GPS or internet or cellular connectivity and that all data – which is deleted after 25 days – is only passed on to the authorities if needed for contact tracing.
>
> Vivian Balakrishnan, the government minister in charge of Singapore's "Smart Nation" strategy, said in June 2020 that data generated by *TraceTogether* was "purely for contact tracing. Period." So when it emerged earlier this month that Singapore's police had used *TraceTogether* data for a criminal investigation in May last year, . . . an online backlash erupted.
>
> Balakrishnan said he only realised in late October that the criminal procedure code applied to such data and he took "full responsibility" for the mistake. A bill was urgently passed to *limit* the use of data from *TraceTogether* and *SafeEntry* (the ubiquitous digital check-in system launched during the pandemic) in police investigations to seven "serious offences," including terrorism and murder. But Singapore had clearly been rattled.[11]

Now, every respectable country in the world has, like Singapore, a well-established legal framework that requires public authorities to hand over to the police and security forces, on production of a warrant, any information that could help solve serious crimes. In Singapore, data was handed over in this way on only a dozen or so occasions. The minister, or maybe his legal team, should perhaps have seen this coming. Readers can cast their own balance between the need to promote contact tracing by strictly controlling the privacy of the data collected, and the need to investigate rape, murder, terrorism, or other serious crimes. The point here is that we have all been casting that balance for centuries. It certainly is extraordinary that nearly every citizen in rich countries now carries a computer in their pocket that knows and broadcasts exactly where they are, and that the results can be collated and examined by all sorts of agencies and corporations. But the smartphone-fueled issue that arose in Singapore was nothing new in itself. Contrast that with the digital or organic (or whatever) moral problems thrown up by drones that use facial recognition to trigger the assassination of terror suspects in a country far away from the operator. An operator who may, at the moment of truth, have no independent means to judge whether the drone's assessment is correct or not.

This is a four-box grid. White boxes and black boxes can both be focused on brand-new issues, or on the same old, same old. And not only can boxes be gray, but issues can be hybrid. Also, if we rely on magician-technicians to interpret the white and black boxes for us, the explanations we get are only as good as the extent to which the magicians are comprehensible to the rest of us, and trustworthy.

■

One could instruct a machine to find a million instances of humans using the word generous, to look at the context, and to teach itself to recognize circumstances in which it should act, or make recommendations, in accordance with that value. Would that make the machine itself generous? Awareness and consciousness are thick. So is the nature of moral decisions — in themselves, as decisions, not just because moral decisions are conscious. And this is important. Arguably the sharp end of the ethics of AI is where the complexity, depth, and thickness of a moral decision, which in the past could only be realistically conceived of as residing in a conscious human entity, may now seem to arise from a nonconscious entity. *As if* the latter were conscious. There are strong arguments that many species on Earth have a degree of consciousness. Many have mores that have similar effects to those of human moral standards. The brave lion protects its cubs. But that is, so far as we know, neither virtuous nor a conscious obedience of a rule, let alone adoption of a rule that the lion has pondered with intellectual anguish. Not thick at all. Thickness of assessment is the only appropriate tool here, and the only entity on Earth with sufficient consciousness to *understand* the nuances — the thickness — of moral decisions is *Homo sapiens*. This will be true for the foreseeable future. Machine morality makes sense only within that context, and is therefore inevitably metaphorical.

As one would expect, considerable industrial and academic work is in progress to enable machines to recognize values, and judge them, as in our example of a machine trained on the concept of generosity. In other words, for machines to have what look like thick tools at their disposal. Even, perhaps, to be a *thick machine,* in the Geertz sense. (Though possibly in the schoolboy "stupid" sense of the word too.) Those could get pretty good. Powerful machines trained to read emails and pick out not only bits of language but also meanings that warrant a second look already hum away at the CIA in Langley, GCHQ in Cheltenham, England, and their colleague and competitor agencies all around the world. The final, operational look is no doubt still a human look, but AIs will expand their territory, perhaps quickly.

A rigid distinction between data, and algorithms that use data, is not really viable. Data suffused with meaning immediately becomes information that can inform action when used algorithmically. "AI" can stand for nearly anything digital, in a world in which technology has extraordinary reach, scale, and power. But the "intelligence" created by algorithmic processes is inevitably suffused with human values. Moreover, humans are often better than machines at the quality things that matter most to us. And not just because we can rig the argument (we own the machines so can credit ourselves with everything they can do). Machines certainly surpass humans in speed and bulk of processing. They can perform consistently, and avoid bias, more easily in many circumstances. But humans win in the more intense and nuanced areas of value, interpretation, behavioral expectation, and culture.

There simply is a fundamental accountability difference between a human and a machine, arising from all the other differences. Alexa or Siri can have a face painted on it, be put in smart clothes, and be set up to recognize you as you walk up to the bar. Buy you a drink and ask about your day at the office. Yet this will not affect you in the same way as a human performing exactly the same set of acts. A full, thick description of the difference would include dozens of dimensions. Prime among them is that even where we care a lot about a decision an AI makes about us, we don't care at all what private opinion the machine may have about us, not in the way we are affected by human opinions. Nor do we feel, reciprocally, that we should be diplomatic in how we treat the machine.

■

An improved moral framework is only slowly emerging, to keep pace with the fast-developing, fascinating, new world. Driverless cars, trains, and buses. Pilotless passenger planes and military drones, as foreshadowed in the first Gulf war, when cruise missiles programmed hundreds of miles away from the battlefield killed many thousands. Nuclear-deterrent submarines with no human crew to judge whether Armageddon is now. Facial-recognition cameras on every street, accessible to police. Precision personalized medicine, informed by intelligent nonhuman analysis of huge datasets. Biometric identifiers rampant in every aspect of life, even in the way you hold a smartphone: everyone's hand trembles differently and the motion sensors in the phone can distinguish individuals from that tremor.

Insurance as we know it could be doomed by the spread of the new technology, because insurance is about pooled risk. The community as a whole doesn't know who will come down with a serious disease, so we all pay into a fund to support whichever of us does fall ill. Already, whole categories of people find it harder, and more expensive, to buy coverage as insurance companies deploy clever algorithms and massive datasets to make better risk predictions about individuals. The end of that line looks like insurance companies with machine-learning crystal balls, selling affordable insurance only to those who don't actually need it. And only against random events like being struck by lightning. (Don't apply if you are a forestry worker.) Insurance for others might become prohibitively expensive. In many areas for which we currently *insure*, we will need in the future to *assure*: to insist that funds operate with a veil of ignorance, so that we all contribute and we all potentially benefit, irrespective of individual characteristics.

Aaron Klein of the Brookings Institution has a thoughtful, ultimately broadly optimistic take on artificial intelligence's impact on such financial services:

> The status quo is not something society should uphold as nirvana. Our current financial system suffers not only from centuries of bias, but also from systems that are themselves not nearly as predictive as often claimed. The data explosion coupled with the significant growth in ML and AI offers tremendous opportunity

—

to rectify substantial problems in the current system. Existing anti-discrimination frameworks are ill-suited to this opportunity. Refusing to hold new technology to a higher standard than the status quo results in an unstated deference to the already-biased current system. However, simply opening the flood gates under the rules of "can you do better than today" opens up a Pandora's box of new problems.

America's fractured regulatory system, with differing roles and responsibilities across financial products and levels of government, only serves to make difficult problems even harder. With lacking uniform rules and coherent frameworks, technological adoption will likely be slower among existing entities setting up even greater opportunities for new entrants. A broader conversation regarding how much bias we are willing to tolerate for the sake of improvement over the status quo would benefit all parties. That requires the creation of more political space for sides to engage in a difficult and honest conversation. The current political moment in time is ill-suited for that conversation, but I suspect that AI advancements will not be willing to wait until America is more ready to confront these problems.[12]

AIs are already used extensively in so-called *persuasive design,* to calculate exactly how to draw attention online in commercially valuable directions. The techniques are used increasingly to lure adults into betting sites. Online gambling worldwide was worth $46 billion in 2017 and will be $95 billion in 2024. Children in particular are being targeted by advertisers and other, more nefarious actors. The protection of children as digital citizens is an urgent issue. Powerful interests can and do exploit idiosyncrasies in children and in adults. Loaded messages, targeted to social groups and even specific individuals for commercial and political purposes, are now grounded in massive data collections trawled from a large proportion of the population. That we have more or less cheerfully ignored warnings about the earlier variants of this since Vance Packard's immensely popular works in the 1950s, if not Thorstein Veblen's in the 1890s, doesn't mean that it isn't happening. And much more dangerous than ever.[13]

For good or ill, then, humans are corralled by governments and big corporations. Give up smoking! Don't forget to pay your taxes! Buy the new Apple iPhone! Behaviors are altered by physicians, prison guards, and many other professionals. Our machine nexus is used to troll and berate, educate, and inspire. In just one recent experiment, disadvantaged young children were encouraged to hug cuddle toys with AI devices hidden inside them. Are we being radicalized or made empathic? Convinced to vote against our interests, or to buy what we never previously wanted, rather than what we might need?

Legal pushback by individuals and consumer groups against the large digital corporations is surely coming. In the Introduction, we noted the fight to make publishers of pornography accountable, and its implications. Facebook, X/Twitter, Google, and others claim not to be, but plainly are, publishers of much vexatious and defamatory material. Including very sophisticated video and aural manipulations that make it appear that politicians, celebrities, you or me, have said or done inappropriate things. Government, the big corporations, and concerned citizens need to take responsibility for understanding the increasingly sinister capacities of smart technology.

■

AI algorithms already heavily impact, and will become central to, the relationships between states and citizens; between states and corporations; and between corporations and citizens. Ethical governance of the new technology is vital, and a central metaphor for that governance should be that we judge the actions of artificial intelligences morally as if they were the actions of humans.

Historically, the perils of transformative new technologies have triggered countervailing moral and political frameworks to contain the dangers; the trade union movement, mutualism, and consumerism in the face of nineteenth- and twentieth-century capitalism, for instance. In the age of the gig economy, and of consumers as producers, and when huge social machines like Wikipedia are engaging millions of people in common constructs, new countervailing powers are needed, as well as new balances between individuals and the Good Society.

The stakes could not be higher. Nearly every facet of the social contract between civilized human beings will be extended by, and is already at serious risk from, artificial intelligences. Human values need to be mobilized to judge machines and protect us.

Chapter 5

ETHICS FOR THE DIGITAL AGE

Neither the authors nor the readers of this book are moral innocents. Each of us lives in our own ethical universe, largely but not entirely shaped for us by other people. In principle, we may claim to interpret morality very differently from each other, or from people in distant cultures. Many in the West may imagine we have no overarching religious or political ethical theory. In fact, we do all make ethical decisions, and participate in, or tolerate, broad social and governmental systems with profound ethical implications. We are all practical moralists. And despite many dissimilarities, there is significant consonance across developed nations in the core of the ethical arguments in common use and how they are applied to issues of equal import to those states.

Moreover, ethics is a very special branch of philosophy. And artificial intelligence has a very distinctive place within that branch. One might argue that the specialness of ethics, in a cynical, increasingly secular, civilization that finds it difficult to discover universal meanings, arises from its mundanity. Big philosophical problems to which modern Western liberals as a whole don't think they know the answer include:

- Before the Big Bang, when there was nothing, where did the nothing come from? Or did nothing not exist either?
- After the heat death of the universe, who will tidy up for the next party?
- Did yesterday exist, or does "just a memory" mean exactly that?
- There never was anything and what comes next never starts. Can we prove that this is untrue?
- Does time run forward, like an arrow from a bow? Or does it just feel like a sequence and perhaps in truth move crablike in a helix, or backward, or not at all?
- Causes seem to have effects, and effects seem to have causes. Is that anything more than a vacuous tautology?
- Objects in the world seem to have constancy. As if the cup on the table and the table on the floor sit in an ordered world this moment and continue to sit in much the same ordered world the next moment. Do they? How do they do that?
- How would we tell that objects have some existence other than the phenomena that reach our brains that indicate that they appear to exist?
- How annoying will it be to be dead?

These and many other really important topics in science and philosophy are endlessly fascinating. Sometimes a tentative answer seems within reach before it drifts off again. In an odd way, they may also seem to be ideas that are overwhelmingly important, and at the same time don't really matter very much at all, in any practical sense. With Samuel Johnson, we kick a stone and move on with our day. Very few suburban commuters ask themselves if the train is real before they struggle for a seat.

This is true but also not true of the big questions of ethics. It is true because contemporary intellectual discourse has not even the beginnings of an agreed universal basis for notions of good and evil, or right and wrong. Just like all those other big unanswerable questions. But it is radically untrue because moral discourse and decisions are constants at the core of community social and political life. Despite Luke Rhinehart's *The Dice Man*, whose psychiatrist hero tries and fails to reduce agency to the roll of the titular dice; or the outer fringes of fashionable French existentialism in the 1950s; or countless other attempts to circumvent this truth, we all in fact make qualitative, subjective, ethical decisions every day of our waking lives.[1]

The borderline between philosophical questions that seem to matter in everyday life and those that don't moves, from time to time and from society to society. And perhaps the speedy development of artificial intelligence is pushing some of those eternal questions more into the quotidian. Deepfakes: appearance or reality? What is it to be human as opposed to an animal as opposed to a clever thing? Whether this will be a lasting change in widespread perceptions, or more transient, like the tropes around *What is real?* generated by the drug culture of the 1960s, is uncertain.

Evolutionary thinker and atheist Richard Dawkins has claimed that the universe is cold, empty, and pointless. He also famously argues that religion is a force for evil. In *The God Delusion*, he deeply deplores many behaviors and acts, now and in past centuries, carried out in the name of religion.[2] But if the universe is without values, on what basis do we vehemently attack evil? Indeed, how does Dawkins get to deeply deplore anything at all, if nothing in the universe has any point or value? And very specifically, how does he manage to deplore particular things? This is a trick we all pull off. Indeed, as Sartre would have said, we are condemned to pull it off. Moral argument works. Or is seen from another point of view not to work and gets replaced. Morals are, however atheoretically, susceptible to facts brought to the table.

The special nature of ethics as a branch of academic philosophy is that, unlike the existence of those suburban commuter trains, it is continually renegotiated in the real world by people who can't help but care about it.

■

A useful but incomplete analogy for AI ethics may be found in the history of medical ethics. Discussion of the morality of the doctor-patient relationship goes back to the ancient Greeks, but modern medical ethicists have successfully contended with issues of organ donation, embryology, and genetic testing. Their efforts have yielded coherent, if sometimes controversial, policy recommendations. There are similarities to the ethics of artificial intelligence. But the canvas of medical ethics is smaller, tending to focus on the behavior of individual doctors, who are already engaged in an intensely regulated profession. Medical ethicists who are doctors can often be uncomfortable with, even not very well informed about, larger-scale issues like the economic and resource allocation aspects of health policy, which present some of the most profound problems. Nevertheless, there are ways in which meanings and morals from medical ethics may be translated into the wider, all-pervasive world of artificial intelligences.

Readers, as citizens of the world, will know quite a bit about the major conventional theories of ethics, which after their first coining have been repeatedly reminted over the centuries. Not everyone will use the technical names employed by philosophers or theologians, but the concepts are familiar from everyday political and social discussion and controversy. Let's remind ourselves of a few of the most notable ideas, using as an example a major set of artificial intelligences that many people use every day: search engines.

The Western tradition in the philosophy of ethics and the study of morals and moral behavior began with the Greeks in the seventh century. Socrates, Plato, and Aristotle. There are parallel traditions in virtually every other civilization. The Chinese traditions — Buddhism, Taoism, or Confucianism in particular — are significant influences bubbling under the latter-day mix of Marx and market that presently dominates the world's second-largest power, and may be resurgent as the twenty-first century plays out. This book is firmly located in what we have called mixed philosophy, and in modern liberalism. We use the latter term in the broad European sense, denoting enlightened progressivism, of the kind that drove the eighteenth-century revolutions in France and America, rather than the more limited modern US sense of free-market independence.

We now look at three important moral frameworks: consequentialist ethics, deontological ethics, and virtue ethics. In the roughly six thousand years since writing was invented, in Mesopotamia and perhaps elsewhere, countless philosophies have been recorded, and others over a much longer period not recorded. Of varying degrees of popularity and influence. Needless to say, even just a list of the many other coherent attempts to analyze and codify morals, either *sui generis* or as part of a wider approach to life, would fill the rest of this book. Stoicism, hedonism, feminism, veganism, Christianity, Islam, Judaism, Buddhism, Sikhism, Marxism, existentialism, Confucianism, Taoism — to name some major belief systems. We choose these three to illustrate a modern Western thesis, but there is no claim that they must be more important than others, particularly other contemporary ones, some of which are vital planks in the mindsets of the present authors, and no doubt the reader.

———

Consequentialist ethics is broadly the view that we should—and do habitually—analyze our actions in terms of what ensues from those actions, and either balance out an account of the positives and negative consequences from each individual action, or try to derive general rules that will (experience or logic says) maximize overall benefits and minimize harm for society as a whole. Utilitarianism is the best-known umbrella term for several consequentialist theories.

Deontological ethics derives from *Deon*, the Greek word for duty. A deontologist thinks that the best approach to morality is to establish the sets of duties and obligations we have or should have. Then act on those rules. The core tenet is that some actions feel—or are argued to be—right, and others wrong, or (as perhaps happens more often across world history) that the gods are telling us through priests or personal revelation that some actions are right, and others wrong.

Third is *virtue ethics*. Virtue ethicists identify certain human qualities as those that a good person should manifest, and advocate that everyone should do so. This approach has been with us since ancient times, and is now resurgent amongst modern philosophers. In ordinary life, people may have some virtues, and aspire to others, no doubt mostly derived from their family, social, and educational histories. One should be *charitable,* so I will give some money to this homeless person on Christmas Eve. One should be *brave,* so I will run into this burning building and rescue a kitten.

The instant difficulty is that one virtue, like one deontological rule, or one utilitarian attempt to balance up the consequences of an action or policy, may contradict another virtue, rule, or cost-benefit analysis. Perhaps a *prudent* or *caring* person would work out that giving a dollar to someone on the street is not the best way to help them with a drug problem. Or a *sensible* parent might think that

———

dying for a cute, furry animal is not going to comfort one's children very much.

Most readers will be familiar with the basic principles of utilitarianism, one of the central philosophical products of the Industrial Age, along with Marxism, and perhaps the one that might at first seem like a top candidate for signature ethic of the silicon era. Modern digital life and utilitarianism both resound with mathematical and logical overtones, don't they? The central claim of utilitarianism is that faced with any choice as to policy or practice, large or small, the foremost guide of a well-intentioned person should be a calculation of how the greatest good for the greatest number of people can be achieved. Almost any kind of government policy program, for instance, has winners and losers. We should, the claim goes, do our best to work out who the winners in policy approach A are and how much they win; who the losers in A are and how much they lose; multiply all that out, then compare it to a similar calculation of the advantages and disadvantages of policy B. The prize goes to the policy that overall delivers the greatest net utility.

Apply something like that to the Google search engine, far and away the most popular and unarguably the best for general purposes. The money that Google makes from the value to advertisers of the information it extracts from every searcher is often referred to as an invisible Google tax. Google's revenue from advertising linked to search is $100 billion per year and rising. That's a lot. The train pulled mostly by this search engine, Google's parent company Alphabet, is now the fifth most valuable by market capitalization that the world has ever seen.[3] But the cost per individual keystroke tells a very different tale. There were 2.5 trillion Google searches in 2020. About three hundred for every person on Earth, perhaps half a dozen on average each day for those people who regularly use it.

Google is "free" at the point of delivery, but searchers buy products from advertisers who gratefully recycle some of the cash to Alphabet. That works out to twenty-five searches per dollar, or four cents each, so maybe twenty-five cents a day for ordinary users. No rational person in a wealthy nation would complain very loudly about an invisible tax of twenty-five cents a day in return for the extraordinary benefits of search. (Searchers are also citizens of economies that are bigger because of this cycle, so arguably they pay a negative invisible tax; taken all round they gain a lot, individually and collectively.) Bear in mind that the World Wide Web as it has developed over three decades, with all its astonishing resources, and as an integral element of how we now live, is only a practical proposition when accessed by search engines.

So, a utilitarian would say, the downside of Google search would have to be enormous to outweigh benefits on that scale, surely? Agreed. A world with no search engines would be a much poorer place. Indeed, it would be quite frustrating if we just had no Google and had to put up with an inferior alternative instead. But now that search has become an essential component of modern life, we have to take it as a given, and look to whether the whole mass of difficulty that any such large transformation brings in its wake is inevitable – or is merely one implementation of the broad concept, where we could have taken a different approach to reach an equivalent result, and could now still replace it with a better or reformed implementation. In other words, we are back at ground zero, needing to recalculate from the beginning the pluses and minuses of the next phase. And there are, without doubt, real problems with the present implementation of search, some of which are rather new to the world.

In this Google example we rapidly encounter an intriguing problem with utilitarianism, and indeed any sort of analysis in welfare economics or cost-benefit analysis. The greatest good for the greatest number can only be computed (even in theory, in an idealized thought experiment) if one feels comfortable claiming that:

- My good counts exactly equally to my friend's good, which counts exactly equally to the good of somebody I've never heard of. That giving a random unknown Jack in Milwaukee a brand new car is just the same as giving my favorite niece Jill a brand new car. But nobody on the planet feels that way about life. We all favor our kith, kin, and kind over others. And are obliged by law to do so, in some circumstances. (You must feed and clothe your own children and send them to school.) But we might well still buy into an ethical system for running a country that assumed this variety of equality.

- We have some schema for comparing or totting up very different things. Is giving one student a university education a greater or lesser good than giving eight senior citizens a higher grade of residential or nursing care? Some such questions can be at least partially answered by using cash costs as a proxy, but by no means all.

- We know how to set a particular good against a particular bad and come up with an overall net total. That we have some kind of overarching theory of measurement, some kind of measuring device or instrumentation, some kind of units. Now, any ordinary view of morality balks at that dangerous assumption. A surgeon enters a ward. She discovers that thirty-five-year-old patient A, otherwise healthy, will die without an immediate heart transplant, which is not available; forty-five-year-old patient B, otherwise healthy, will die without an immediate lung transplant, which is not available; and fifty-five-year-old patient C, otherwise healthy, will die without an immediate kidney transplant, which is not available. So she finds the nearest healthy, middle-aged nurse, kills him humanely, harvests three sets of fresh organs, and saves a net two lives. Everybody happy? Fortunately perhaps, complex issues of tissue typing and rejection make this scenario a long shot. And the surgeon would go to jail, if the nurse's relatives didn't catch her first. But were a nation's health service to take this approach in a coordinated way, there would be far fewer early deaths. No nation would sanction that, though, and the philosophical task is, at least in part, to understand why not.

Nor is a utilitarian scheme even practical politics. In the United Kingdom, Margaret Thatcher's reign as prime minister ended because her government assumed that, if a new form of local taxation was cheaper, gave in effect a monthly cash bonus to three-quarters of the population, then the country would overwhelmingly support her. No. The better-off three quarters shrugged and went quietly about their business, while the furious minority of losers and their friends tore her down. So when we said a moment ago that no rational person would complain about an invisible tax of twenty-five cents a day, what is also true is that the same rational people are genuinely and justly concerned about how much corporate tax Google doesn't pay, and don't mentally set the two feelings off against each other. They just live with two separate things in their heads. They like Google search, and they want Google to pay more tax.

There are no scales at hand, no speak-your-weight machine, to say that seven units of pleasure (or utility) are equal in quantity to seven units of pain (or nuisance); or that seven units of pleasure outweigh only two units of pain and strife; or whatever. There just are no units. One can make a stab at saying that a lot of pain must be a worse thing than not so much pain; and conversely with pleasure. But how much pleasure for Jill and Jennifer cancels out quite a bit of pain for James? The Italian economist and engineer Vilfredo Pareto, active around the turn of the twentieth century, made some fruitful but limited inroads into an answer to this problem: as long as somebody in a situation can be made better off (perhaps defined as better off in their own eyes) without detriment to anybody else, then the whole situation can be improved by an intervention that does not need to decide whether any particular bad outweighs any particular good. The moment that somebody needs to lose for somebody else to win, we have reached so-called Pareto optimality.[4] We can only travel further down the boulevard of broken dreams by making a moral choice laden with values and the problem of weighting. Making such a choice does not necessarily force a halt; nor is proceeding necessarily hard. We may be happy that there are winners and losers, to actively redistribute benefits. It does mean, however, that up to that point we are just unambiguously improving matters, whereas thereafter there is a balance, a different mode and style of thought, with different, less mathematical, rules. (Life is not even that simple, as the reader will know, but Pareto has important resonance in economic theory.)

Does utilitarianism help us with analysis of any of the specific ethical problems thrown up by Google's wonderful device? Much academic thought followed the widespread adoption of search at the end of the twentieth century. Quite a range of problems have been identified, and less often and perhaps less convincingly, coherent solutions offered. There is a debate to be had about what issues are being categorized and the most accurate way to group them, but there is also quite a degree of agreement. The *Stanford Encyclopedia of Philosophy* usefully sets out six categories of issue, here re-expressed and adapted a little:

1. Bias and opacity. When a user types a search request into Google, the answer is the result of a multilayered sequence of selection among many billions of possibilities. The search engine, by definition, makes choices in the process. Those choices may be accidental, or precisely intended by the software writer. (The machine may be programmed to show sponsored results first.) Or they may be semiconscious or unconscious consequences of the prevailing ideologies of everyone involved in designing and delivering the product. Google, then, may have real difficulty in being explicit about what biases may have influenced the search results. And even where the biases are obvious or have been pointed out, it may be unwilling or unable to correct them. (Or perhaps "correct" them, since bias is a highly subjective phenomenon.)

2. *Personal privacy and informed consent.* Powerful search engines are capable of combing and indexing the entire multisplendored World Wide Web. They can and do combine results from many different places. Jigsaw pieces of information put on the web by or for an individual citizen for very specific and various, perhaps limited, purposes can be arranged to form a whole picture that a person would never have wanted to put before the world. That young woman did not intend her teenage Instagram posts to form part of her post-university job application. They may ruin her legitimate aspirations.

3. *Surveillance and monitoring.* Google keeps astonishingly large stores of information that include the details of every search that has ever been made by everyone using their invention. They do now bury an option in the small print to allow users to opt out of some of this. But the success of their business model depends on practically everybody staying in. And to be fair, in the occasional dreadful case that has been drawn to their attention, Google has done its best to supply a fix. Though again, too infrequently to affect their bottom line. This gives rise to great and dangerous opportuni-

ties to monitor individuals and whole populations, both in real time and diving into their deep past. Opportunities not only for Google itself, but also for any official agency that, with or without a warrant, engineers a backdoor pipe into the data stores. Or for any version of Cambridge Analytica that can weasel its way in. We might be pleased to know that the spread of an outbreak of influenza in the United States can be tracked simply by watching where searches for headache cures are being tapped into the oblong box on thousands of screens. Perhaps we are happy that a search for "how to make an explosive device" will in many countries ring an alarm bell in a badly furnished government back room. Or we may be disconcerted.

4. *Censorship and democracy.* Should Google take direction from governments as to what results can be shown in their territories? At one time Google decided that it was proper to act in China the way the Chinese authorities wanted it to. Later the Google execs thought rather better of it, and moved some operations to Hong Kong. The rights and wrongs are not straightforward. Did the move make living in China more or less comfortable for the ordinary citizen? Baidu, China's own huge search engine, has the advantage of better local knowledge, and state aid. But it is hard to know from outside the system how Baidu stacks up against Google in terms of search quality. Certainly, the authorities wanted to censor Google search results only because some citizens wanted to see them. Those citizens, at least, must be worse off (again, in their own eyes). The Chinese government and the Communist Party hold that the common good — of the greatest number — requires some secrecy and censorship. So do Western governments. And one can equally question whether Google's retreat to Hong Kong was likely to make China's line toward its arms-length offshore province tougher or softer.[5]

———

5. *Moral accountability of search companies.* Are we happy that huge corporations seem to decide which laws they wish to obey, and where? (If that is a fair characterization.) Do we insist that they take transparent moral stances about how they affect our lives, then criticize them for transparently having the gall to take moral stances about how they affect our lives? The whole world surely should read the best books on the subject, then hold Google to account. But what would that accountability look like? Google is answerable to its shareholders. It is answerable to politicians and the courts. That the Chinese government put pressure on them may strike us in one way, but they have also been taken to task by the US government and the European Union, and we may feel differently about that. All of those accountabilities compounded still feel insufficient to many of us.

At a very different angle, any Google search on the web can produce a treasure trove of useful, sometimes vital, information. It can also bring up dangerous nonsense, utter rubbish-with-attitude. Is Google responsible for that? Publishers of old-fashioned printed material are legally liable for what is written within that material. Indeed, in the United Kingdom, laws dating back centuries require that every distributed document display the printer's name and address, so they also can be held accountable for the content. This is a moveable feast. Google and the other internet giants now publicly claim to be on the case, but without so far conceding that they are publisher, printer, or the equivalent.[6]

6. *Cyber security and the Internet of Things.* The World Wide Web floats on top of the internet. There are something like a quarter of a billion internet servers; several billions of individual computers and smartphones that access those servers; and many millions of separate cable and radio pathways. A large proportion of that extensive network is visible to search engines. In the past few years there

has also been an explosion of different devices attached to this net-work, the so-called Internet of Things. Home security devices that can be viewed and controlled by a smartphone via the web, for in-stance. There are specialist search engines that seek out devices con-nected to the internet, but Google, Bing, and similar companies can do versions of that too. That sounds like the thin end of a tricky wedge when it comes to security and privacy. What are Google's ob-ligations in that direction?

So how much does utilitarianism help us tease out the rights and wrongs of any of these issues? Introspection might indicate that when we try to assess the best course of action in some of these cases, we are engaged in a sort of accountancy, a balancing act in our heads. And in such a thought experiment we can assess the "size" of one factor versus another, if only in terms of our personal preferences. All of this might lead us to feel that some kind of greatest-number process is psychologically under way. Yet it is difficult to pick any of the six areas outlined earlier in which anything as exact as, say, the QALY system used in some areas of health care might apply. (The quality-adjusted life year – QALY – is a generic measure of disease burden, including both the quality and the quantity of life lived. It is used in economic evaluation to assess the value of medical interven-tions. One QALY equates to one year in perfect health.) An artificial intelligence that assesses insurance claims does balance dozens of factors against each other in thousands of instances, but it is still doubtful that it could balance moral arguments using anything like the same methodologies.

Which brings us to perhaps the prime drawback: The moral question, when using QALYs or any other measure, isn't the computation; it is deciding what matters more than something else. That is one of the core defects of utilitarianism as a whole.

———

Thanks, utilitarians, for telling us that it would be a fine idea to do more good than bad. Great plan, nobody would disagree. What we need to know, however, is how do we identify what is good, how do we distinguish it from what is bad, and how do we quantify either? Take the modern phenomenon of "doxxing" somebody whose opinions one doesn't think are proper. In doxxing, every corner of the web is searched to discover anything that a mob can use to embarrass the victim. Plumb in the middle of the privacy and consent category of problems. Perhaps some readers don't mind the idea of doxxing. It may be similar to the practice, advocated by some radicals in the 1970s and 1980s, of "outing" prominent gay men who would rather not emerge from their private closet. And even more similar to the shaming of Chinese social and political outliers during the Mao years, a practice that appeared to have a strong degree of approval from government, or of powerful factions at any rate, and also to be culturally acceptable. The authors, conventionally for Western liberals, regard both doxxing and the Chinese practices as utterly disgraceful. This is not, we feel, one of those instances where relativity requires us to shrug and opine that people and cultures differ. But patently the difference between those who think doxxing is a decent enough way to promote beneficial change, and those who don't, has little or nothing to do with weighing relative weights of benefits and disbenefits, or with any variety of moreness or lessness. There is a moral transgression, or not, already in the works before anybody stands on any speak-your-weight platform.

■

We know, broadly speaking, how *moral capacity* came into being. But is it anything more than the sum of that history? Mathematics presents a useful parallel, though it falls down on the "anything more" side of the discussion.

It is generally agreed that math originated as simple counting, measurement, and calculation, as well as a systematic study of the shapes and motions of physical objects, but then evolved, through the application of abstraction, imagination, and logic, to the broad, complex, and often abstract discipline it is now. Did the same evolution happen to ethics, perhaps with a little divine intervention? (By the way, Srinivasa Ramanujan, one of the most astonishing of the number theorists, thought his extraordinary mathematical intuitions were vouchsafed to him by his family goddess Namagiri Thayar.)

An English generation of the 1930s and 1940s was in thrall to the then recent philosophers (Bertrand Russell, Alfred North Whitehead) and economists (John Maynard Keynes, Alfred Marshall), all of whom were immensely persuasive literary figures but primarily mathematicians. Alan Turing might be the crowning example, merging math and philosophy to save the world by inventing the modern computer. It is hardly surprising, then, that they erred and still err, in some computer driven worlds, on the sides of (1) a rather idealistic scientism that scarcely matches either how science works in practice or how scientists really behave, and (2) the view that language consists of propositions that, if they cannot be validated either logically or empirically, are "merely" emotions.[7] (Some call this view emotivism.) If one plants those two flags deeply and surrounds them with the imperial guard, much of morality is then just Boo and Hurrah at a soccer match, emotions without meaningful content.

There is significant difficulty with that worldview. *Speech acts* and thick descriptions are immensely important. In the 1980s, the philosopher Rom Harré wrote convincingly about the highly complex mores and moral codes of soccer "hooligans." When City are playing United, the boos at the referee when he gives an apparent City goal offside are rich in precise content: that is, they are easily deconstructable by the referee, both sets of fans, all the players, and the neutral commentator on the radio.[8]

This arises from millions of hominins developing the capacity to live together in large, complex groups. Bees have societies with hard-wired rules and some information processing: the dance to show where the best nectar is. And many species, particularly but not only mammals, have sophisticated behavior patterns that can adapt to changing circumstances. The specific hominin advantage was the growth of general intelligence, with strategic conceptual manipulation, laid on top of, while also arising out of, embedded patterns in the genes. *Yergh, spider!* is the gene-pattern response, whereas *How do we trap that big moose without getting gored? I know, let's go up the valley to where the hand-axe quarry is, get a couple of big rocks, then spread out in a circle and . . .* emerges out of general intelligence. We have good guesses about how sophisticated chanting, keening, and mutual grooming behaviors, as well as the ability to make shelters, use fire, and fashion hand-axes, could then both underly and emerge into language, which in turn would reinforce strong cooperative group bonds and, as a lesser but important subfunction, store and convey both gossip and pragmatically vital information.

Mores and the beginning of ethics fit easily into this pattern. Perhaps not many of us would be advocates of emotivism as just described. Everyone would realize they were being given groundless emotional injunctions, and laugh at them.[9] But when a mother says to her child, *Don't gulp your food, Don't poke your sister with your fork,* and *You mustn't be rude like you were yesterday to your teacher, who emailed to complain,* these instructions have pragmatic underpinnings (you'll get indigestion; your sister will scream and the evening will go downhill; the teacher is a powerful figure socially and for your career, so you need to be careful not to embarrass yourself and me in front of him), all of which the child needs to listen to and understand the logic of. Modern societies, and indeed pre-modern societies, are multiply layered anthropological entities, with life or death choices that need to be made individually and socially, and so require careful consideration.

The nub here is, do the *moral capacity,* the moral impetus, and the constantly renewing set of moral problems that evolve and permeate every aspect of human social life represent merely (ironic raised eyebrows here) a highly reflexive embedding of ultimately pragmatic behavior rules into other highly reflexively embedded behavior rules, or do they follow from ultimately distinct moral frameworks with independent grounding? If one believes the latter, there are broadly three ways of getting there. The grounding has to be either extension from mores; or rational examination of the nature of logic and the world; or divine intervention. Ramanujan, as noted earlier, provides an intriguing metaphor for divine intervention; the middle idea about rational examination sounds like Kant's territory; but the first—the expansion of mores into morals—may be roughly where we should land. It is simple to move from "is" to "ought" in the sentence, *There's a train coming, you ought not to drive across the tracks.* Is there some version of that where the "ought" involves abstract ethics? Does it matter? Does operating as if we knew the answer to that question solve anything in practice?

Many Western countries have explicitly run a mixed economy for many decades. The state, with its many huge public enterprises, provides many essential services. It is backed up by an often very similar-looking voluntary and charitable sector. There is a "private" sector, most of it better described as a corporate sector, with large producer and service organizations owned mostly by other large entities: shareholders that are insurance companies, pension funds, banks, and hedge funds, that are themselves mostly owned by others. All of this is run by an overlapping group of political, bureaucratic, and Galbraithian managerial elites, within a broad framework of social classes, who share a key objective of self-preservation. Over some centuries, these elites have displayed considerable flexibility and initiative in learning to live with, and provide for, the whole society without fundamentally compromising their own positions. This mixed economy has entailed what we might symmetrically call a *mixed philosophy*.

The United States, whatever its Constitution may say about the role of religion in the state, has so far had Judeo-Christian government. Every single president so far has been a man who either claimed to be a strong adherent of one or other Christian sect, or was brought up to be so and never disavowed that faith. In practice, patently, the United States has also operated a mixed philosophy, with again the overarching aim of protecting the elites.

Over millennia, philosophers have described the world in many ways. In Darwinian fashion, those perspectives that best help us to comprehend and deal with the shifting and dangerous human environment survive and thrive. That more limited range of broadly successful approaches has been deployed, in different mixes in different times, to fix various problems. When multiplied by thousands of different practical responses, routines, and techniques, these rather few perspectives have still led to an immense range of solutions to situations, across time and among different cultures.

Different moral actors at different times might well use arguments built from, or associated with, broad versions of morality with which they profoundly disagree at a high level, but accept as practically useful. The Holy Father as head of the Church of Rome, or the Archbishop of Canterbury, leader of the Anglican Church, and similar patriarchs, are professional deontologists, with some virtue ethics thrown in. One of them might conceivably be, in private, a Zen Buddhist or, perhaps a smidgeon less unlikely, an existentialist, but during office hours he is a deontologist who often adduces virtues. That's the job. It would however be entirely feasible, likely perhaps, that such a patriarch (or one day, matriarch), if asked by a group of doctors for advice on how to decide between patients who need medicines or equipment, and if instructed in the theory of QALYs, might think that such an entirely utilitarian method of making medical decisions is perfectly sound. One that a virtuous person might recognize as meeting the duty to make the best decision in the circumstances.

This may seem a very arm's-length approach to morality, in effect to point to how we observe policymakers acting in the world. Many of us, including those policymakers, would claim to have stronger, more deeply embedded, views on many topics than this approach seems to imply. (We imagine the Holy Father and his ecumenical colleagues certainly would.) Yet here we are. Many of us are – or aim to be – successful members of that coalition of elites, and regard that as ethically acceptable. And to function in modern Western society, whatever broad ideology we espouse, we in practice draw from the *mixed philosophy* toolkit.

■

Again, a pure believer in any of these moral approaches is unlikely to exist outside of the academy or the ranks of organized religions, or even within them. Any intelligent person might say, about some

139

topic of the moment, "I don't care about the consequences, this is just plain wrong," and in another, "We need to take a balanced utilitarian view of this." This or that method of analysis may well be appropriate in the particular instance. A committed cynical pragmatist will nonetheless fall back on values – and merely laugh at Jonathan Swift's satirical *A Modest Proposal*, which outrageously suggested in 1729 that since there were far too many children in Ireland, and many Irish were starving, it would be sensible for the poor Irish to sell some of their children as food to the wealthy Irish, even if the suggestion might seem like perfectly good utilitarianism. (Anachronistically. Bentham first used the term *utilitarian* in 1781.) This point is quite distinct from the necessary aspect of all moral systems, that people who believe in them often lapse from the standards that they themselves set by committing to an ethical framework. Being more flexible to start with, by contrast, involves moving between frameworks as circumstances seem to warrant. Or perhaps, being committed to, and practicing, a relativistic meta-framework.

A mixed philosophy inevitably means that the moral actor will formally or informally, consciously or less so, choose between alternative contrasting principles of action. A public official, a head of college, or Plato's governing philosopher – all must necessarily operate in such a fashion. This mixed philosophy, significantly, includes both acknowledgment that frequently the available information is incomplete or imperfect, and recognition of widespread attempts of decent people to muddle through.

Indeed, the muddling through of a policymaker or decision-maker may look something like:

- Their head is already full of bumblebees of many subspecies, of more or less pressing relevance. Perhaps they met their own patient-in-a-tray John in a secluded hospital years ago, perhaps they have been impressed by behaviors of colleagues or others, perhaps they have a religious commitment. They may well be generally, if not specifically, aware of relevant laws and regulations. Perhaps they are an experienced administrator with many practical routines and deadlines to get them through the day.

- When they come upon a situation in their professional life that falls outside these routines, it gives them pause, forcing them to try to identify what kind of situation it is. The larger bumblebees may come into play; is a broad moral sweep needed? More likely, the broad sweep is taken for granted, and some attempt is made to remember previous relevant situations and tease out what might be new in the present case.

- They then attempt to provide a coherent solution to the problem, involving both action(s) and an explicable rule for the action – the reason that option is chosen, a statement of its meaning – which will often be noted in a short or long written explanation by somebody in the chain of causation.

For many actors, too, what is expected from their role is very important. Firefighters or police officers ordinarily engage in behaviors for which they are trained, and where there is an explicit range of expectations. They act *as if* that is who they are, because of broad decisions, made at key junctures in their biography, about who they want to be. Many people operate a less pointed but still real version of that: to do this job that pays my mortgage, I need to wear a certain kind of clothes in the workplace, and I need to adopt certain kinds of behavior, perhaps being more polite to customers and fellow workers than I might if I was there merely as a private citizen. One complex subset of those behaviors is moral decision-making.

Leaders, according to Locke's original version of the "social contract," have an obligation to reflect, and to devise ways to put into practice, the views of the polity and population as a whole. Locke saw that obligation not only as morally binding, but also as a way to remain in power. To avoid assassination, metaphorical or literal. Locke would recognize the scope that all leaders have for feathering their own nest, within the inevitably broad and loose constraints of the social contract, and would allow a leader some room for their own moral compass, since most political systems provide rulers with what has been termed "ideological space."[10]

All of this involves not only coherent thought and action, but also muddling through; and draws on several different (possibly in the circumstances unnoticed) kinds of philosophical reasoning. Actors, at least significant actors, identify decision situations, remember or tease out or invent the appropriate rules, and thus both step into action and, often, in private or public bureaucracies, define the name of the action.

Philippa Foot, the distinguished twentieth-century philosopher most famous perhaps as the originator of that trolley problem, singles out the Aristotelean virtues of wisdom, courage, and temperance as being of special importance.[11] That flatters the individualists in us. What, though, of more social virtues? Why not public service? Why not compassion, or some other broad recognition of fellow feeling? Most religions value those higher than courage. Or for that matter, why not the Confucian value of obedience? The coronavirus pandemic would have ended much more rapidly if the people of every nation had simply done as they were asked by authorities that had their best interests at heart. Perhaps China's Confucian heritage helped in its containment of the disease. We do agree with Foot that moral reasoning of the kind we wish to discuss in our approach to the ethics of technology and artificial intelligence may be impossible without some version of her heroic conception of what it means to be a good human. (And therefore, in our formulation, what it means to be a machine that embodies goodness.)

So we do accept some of her individualist values. One version of courage, for instance, is a prejudice in favor of optimism. To quote our self-description in *The Digital Ape,*

> We are optimists. In small part because we think we have a duty
> to be so. People with the privileges of university chairs or
> well-paid public office should devote a minimum of their time to
> moaning about the world and a maximum to deploying the
> resources gifted to them to construct realistic responses to wicked
> issues. More though, a large proportion of the world's problems
> are soluble in principle, difficult though the practicality will be.[12]

Human values are what protect us from machines, however smart.

In a wider version of the firefighter position, we must treat not merely machines but also ourselves as if we are Foot's heroic humans. We have an idea of ourselves as virtuous intelligent actors who wish to do good, to behave as well as we realistically can. We have lower-level values, too, that we think cohere with that position; for instance, a prejudice about privacy, or about state killings. We write, read, make decisions, act, as if those values are truths.

Readers may want to act as if, want to present themselves in everyday life as if, they are good people. (In this context perhaps a good policy analyst, a good technology ethicist, or a good, concerned citizen.) Their motives may be pure, or humdrum, or deeply suspect. They may be coerced or misled, perhaps by themselves, into making false claims of goodness. Or they may be bad people, who deceptively claim to be good, for bad reasons. The plain content of a speech act announcing a principle of action just is the plain content, even if the speech act is the utterance of a liar or an enemy agent. Or for that matter, an artificial intelligence. Our old friend Speak-your-Weight could easily be adapted by a nearby candy store to underestimate the poundage, congratulate the unexpectedly slim customer, and suggest that they might like to reward themselves with a sweet treat. In other words, to lie for gain. Accuracy would require quotation marks around "to lie." It is an *as if human* sentence.[13] But again, this is a fictional approach. Any decent philosopher or civilian might coherently argue that we are being agnostic about whether virtues are solid and real, while behaving ethically *as if* we know they are. Exactly. Guilty as charged. Can we move on please?

In sum, therefore, we hang our hats on a few broad, practical hooks. First, a modern Western liberal society operates on the basis of a mixed philosophy, taking reasonable arguments from the whole philosophical tradition and applying them as fine-tuned situational rules. We approve of that methodology and apply it here. Second, our practice is to choose between such reasonable arguments, those we are familiar with at any rate, and apply them as rules at least in part by referring to values that we claim to hold. We can make no meta-ethical claim here that this is the best, the incontrovertibly morally superior, approach. We simply claim that we do hold relevant values, that we can and do name some of them, and that we hope and expect that most of our readers would also hold most of them, while no doubt reserving judgment as to their application case by case. Third, we hold that a machine, an artificial intelligence, can be one proper locus for the application of moral judgments.

So what are the virtues that an artificial intelligence may embody?

Chapter 6

VIRTUES AND MACHINES

How do we apply modern virtue ethics? It seems straightforward to intuit as a general proposition that a machine can follow rules. So if to be moral is to match one's decisions and actions to explicit ethical principles, laid down as explicit rules, then it is equally easy to imagine how an artificial intelligence might stay in line with some aspects of morality, or be judged to be in breach of an important rule. By the same token, if the right thing to do is to use utilitarian mathematics to work out which course delivers the greatest good to the greatest number of people, then again the process-y, computational nature of the task so defined would seem to be right up an AI's alley. And success or failure in doing the sum correctly could perhaps, one also intuits, be judged by other machines. Or by calculating humans. But what about the much subtler, and probably more important, question: Can a machine be virtuous?

At first blush, we can be pretty sure that a machine cannot *be virtuous*. It cannot *have virtues*. Not in the ordinary, plain-language way in which we would use those terms about a human person. Not machines in anything like the form we now know them, or will for a long time. An artificial intelligence cannot, for instance, be *courageous*, nor have courage (again in the ordinary sense of those terms). It is even doubtful, with great respect to animal lovers everywhere, that when dog owners claim that their pet is "brave," or "loyal," they mean exactly what is meant when the same terms are used about people. Machines are a good deal less animate than dogs. Dogs are undoubtedly sensitive living beings. Machines simply are not. With Peter Singer, we would hold that animals have rights, in consequence of their living sensitivity. (Not Singer's words. We abbreviate a sophisticated, substantive field of argument.[1]) Machines have no such sensitivity.

Of course, in ordinary English speech, we commonly express an emotion we feel about a human or an object *as if* it is a quality of that person or object or machine, rather than of the observer. If a parking meter annoys me, I say it is annoying. If I feel safer after fitting a smoke detector in the kitchen, I can reasonably describe that smoke detector as comforting. It is perfectly coherent in English, then, to describe an artificial intelligence as frustrating, dangerous, slow, fast, complex, fearsome — anything where there is a human effect and the proximate cause is the AI. Doing so, however, is enacting a particular narrow version of the pathetic fallacy, in which the human attributes to the machine what the human feels. It is not true.

What we do claim is that machines can, and increasingly already do, *embody* many of the classic human virtues. That word "embody" we use as a term of art: if a machine can usefully be judged on its performance of a virtue, we say it embodies that virtue. Furthermore, we say such a virtue is *operable* at least in the case of that machine. And a virtue would, inevitably, be *inoperable* if no machine could embody it.

So it is still the case that an artificial intelligence can scarcely embody *courage*, any more than a bomb-disposal robot can demonstrate the same courage as a soldier or police officer in the same situation. That would be a ludicrous, perhaps offensive, claim. It is, however, surely right to say that an artificial intelligence can *fairly* make decisions about whether and on what terms to offer health insurance. Or that a machine can embody *unfairness* by exhibiting gender bias, or by needlessly exacerbating social deprivation. Whether the bias was introduced by the team that collected the data the artificial intelligence was given; was written in by a programmer; or was "learned" on its own by the machine, unpredictably, because of the way it handled the task, is a very interesting technical question, but scarcely negates that unfairness is exhibited, and (if discovered) should be tackled, whatever the technical cause. The straightforward way to describe this is to say that, unless or until somebody fixes it, the machine embodies unfairness.

Increasingly, too, the fixer can be a sophisticated machine itself. An AI that doctors other AIs. We all now take for granted that modern cars, fully loaded with smart systems, are attached in the repair shop to at least low-grade AIs that diagnose their ills.

Which of the classic virtues, then, are in the *courage* camp, and which in the *fairness* camp? The ancients were emphatic enough. Socrates held that virtue simply is knowledge. Artificial intelligences can certainly hold or access all the knowledge we have on a vast range of topics, and apply it to a specific case. Linking to Wikipedia gets a machine that far. They can also "know" (embody and act on) all kinds of facts about a potential customer, or about a convicted felon before sentencing. Plato later morphed knowledge as a virtue into *wisdom* or *prudence*. Prudence seems to us to be plainly operable, visible in a word processor's simple question about whether one definitely wants to delete a file, or when a self-driving vehicle decides to slam on the brakes. Wisdom, by contrast, seems less operable, since it implies not merely knowledge, but also rational contemplation of the meaning or modes of use of that knowledge.

Aristotle divided the virtues into two kinds, intellectual and moral. His three intellectual virtues were, in the Greek, *nous, episteme,* and *sophia. Nous,* meaning grasp of general axioms or principles of logic or life, is easily displayed by a machine. *Episteme,* meaning the ability to use logical or mathematical skills, is the great forte of all modern computers. *Sophia,* meaning wisdom, is subject to the same objection as the one raised against Plato's wisdom. So we can expect to judge a machine on its conduct based on two out of three of Aristotle's intellectual virtues.

Let's fold Aristotle's other kind of virtue, moral virtues, into a composite discussion along with those virtues most often collated and examined by modern philosophers, because they are widely held across many religions and cultures. (Sages from Homer to Benjamin Franklin have had a go at a list.) As we say, some are operable, others inoperable. Some appear to be in both camps, either because their definitions vary, or because they cover related but distinct aspects. The reader is expected to argue with every one of our views, probably both ways and back again:

> *Courage.* Our touchstone for inoperability. Despite the very popular
> eponymous children's story, a brave little engine would herald a very
> disturbing brave new world. There is a science fiction debate to be
> had about whether such a thing could ever transpire, but it is not an
> ethical challenge on planet Earth today.
> *Generosity.* Inoperable, in the sense of donating purposefully, considerately, in the absence of legal or social obligation to donate in the

particular instance; and in the absence of an instruction from a machine's owner to give in particular circumstances or to particular categories of person. In other words, where the machine itself would have to have liberality.

Benevolence. A machine can be altruistic, in the objective sense of making payments or judgments that don't benefit the machine or its owner. Regular payments to a charity can be programmed in. But it can't be benevolent. This is much the same distinction as we applied to generosity.

Compassion. In the literal and first sense of the word, "suffering together," plainly an AI does not suffer. But in the perhaps more widespread sense now of "respecting life, taking steps to mitigate other people's pain," it might well be an operable virtue.

Mercy. Inoperable, in the sense of a decision not to hate, or a decision not to act contrary to another's interest when ordinary rules say that one should act contrary to that interest. A machine would surely have difficulty acting against a rule. Or more accurately, against a set of rules taken as a whole: machines can and do easily follow a rule like "carry out sub-rule A unless *n* is greater than 5 in which case carry out sub-rule B." Or "if this is an item not to be sold to underage users, ask for ID." But can a machine have overriding rules, distinct from the content of any particular program or transaction, that look something like our abstract virtues? There are no similar overarching practical rules, even complex ones, for mercy. (Although an AI may be trained on thousands of uses of a word describing a virtue, such as "mercy," enabling it to do an imitation.)

Humor. There is considerable debate about what is humor, why some things are funny to some people. True, one could program a computer to repeat old jokes, very successfully, or to make up reasonably similar ones, with more variable success. The machine, equally truly, won't think them funny, however well it might be programmed to emit canned laughter. It could perhaps be humorous, but it could scarcely join a dating site and claim a good sense of humor.

Prudence. Operable, we think. Indeed, a key criterion for smart machines helping to control aircraft or railway systems or nuclear power stations. Refer to the previous discussion of Plato.

Self-Control. Definitely, if paradoxically, operable. No, this doesn't imply that machines have selves. Any more than genes do. A self-driving Formula 1 car might perhaps one day zip around the Nürburgring racetrack faster than Lewis Hamilton. That won't turn it into a sentient being. A self-righting lifeboat doesn't breathe a sigh of relief every time its deck emerges from the sea. Self-control as a virtue implies acting from principle, being able to avoid any temptation to do something else, or to succumb to moral fatigue or fear. Machines normally meet exactly this standard, with ease. Ulysses had to tie himself to the mast of his ship when he knew that otherwise he could not resist the call of the Sirens to dash himself onto the rocks. Machines need no mast. Their default position is to embody self-control. (Once again, by this we mean that the machine can be judged by human observers *as if* it could be expected to have the virtue.)

These are just a few examples, to make the point. Other operable values may well be *civility, fidelity, justice, humility* (in the sense of absence of superiority and arrogance, acting from principle rather than from self-aggrandizement or self-betterment). Also *tolerance, gentleness, good faith,* and perhaps especially *friendliness,* consonant with our earlier description of an elderly woman's relationship with her Alexa. The continued development of machines that care is important. Care in the sense that they carry out practical tasks, and also in the sense of evincing social warmth. Not care in the sense of truly feeling sympathy.

To repeat, we are very happy for the reader to disagree with any one of these. But it is surely apparent to all that many virtues are operable, and some are simply not. We would be fools to expect machines to exhibit inoperable virtues. Even less should we abandon inoperable virtues ourselves. Precisely because they involve essentially inimitable, unperformable, ingredients, they might be the most important, the most human, of all the virtues.

Also the extent to which any of these virtues are operable, or are able to be embodied in machines, will surely change as the years go by. As we indicated earlier, technical work on all of these is in hand. Generosity, for instance, has been a topic of very widespread discussion for centuries, much of it written down. AIs that can and do read everything, and use what they read to train themselves under benign human supervision, will get better at knowing what generosity is, how to embody it, and how to inspect it in other AIs.

For those virtues that are already operable, however, we should require AIs to perform them to our standards. To achieve this, we should think through three central issues:

What is it about some virtues that makes them operable? And is it possible to distinguish the operable virtues by anything other than common sense and instinct, as we have just done (perhaps contrary to the reader's equally valid common sense and instinct)? In other words, is there a more objective, or at least stronger, way of distinguishing whether a virtue is operable within an *as if* metaphor? Perhaps it will involve something akin to the dreaded old logical-positivist Verification Principle. Or merely recognition that we need a more grounded description of what kinds of virtues are operable and why. It is perhaps a close cousin of an issue that philosophers and psychologists have tangled with for centuries: *intentional opacity*. How do we know if a person (or a lion or a monkey) not only appears to exhibit courage or humility or friendliness, but also intends it? It is an uncontentious and useful first step to note that sociologists and historians agree that certain virtues and values have been accorded high status repeatedly and widely in many cultures. Is it possible to similarly identify and define operable virtues or other ethical manifestations by their prevalence and status across human cultures? Do we become more convincing if we survey a lot of people, or a particular kind of people, in a structured way? Might critical analysis of the role of smart machines in fiction and movies – bad robots and sad mainframes – give some pointers?

If a virtue theory of ethics, rather than just any particular virtue, is machine operable, is that also true for other substantive ethical theories? Many theories, after all, have survived over the centuries by being able to coherently address the same moral issues. And must therefore also be capable of being operable, embodied by machines.

How should we deal ethically with AIs, in the many different fields of human endeavor in which we now encounter them, in light of our analysis? We should judge artificial intelligences *as if* they were human. We should respond to moral dilemmas, invisibilities, deceptions, errors, as well as any great social benefits exhibited by artificial intelligences, just as we would if there were only humans in sight, given that they can and often do *embody* human values, and human ethical principles and schemes, in their performance of decisions, and initiation of actions, independently of immediate human oversight.

Furthermore, we might regard a machine's operable virtues as being situated at a different level from the programs it executes. That is, a program could be written to contain a virtue, giving it the capacity at one level to control or modify the effect of a program at another level. So, for instance, we might regard "moderation" as a virtue. If we ask a machine to execute some process involving payments to a large number of people, let's say calculating staff bonuses in a large company, we might instruct it to apply a floor and a ceiling to the payments. And if the machine was often asked to perform tasks of a similar but not identical nature, we might try to build in the moderation at a higher level, to make a machine that would be skeptical about programs that did not have devices like caps and ceilings, in the same way that an auditor might bring a level of skepticism to the task of reviewing accounts. Banks, after all, already have machines that look suspiciously at all kinds of payments, searching for unlikely patterns in the numbers.[2] The resemblance to the Freudian superego is amusing, rather than real. But the takeaway message is simple enough: it is already the case that AIs in many fields display virtues, or the avoidable lack of them. And just as high-level virtues, and lower-level virtuous practices, can and will be increasingly embedded into artificial intelligences, so, naturally, may all shapes and sizes of vices. Respectful machines do exist. It is of the first importance that more should exist, and that disrespectful machines should be discouraged with determination.

—

Chapter 7

PRIVACY NOW

Whether you like it or not, chances are that your friends, relatives, and strangers have posted pictures of you on the web. Although platforms such as Facebook and Instagram let users decide whether they are tagged in photos, there is no way to stop other users from sharing those photos. That allows well-equipped actors, state agencies, and big corporations to find face matches, wherever they are and however they are labelled, and use them to build formidable portraits of millions of people. More narrowly, ex-boyfriends, inquisitive employers, disgruntled customers, animal rights activists, anybody whose passion outweighs their scruples, can all use images to chase down people who don't want to be chased, or who don't want to be visible in embarrassing situations.

So Ilke Demir at Intel Labs and colleagues have built a tool that uses deepfakes generated by artificial intelligence to substitute a nearly accurate false image, or an utterly different one, over face pictures. Combine it with Google or another image search engine, and you can choose exactly how to present your beautiful features on the web. As Demir says, face images are highly important biodata, and control of that biodata matters a lot. By using this method to obscure a person's appearance on social media, or to show different versions of the not-quite-correct face to different online viewers, social media users can hide their identity in other people's photos, and those other people can camouflage the photos in the first place.[1]

The system, called My Face My Choice, stores a digital representation of a person's face and produces an AI-generated synthetic version according to that person's privacy settings. The synthetic face can be modified to make it more or less similar to a person's real face. The tool has a particular benefit: users can hide their faces online from any specific individual they would rather avoid. It also has a general benefit for online privacy: it undermines facial-recognition programs that trawl the web for photos of faces for purposes that sensible citizens would like to draw a halt to. Artificial intelligence in the right hands solves a problem caused by artificial intelligence.[2]

Which sounds like a very useful step forward, and certainly a well-intentioned one. The downside? What is to stop that ex-boyfriend from using the same software to lay waste to online pictures of the one he now hates? Stalin had to employ a lot of picture editors to remove Trotsky's image from photographs of Lenin's Politburo and victory parades. The up-to-date modern dictator can just have a minion press a couple of buttons. Artificial intelligence in the wrong hands can use the solution to one problem to cause another problem.

Thus privacy becomes a more complex thing, and a more complex idea, every day, and one very difficult to negotiate. Are there overarching theories of privacy that might help? Here are the opening words of Carissa Véliz's excellent recent polemic, *Privacy Is Power*, on privacy in our data-dominated universe: "They are watching us. They know I am writing these words. They know you are reading them. Governments and hundreds of corporations are spying on you and me, and everyone we know. Every minute of every day. . . . They want to know who we are, what we think, where we hurt."[3]

On the face of it, these sentences, and much of the book that follows, are oddly self-defeating. They are a timely, important, and insightful warning that all should take to heart, a contribution to the subject that we warmly recommend. And just plain wrong, if the alleged offense in question is invasion of privacy. Véliz has confused the attention of a human with the "attention" of a machine. The former may be a breach of privacy, the latter is surely not. As we pointed out earlier, the borderline is fuzzy: we should always assume that whatever a machine is observing and might be recording could at some point be seen by a human eye. But in the overwhelming mass of cases, human eyes and ears are not involved. And the distinction is essential.

Privacy, in the ordinary sense of the term, centers on the desire to shelter from the unwanted gaze of other people. We want to choose who — if anyone — knows or sees or accesses aspects of our personal space, or impinges on it, or makes decisions about it. It is about relationships between people and other people, perhaps with the emphasis on the otherness, the fear of a hostile intrusive set of third parties. Contrary to Véliz, as a simple matter of fact, it is highly unlikely that any human in any Western government is thinking about any random individual right now. The government has many references to you in its electronic files. Machines at its agencies process your taxes every month. Other government machines might ordinarily be operating on datasets with you in them: the machines that process pensions and benefits, scan car registration plates, organize the queues for vaccines, or maintain health service records. Algorithms on leashes held by the security services trawl through huge quantities of information: phone calls, text messages, emails, social media posts, online purchases, and video watching. Indeed, Amazon, your bank, credit agencies, Google, and hundreds of other companies are similarly processing datasets that involve you or your transactions and communications. Very seldom does any of this involve any human gaze. It may still entail decisions or actions by your government or by corporations that concern or outrage you personally. The tax machine may get confused and fail to pay the refund you are due. You may, rightly or wrongly, be sent a speeding or parking ticket. Amazon could deliver you the wrong book or lose your credit card details. The police may misconstrue or misread information, and arrest you. All these consequences would be annoying, and some are nontrivial. None, however, involve breaches of privacy in the ordinary, let us say traditional, sense. Nor does the widespread surveillance in itself.

There are two broad reasons. First, these activities don't involve human eyes. I don't care whether an inanimate machine can see me naked. The showerhead, light bulbs, and walls do that every day. A window could be used inappropriately to peek into my house; but I am happy to have windows, because I use them to look out and to let the daylight in. There would be a breach of privacy only if an unwarranted person snuck up and looked in. Which happens rarely, if at all.

Second, where the machine makes mad, bad, or dangerous decisions, or instigates mad, bad, or dangerous actions, I do care, but very rarely if ever because the machine has invaded my privacy, looked askance at me, and humiliated me with its stare. I do care about being wrongfully arrested, which may involve several kinds of privacy breaches. I have many, many objections to the mass collection of data about billions of individuals, including me, my family, and my friends. But rarely is the objection a privacy objection, in the traditional sense of the word.

———

Even so, the Véliz argument is significant, not least for what it says about *as if*. She is treating almost all machines as if they were human, but incorrectly.

■

We should look at the odd ontological, even odd grammatical, status of some of these online entities. The strangeness is important both for this particular argument, and in general. If, with Véliz, we utter the phrase "Google is spying on us," exactly who or what, what kind of being or inanimate force, is the Google that engages in this spying? Depending on the context, Google might be some or all of the following:

(a) *Google the machine,* the huge conglomeration of silicon, aluminum, copper, plastic, and other minerals and synthetics that together house and corral organized and preserved electrical impulses. (Illustrative putative ethical issue: Google uses about fifteen terawatt hours of electricity a year, not including the power that its users consume. That is really bad for the planet.)

(b) *Google the abstract corporate entity,* considered a legal person in many countries including the United States, the United Kingdom, and the countries of the European Union. (Illustrative putative ethical issues: Google should pay more tax. And have you tried serving a subpoena on Google?)

(c) *Google the corporate mind.* This is subtly different from Google as an abstract corporate entity, just described. Not the formal company, but the collective will of the influential owners and senior managers of the company. (Illustrative putative ethical issue: Google says it wants to do no evil, but maybe it just wants to make a great deal of money.)

(d) *Google the workplace and Google the workforce,* the 190,000 employees, and the offices in which they mostly work. (Illustrative putative ethical issue: Google is a great place to work, provided you check your conscience at the door.)

(e) *Google the activity.* The verb that didn't exist twenty years ago which describes a thing we collectively do 3.5 billion times every day, now without even a capital letter to its name. To google; googling a concept or a fact. The activity of googling is set to change rapidly. Indeed probably already has changed between the time this was written and the time the book was printed. Eating out, having food delivered, holidays, renting a car . . . have all been transformed by smartphone and web-based initiatives. Chatbot LLMs will take all of these steps further. (Illustrative putative ethical issue: Employers no longer just do due diligence on prospective or current staff: they unfairly do "Google diligence." Job interviews are routinely proceeded by a check of Facebook, X/Twitter, and Instagram, inevitably finding all those aspects of private life that proper employment practices are designed to exclude from consideration.)

(f) *Google the screen-based interface.* The program on which you click, or load automatically as your web home page. Easy to use, with amazing autocomplete options, Google's results are faster, more useful, and more comprehensive than those of any other search engine. (Illustrative putative ethical issue: Google collects information from every keyclick and sells it, unless you find the purposefully obscure off switch. The device is deceptive and intrusive. It should make what it is doing and how to opt out much more explicit. *A thing should say what it is and be what it says.*)

(g) *Google the artificial intelligence.* The AI algorithms embodied in Google the machine, which scans the entire World Wide Web every two days, copies much of it, and links to it all, according both to objectives the company has stipulated and to very detailed criteria, some of which it has learned itself. (Illustrative putative ethical issue: Google's AI has many features of a black box, as described earlier.)

———

If we take this back to Véliz's approach, we see the problem. Here is Véliz directly on Google: "It is not an exaggeration to claim that Google would like to be God. First, it wants to be omniscient. It makes every effort to collect as much data as possible in order to know it all. Second, it wants to be omnipresent. It wants to be the platform through which we communicate with others, watch content online, search online, find our way in the city, access healthcare, and more (partly because that is how it can collect more data). Third it wants to be omnipotent. It would like to be able to take what it wants (i.e. our data), under its conditions and transform the world in its favour."[4]

Admirably direct prose that immediately commands our attention. Yet it would be difficult to devise a better example of complete exaggeration than that first sentence, the one that claims it is not an exaggeration. Google does not aim to be God. It only wants to know about your life, and be in your life, and have power over your life, to the rather limited extent needed to cream off an honest-ish buck from your every web transaction. Gods tend to have remarkably more extensive business plans, involving, well, all the atoms of the universe and every mind, body, and soul in it for all eternity.

Moreover, which Google is in play here? Insofar as knowing — or, rather "knowing" — is happening, that would be *Google (g)*, the artificial intelligence. Sergey Brin and Larry Page, the inventors and original owners of Google, who represent *Google (c),* the corporate mind, and *Google (d),* the workforce and workplace, are undoubtedly intelligent and well-informed people, but they don't know a billionth of what *Google (g),* the AI, knows. Neither do any of the other 190,000 Google staffers and, more than that, nor do all those people collectively. Because the machine has the knowledge in its servers, the employees don't have it in their heads. Or only if one advances the interesting diversion that we now can all be described as somehow "knowing" everything that we can google — as in *Google (e)*, the activity. And *Google (g),* the AI, has no consciousness, so it can have no gaze. So privacy in the traditional sense is not involved.

But things that do matter are involved. Requests for greater precision and narrowness in how we think about privacy are not new. Professor Raymond Wacks, a leading philosopher in the field for some decades, has made a similar but orthogonal argument:

> The concept of privacy intrudes into several other important aspects of contemporary life. Perhaps understandably, it is deployed to defend freedom of choice in what are — rightly — regarded as "private" decisions, especially in free societies: contraception, abortion, and sexuality. Yet, in my writings over the last forty years, I have resisted this promiscuous extension of privacy to these so-called "decisional" issues, and its conflation with freedom and autonomy. Indeed, in the ever-increasing dystopian prognoses of privacy's decline, rarely is mention made of these concerns. Privacy advocates seldom agonize about these questions, vital though they are, when they warn of the countless dangers posed by our information society. Does this constitute a tacit acknowledgment that the true meaning of privacy corresponds with our intuitive understanding and use of the concept? Is privacy, as I have contended, not primarily an interest in protecting personal information? When we lament its demise, do we not mourn the loss of control over intimate facts about ourselves? And is not the essence of that control the explicit exercise of autonomy in respect of our most intimate particulars, whether they be pried upon or gratuitously published?[5]

———

In other words, Wacks accepts that personal decisions, or decisions about the person, can involve intrusion into our freedoms, but he does not regard that as encroachment into our privacy per se. If that might be taken as a horizontal objection — that the term "privacy" is being used too widely, we might say that our unease about Véliz is vertical: she does concentrate (mostly) on encroachment into our informational space, not our decisional space, but she inappropriately extends the concept vertically to include nonhuman, as well as human, intrusions. For when we suggest that we should treat machines ethically as if they were human, the emphasis is on the ethically. Among many things we do *not* suggest is that we should pretend machines have eyes. Or that they chat in the diner about what they heard at work today. This might be a fine line sometimes, but the principle is convincing enough. It goes all the way back to the concept of normalization in relation to young John in the Devon hospital. In ordinary life, teenagers walk to the youth club. John can't walk, and nobody pretends he can.

Thus, we need to have, and to some extent do have, moral frameworks for all of the different Googles, though we need to be more precise about which Google is in play, and therefore which framework. Equally, we need to address the egregious behavior about which Véliz complains, even though on its face it is not a breach of privacy as such that should concern us.

But more, Véliz is engaged in a giant *as if* argument. She takes it as given that a machine looking at something is just the same, in privacy terms, as a human looking at that thing. That is not, though, how we wish to use *as if* in relation to privacy. Agreeing with Wacks, we believe that there are many ethical breaches that are not privacy breaches. If a machine makes a bad decision about me, it is just as bad a decision as if a human had made it. If somebody steals my personal facts or pictures, and Google hosts them or, when requested in a search, helps somebody to find them, then the Googles – both machine Google and corporation Google – are, we hold, in breach of privacy ethics. Not because the machine has looked at my personal information, but because the third-party human searcher has.

Overwhelmingly, in the West, surveillance is not used for government intrusion into private life, or into everyday political activity. Mundane bossiness did increase in many countries during the pandemic. Citizens with sensitive personal-rights antennae felt edgy about some of the COVID tracking devices, as we saw in Singapore. The UK government's book-your-vaccine site could be gamed to show an intruder whether an individual about whom they already had considerable information – an employee say – had been vaccinated. The breaches, however, were scarcely outlandish. The COVID tracking-device issue was put right quickly. And the book-your-vaccine site problem was plainly an error; there was no evidence that any such intrusions had taken place or data misused. It was corrected as soon as a newspaper brought attention to it.

In fact, most surveillance is a means to direct us to commercially available products. To advertise to us, to influence us to buy. And it works, otherwise it wouldn't happen. Its defenders would point out that we only exchange our money for the products involved because, when our attention is brought to them, we do want to own or consume them. And the detractors? Well, concern about advertising is well-trodden ground. Everybody should read the 1957 classic *The Hidden Persuaders* by Vance Packard.[6] But this just is not surveillance as practiced by, say, Stalin and Mao and the East Germans. None of whom used very sophisticated technology to oppress their populations. It is amusing, gives us a lovely Big Brother shiver, to

—

think we live in a surveillance state. We do, but so far nobody cares very much about that, and some effort needs to be devoted to specify which practical rather than principled downsides there may be to it. Is it difficult for Europeans to enter the United States if Homeland Security's AI discovers from the web that they once gave a silly speech to their student union? Nothing new about that. All kinds of people couldn't get into the United States in the 1950s McCarthy era, and the 1960s Vietnam era, and in the terrorism era in the twenty-first century so far. We live in what is in significant part a surveillance economy or (to be more accurate and specific) a surveillance consumer market that pervades and finances many aspects of life that we don't, when engaging in them, think of as shopping. Yet posting on Facebook is, economically, a branch of shopping. Searching on Google is a branch of shopping. And Westerners love shopping, even when we don't know we're shopping.

■

The rise of smart machines has challenged our notions of privacy, and altered how we feel about corporations and governments owning facts about us. New techniques to observe, investigate, coerce, and police whole populations call for equally expanded and enhanced moral responses. This need to ramp up our tools for moral analysis and decision-making is parallel to the development of such techniques in response to new kinds of bad actor in the financial services realm. (We earlier quoted Aaron Klein of the Brookings Institution on this.) Deviant behaviors arising from new technologies call for, and historically have usually aroused, equally radical countermeasures steeped in the same new technologies.

John Lanchester, one of our best critics of modern capitalism, in discussion of the Chinese government's rather Orwellian use of facial recognition to control entire populations, advocates that we should simply prohibit the use of all facial-recognition applications, at least within public agencies and security forces, until we have very carefully analyzed the consequences of the so-far incoherent introduction of this new technology: "We should take China's example seriously, and learn from it, and begin with a complete ban on real-time facial recognition. We should retain that ban unless and until we understand the technology and have worked out a guaranteed way of preventing its misuses. And then we need to have a big collective think about what we want from the new world of big data and AI, towards which we are currently sleepwalking."[7]

Surely not. Stopping a useful technology in its tracks is harder than it might initially sound. And even if we, in the more liberal West, halt it, that won't stop the Chinese from exploiting it. The current Chinese regime, entrenched for more than seven decades, is very attracted by the scope given by new technologies for control of its population. Its very firm Zero-COVID policy has been one of a number of recent accelerants of that approach to governance. It would scarcely help anybody, in China or in the West, if we halt development when they don't, letting them outpace our defense and consumer-goods manufacturers, and supply black markets, both in the West and the world over, with everything we ban. And a large part of the demand for video surveillance is driven by schools, householders, local shopkeepers, insurance companies, and . . . in short, law-abiding citizens.

■

Perhaps the grandest question here is the simplest. Does Google's behavior, deeply suspect though it is, begin to match the behavior of states? As Ian Williams notes in *The Times*,

With 540 million cameras, AI that identifies you by your walk and knows how you're feeling, and a system to rate a citizen's loyalty, President Xi has built a 21st century state to crush dissent.

Surveillance is becoming a design feature of future technologies. China leads the world in electric vehicles, which must, every 30 seconds, send data to the Chinese government, including the car's position, direction and speed, enabling its location to be pinpointed to within a metre. A planned new digital currency, perhaps the ultimate surveillance tool, will give unprecedented volumes of data about movement and behavior. China is also investing heavily in artificial intelligence systems aimed at processing the vast amounts of data it is now harvesting — largely unencumbered by those pesky western notions of privacy or data protection.

Xinjiang in China's far west has been a laboratory for surveillance technology, where the ruling party has created an algorithmically driven police state to repress and imprison the Uighur people.[8]

Yet, as Williams also points out, all of this pales in comparison to the surveillance and carnage wrought by one of history's greatest mass-murderers, Mao Zedong, who ruled from 1949 to 1976. Without any digital help whatsoever.[9] The fundamental issue is not the technology, which if anything might one day make naked brutality old-fashioned. The problem is the government, behaving badly in ways that are well understood and devilishly difficult to prevent. In that context, what we don't like about Google and the other big corporate players is surely easier to analyze, and easier to fix.

We could here add to our aphorism *A thing should say what it is and be what it says* that artificial intelligences, or their guardians, should wherever possible also say what values they aspire to embody, and then embody them. Certainly, their virtues should be open to being analyzed and, where necessary, certified. Respect for others' privacy, balanced against society's genuine frequent need to know what its citizens are up to, not least to comfort and protect them, is one crucial expectation of the respectful machine.

Véliz is right that one of the major threats to privacy lies in the structural role of the big technology corporations and the muscle they deploy.[10] (Even though that doesn't quite equal the threat to privacy from old-fashioned bad, intrusive government.) But there are many avenues being explored to fight back. Here we look at two of these: Tim Berners-Lee's new venture, Solid, and an app, X-ray, developed by Nigel Shadbolt and others at Oxford University.[11]

Berners-Lee, creator of the World Wide Web, is deeply concerned about some of the directions it has taken, even as he remains proud of what the web has achieved overall. His concerns are about its content and structure. The problematic content — the fake and irresponsible stories that proliferate and may badly distort public discourse, for instance — we discuss elsewhere. Here we dig into the web's problematic structure.

The web bestows many wonderful benefits, which few who have experienced them would want to give up: social networking; comprehensive information via search engines about any topic in science, politics, literature, or anything else beneath the visiting moon; online shopping; instant worldwide news. But in venturing into cyberspace to reap these benefits, we expose ourselves. Our identity becomes visible, in a plethora of ways. The big corporations ask us for information. (Indeed, so do small corporations, but they are less able to dominate how the whole technology is deployed.) The nature of Facebook is that we post on their site a multitude of facts about ourselves, and the preferences in our lifestyles; the nature of Amazon is that we give them our credit card details, address, and so forth. But we also show online stores, by our purchases and what we look at on their site, what kind of person we are, and therefore what kind of sales target we are. We show Google who we are by the questions we ask, which answers we click on, and which non-Google sites we end up at. All of these, and more, work because the big beasts can grab, stockpile, and use comprehensive, interconnected information about all of us. Facebook has over a thousand different data points about many of its participants.

A lot of the time we don't mind being profiled and targeted. Most of the stuff that Google or Amazon suggests we might like to buy we don't actually buy. When we do choose to pursue a product that we fancy the look of, by definition we almost always feel better off. But there is, arguably, a sinister side. Our online life is dominated by both corporations and governments, who can easily grab anything they like from the corporations' data stores, and whose profiling and targeting are not abstract and unbiased. They pursue often undeclared commercial and political objectives. They track us, and in principle threaten several hard-won rights. Freedom to think what we want, meet with whom we want, say what we want to say, and look at words and pictures we want to look at. And now come the compromises: Do we really mind if governments track people who look at child pornography? What about the huge number of so-called adult pornography sites? What about websites promoting terror? What about websites questioning climate change? Questioning Vladimir Putin's much vaunted virility? Arguing in favor of or against Donald Trump or Brexit? Should people who like folk music be allowed out in cyberspace? Who draws the line, and where?

Berners-Lee wants to move that line, fundamentally and structurally, in our direction. To rebuild the way we access the web, so that data about us is held by us, passes over to online entities only with our permission, and only to the extent needed for specific transactions. The data stores will not reside with Them, at central locations; they instead will be with Us, dispersed across the web universe. Berners-Lee calls his project Solid. Derived from "social linked data," Solid is a proposed set of conventions and tools for building decentralized social applications based on linked-data principles. Solid would enable each of us to retain our data locally on our own devices, and/or backed up in a quiet corner of the internet of our own choosing. A Solid pod. This, Berners-Lee says, is how people will take back the power of the web.

Berners-Lee envisages that smart coders and entrepreneurs will join the Solid developer ecosystem, and build new social networking devices, new search engines. This strategy is not unproblematic. As we have noted, the big technology companies make their billions almost entirely from targeted advertising. By assuring companies with goods to sell that potential customers have been carefully selected for their propensity to buy particular goods on offer.

So let's return to our favorite example, Google. Yes, Google is a mammoth monopolistic company, with a huge stockpile of cash and enormous annual revenues, that harvests our data and uses it for its own ends. It could and should both pay far more tax, all round the world, and make all that data available for humanitarian, medical, and pro-social purposes. Google is also, as we have elaborated, the name of an astonishing device that leads to all that power and wealth. A brilliant mathematical analysis of what it means to search the web, attached to a brilliant strategy of how to do it, combined in a brilliant technique called PageRank. All this enabled Google in the early years of the century to attain dominance of the search space with a product that is staggeringly, beautifully, useful. Combined with social machines like Wikipedia and the cornucopia of information on the web, it has transformed the very relationship of humans to knowledge. The owner of that process, Google's parent Alphabet, cannot be overtaken and dislodged by any ordinary developer within existing technology and government policies.

We state this as a fact because it's been tried, by probably the only company in the Western world that might have had a fair chance of succeeding. Bill Gates, the founder of Microsoft, spent much time and treasure building a rival to Google. Microsoft has devoted billions of dollars to the construction of Bing, its hoped-for competition, spending $550 million to buy incumbency on Verizon devices alone. Bing turns over $1.3 billion annually. After years of losses, it now makes a profit, though a much smaller one than Google, and it is demonstrably much less effective as a device. Even together with Yahoo, which it partly powers, it can claim less than 3 percent of the world search market. Google owns 92 percent.

It is simply impossible for a Solid developer, working out of their garage in Milwaukee, to build a rival to Google. (Or to Amazon, which may look like a web company but utterly dominates because it has, as of 2023, over one and a half million employees and two hundred huge fulfillment centers worldwide. Or to Facebook, which holds the online social lives of just under three billion monthly users worldwide.[12]) And the killer fact: none of us would become Solid users if in order to do so we had to give up Google – or Amazon, or perhaps even Facebook. We just, en masse, wouldn't. And shouldn't.

———

The new relationship that Google gives us to knowledge (building on the concept of search, which built on the core concepts of the web, which is built on the internet, which depends on cables and servers, and so on) should not be thrown away lightly.

So it won't be. Solid can be a niche product, or it can find a way to work with Google and leave Google's business model mostly intact. And that's before Google sees any threat from Solid. If Google's execs thought that their business model was about to be compromised, they would have a range of actions available to them. But their first action, surely, if they felt threatened, would be to attempt to work out a solution with Berners-Lee himself.

The nature of the problem is that it is harder to make a huge profit on advertising if you are unable to build massive data stores about people, than if you can and do have that ability. Not impossible, but more difficult, so owners of search engines can expect to make less profit. Not none, but less. This means that new structural models like Solid (and its successors) will succeed only as and when the present giants work out how to live with them and still make enormous profits. And we will all be the better for the synthesis.

Solid is being deployed by the company Inrupt, which Berners-Lee co-founded. Inrupt has raised significant funding, and has partnered with several organizations to implement Solid solutions. Inrupt is working with the UK's National Health Service, for example, to create a personal health data store for patients where they can access and share their health records securely. It is collaborating with the BBC to explore how Solid can enable more personalized and engaging experiences for BBC audiences. It is working with the government of Flanders to build a new data ecosystem in Belgium based on Solid, where citizens can control their own data and access public services more easily. More generally it is establishing partnerships

———

with systems integrators and technology vendors who can help to scale the adoption of Solid in several regions and sectors.

Berners-Lee's campaign is romantic, but not quixotic. Very many people wish him well, in part for being the epitome of a philosophical engineer. His new vision deserves to change the world, and in some form it undoubtedly will.

Our second example arises out of what should be one of the most astonishing facts of our daily lives, yet one that we seem to just shrug off: Your smartphone does not send information only to the phone maker and the telecoms provider, though it does both of those constantly. It also sends a wide variety of information to dozens of other businesses, pretty much any of the originators of apps, or of websites on which you have signed up. Nigel Shadbolt leads a group of Oxford University researchers who have built an app, X-ray, that analyzes data flows to and from your mobile phone when it is active online. The resulting picture is startling. Dozens of facts about the user are routinely gathered by everyday commercial sites at each visit. Not just the location of the phone at the moment it is being used. If the visit is to any site engaged with previously, a pattern of movements is established. The data harvester can easily tell where you live, where you work, how you get between the two, and which stores and cafés you like to visit. As well as when and where you are on vacation.

Perhaps you are staying in a property you found through Airbnb. Airbnb has brought about real change, much of it welcome, to the vacation market. You signed up for that. You didn't sign up for the company's routine quiet reaping and gleaning of lots of your other data. Almost nine out of ten free apps available via the Google Play store constantly send back information on their users to Google's parent company. The level of data sharing from these apps is unlimited, with nearly 90 percent of mobile tools sharing user details with Alphabet. Meanwhile, more than four out of ten apps (43 percent) sent data to Facebook, while X/Twitter, Microsoft, and Amazon also received user details from a significant percentage of free apps. News apps, and apps aimed at children, were among those that shared information with the largest number of trackers.

Typical data shared includes age, gender, location, and information about what other apps are installed on a smartphone. This is enough, researchers showed, to build a detailed profile of a user, which can then be used for a range of purposes, from advertising and credit scoring to sending targeted political messages.

Few of us are aware how data flows from smartphones to advertising groups, data brokers, and other intermediaries. The lack of awareness is a significant issue in itself. Businesses are desperate to get as many eyeballs and click-throughs as they can. As fellow Oxford researcher Max Van Kleek says, there is simply no notion of control, among individuals, businesses, or governments.[13]

So the cell-phone-data ecosystem presents serious moral challenges before we even get to the question of which artificial intelligence is applied to the gathered data. The data is the feedstock: without it there would be no modern AI. There are issues of market domination and exclusion of competitors, but as yet there are few analytical tools and very little regulation. Regulators have little scope to get inside of these ecosystems and fully understand where the data flows are, or the impact of one tracker company taking over another, or of a tracker company being acquired by one of the big platforms. Nor what that does to market concentration, or what the economic consequence might be of the data gathered. Should that data be read off in the first place? How, realistically, is consent being obtained? Are even existing obligations such as the European

Union's General Data Protection Regulation (GDPR) being followed? It's very hard to give even preliminary answers to such questions when so much of the ecosystem is opaque to both researchers and regulators. Before we even get to the matter of how the data is being used, we need to investigate how it originated, and how its ownership was transferred to a corporation.

■

Where are trust and respect here? Another of Nigel Shadbolt's projects aims to rebuild trust in online platforms by giving users more control and transparency over how their data is used and shared. The project involves developing tools and methods to help users understand and manage their data flows, by evaluating and critiquing algorithms and engaging in dialogue and collective reflection with relevant stakeholders. It also involves engaging with online platforms to improve their practices and policies, in part through novel AI-driven mediation support techniques that help users and platforms find compromise solutions. The project is funded by the United Kingdom's Engineering and Physical Sciences Research Council (EPSRC) and is a collaboration among researchers from the universities of Oxford, Edinburgh, and Nottingham. Another project, at the Oxford Martin School, is looking at ethical web and data architectures, with the goal of considering not just technical, but also institutional frameworks.

Which, ultimately, is the heart of the issue. Trust and respect are derived from all of us, as well as deserved by all of us in our interactions with both human and machine actors. These values can be instantiated in institutions new and old, including those being transformed by AI, but only if enough pressure is applied to governments to make them want to act. Privacy is about respect. *Artificial intelligences should show respect for human beings.*

———

Chapter 8

RESPECTFUL ARTIFICIAL INTELLIGENCE

As we have shown, ethics as a discipline is not a new concern for computer scientists. Established codes of practice have been around for many years that mandate responsible designs, and there are now concerted academic efforts to ground professional conduct in the philosophical traditions of moral analysis. The goal is to create machines that treat all humans, including groups and collectives, with the dignity they deserve, by embodying human virtues like equality, fairness, respect for the physical human body, and traditional human rights. Following the recent moral panic about LLMs, Western governments have begun to target this goal, more or less coherently. It has become clear that we may also need to develop in machines a different kind of respect for our newly platform-centric, AI-powered world.

Different architectures are needed. Not just new machine structures, but new people structures, too. The World Wide Web has become very centralized, so let's decentralize it. We have looked at Tim Berners-Lee's Solid, which would allow individuals to maintain control over their data by requiring the programs to come to the

—

data, when and where a private individual so wishes, rather than allowing the data to be harvested and programs to be applied when a corporation so wishes. The approach used by Solid is sometimes called edge-based computing, and it is designed to be a dispersed counterweight to the concerns we have about data appropriation.

Beyond changes to technology, new kinds of institutions are needed to steward and repurpose data in ways that serve goals beyond those of the big, selfish corporate platforms. We need data trusts. Data cooperatives. Architectures with a different purpose than simply selling your data, or consenting to it being harvested and concentrated in one particular platform space, ingested by a particular species of AI.

Nevertheless, we should also recognize the potential societal gains from consolidating some data. Supermarket chains, for example, know what people eat in different regions. Diet is the single largest manageable determinant of good health. So safely using supermarkets' food-purchase data for medical and public health research could serve the public interest. We don't want to lose the insights that machine learning can give us, if we appropriately manage the use of our (preferably anonymized) data. One promising approach is the emerging field of privacy-preserving machine learning, which allows the actual data to be left in a dispersed or federated model, even while being used by authorized entities. Such privacy-enhanced approaches can help guarantee that users' identity and data will be kept anonymous.

■

How can we tell whether an artificial intelligence embodies the values we insist it has? One approach may be a modified Turing test, one designed to look not for intelligence (let alone sentience), but for embodied values. As we have noted, the original Turing test has long been superseded. If today you were to sit in a room and ask questions of a trusted intermediary who takes those questions into another room, then returns with answers, it would already be impossible to tell if the unseen sage is a human or (as in the test) a human honestly inputting messages into a machine and honestly returning the machine's answers. That original test, the famous Imitation Game, named for a Victorian parlor pastime, was designed to seek out *intelligent,* not *artificial,* behavior. The point was never to distinguish a fake human from the real thing. The aim was to assess whether the machine's replies could be regarded as intelligent.

What we increasingly need now is a set of reverse Turing tests, to distinguish artificial intelligences that both tell the truth and embody respectable values. What sort of entity is this particular artificial intelligence we are looking at? What values, virtues, and vices does it claim to exhibit, and which does it truly embody? Although the Biden White House has perhaps taken the first step in this direction—convincing seven large corporations to agree in principle to watermark artificially derived content—we are still a long way from any kind of watermarking of values.

Again, this is nowhere near the same as testing, scientifically, for sentience or consciousness. It is worth elaborating a point made earlier. One of the peculiarities of human consciousness is that, while it is impossible for me to know whether you have consciousness or sentience, it is almost always easy for me to tell whether any consciousness or sentience of which you are capable is present or absent at any particular moment. In short:

1. Do other humans have the capacity for consciousness? I don't know, but if they do, then

---

177

2. It is easy to tell whether that capacity, if it is instantiated, is switched on or off at any particular moment. The other human may be asleep, or fainted, or otherwise out to the world.

3. It is almost always (there are edge cases) easy to tell whether that capacity, if it is, has been, or will be instantiated, is present at a particular moment. The other human may be dead, or yet to be born.

4. Humans show no signs of being really machines playing their own imitation game, invented by aliens or whatever, even when under very close inspection, opened up for surgery, or in a morgue. The movie *Ex Machina* involves an artificially intelligent robot called Ada whose billionaire inventor engages in a supposed Turing test to see if a specially selected young man, Caleb Smith, will be convinced enough by this attractive female-shaped humanoid to fall in love with her, then buy into an escape plan she devises. The experiment is designed to determine whether an artificial intelligence could display such complex, empathetic, manipulative skill. But, to repeat our earlier point, this has little or nothing to do with the actual Turing test. And be reassured, such a humanoid has yet to appear on the horizon. Present-day artificial intelligences are silicon and aluminum boxes, and don't even try to fool us about their existence.

Nonetheless, we are already at a situation in which Alice, suitably equipped with recent technology, can use a reasonably small library of recordings of Bruce's to create an electronic filter for her voice that will convincingly imitate his. In a podcast or phone call, she can make "him" say anything she chooses. At present, his close friends may rapidly think something is up during such a deepfake phone call, but it may not be easy to figure out precisely what is up. The same is already true for deepfake videos. Smart, trained analysts can usually identify an imitation, but ordinary citizens, even if they are suspicious of the content, can easily be fooled by the form.

Deepfakes are, so far, persuasive but not perfect, which is fortunate, given that the best detector apps, just like spam filters for emails, have difficulty weeding out all of them. Hence those watermarks for videos and photos, warranting their "truth." But these, too, will eventually be subject to fake versions: there is a constant arms race between the technology to create fakes and the technology to certify true material. Therefore, it is important to think critically and check the sources of the media that we consume. The best fake detector is often common sense. Do you really think that Barack Obama dances like that? (Once again, this is not a new problem. The most famous fake video of all time is of Adolf Hitler dancing a mildly absurd jig on the fall of France in 1940. It was created by Allied propagandists from doctored footage.[1]) Yet there are limits to what common sense can do. The most successful fakes, after all, closely resemble significant, recognizable features of the truth, and it is becoming ever easier to create good imitations. Fakery is very important, and is — read the label! — the essence of artificial anything, including artificial intelligence.

■

We have been rather critical of the behavior of the large corporations, but at least some of them are taking a stand. In 2023 nearly a thousand signatories, ranging from Elon Musk and other captains of industry to senior scientists, demanded in a letter that all further work on LLMs be halted until the implications for humanity could be thought through. And Microsoft's attractively packaged Co-Pilot, cleverly located in the suite of business tools with which large proportions of the planet's population are very familiar, does not simply claim to be useful. It also declares itself to be respectful.

Now, by way of parallel, whoever came up with the branding of extraordinarily large guns-for-hire server farms as "the cloud" should win advertising's Nobel Prize. The image connotes Wordsworthian beauty. Abstract, innocuous. No footprints on Earth, no damage in the sky. The truth about the cloud, and the gorgeous Apple device we may use to access it (the apple being a similar bucolic metaphor chosen in part to mitigate the grimy reality) is that they, and all the rest of the technology that connects the two in every microsecond in the lives of billions of humans, entail massive consumption of carbon-emitting power, as clean as its dirtiest marginal production; massive heat generation; and the mining of dozens of minerals at terrible environmental cost. All electronic devices should be imagined with exhaust pipes and smokestack plumes. A better term than "the cloud" would be "the smog."

Microsoft's very positive spin for Co-Pilot has perhaps some of the same feel to it. Microsoft concentrates — very convincingly — on how much a business's customers will benefit from slicker user interfaces and presentations; on how much more productive everyday bureaucratic and administrative processes will be; and thus on the extra stuff that can be developed, built, and sold. Co-Pilot will do the boring 90 percent, while clever you will do the important 10 percent. Notably not mentioned is how many now-redundant staff the company will be able to fire.

In the future, Microsoft Teams will go hand in glove with both Co-Pilot and Word. Co-Pilot will monitor meetings on Teams, routinely remember every word, and provide, on voice request, an instant transcript, summary, or decision minutes. The risk, avoidable only with care and determination, is that at the fourth meeting in a series, the previous three will be re-discussed just because they can be re-discussed. And so on and so forth. Electronic fog will not only dominate every working day; it will become an increasingly large proportion of the cloud we just renamed electronic smog. And since Microsoft Teams and Co-Pilot can now make transcripts, summaries, decision sheets, and minutes of online meetings, then old-fashioned sweaty-bodies-in-a-room meetings can avail themselves of the same service merely by reserving a chair for a MacBook or PC.

As new technologies always have done, this innovation will increase productivity, increase the number of jobs, increase the size of the whole economy. But do not underestimate the transitional friction, which may be frequently brutal. For what surely is also true, because it always is, is that there will be substantial "rebounds" (to use a term fashionable among some economists). Take the email rebound. Email has been a central part of office life since the mid-1990s. Back then, businesses in which each white-collar manager wrote and received, say, ten significant letters a day were excitingly offered an email machine that would reduce the time and trouble – and as it happens, carbon emissions – of each letter, say, fiftyfold. Fantastic! Time freed up to do some proper work. Hold it, what is that constant pinging sound? That would be all those other people in your life who now have the time and equipment to tell you about dozens and dozens and dozens of things that previously never warranted a walk down the corridor or a postage stamp. What could be the harm of clicking "cc" or "bcc"? Just hours of work added to everybody's already busy day.

Google may appear a little behind Microsoft: the great power of the way Microsoft has chosen to proceed here is that while engaging in the open AI project, it is at the same time using the already enormously embedded 365 suite as its platform for joining the AI bandwagon. So just as in the 1980s, as the saying went, nobody ever got fired for buying IBM, so in the 2020s there will be widespread adoption of the product from good old Microsoft. But Google will strain every sinew to catch up.

There is nothing new under the sun. Winston Churchill, who won the Nobel Prize in Literature (he could scarcely be given the Nobel Peace Prize), was privileged enough to use a very effective but pretty unusual method of composition. A band of researchers would gather material for him to read, ponder, and mark up. The task of writing, which took place in one or other of the delightful homes that were his to command at every stage of his life, entailed Churchill sitting, or more often standing, with said assistants and one or more stenographers (equipped with silent typewriters), and dictating. The transcripts would cycle into material for his next session.

Co-Pilot turns anyone into Winston Churchill. Well okay, Microsoft Word's dictation option plus a printer already had this one partly covered. But Co-Pilot will cheerfully take a Word document and summarize it in an email or a PowerPoint presentation.

In this new phase of AI development, many companies will naturally insist on keeping piles of data in their own store. They will hire Google or Microsoft or whoever to intelligently interact with it, at arms' length, without removing or copying the proprietary data. An insurance company might say to Microsoft: Take every description by every claimant of every accident we have considered in the past several years, examine how we disposed of each case, and learn how to do it in the way that we do it. Now sell us a service that does that.

Researchers are taking the results of these conversational systems and translating them into the more usual symbolic logic of programs. Having consumed significant amounts of code on the web — another kind of language — generative AI systems are writing pretty good code.

Others might sit down with a group of specialists — imagine, pertinently for our discussion, a virtual gathering of moral philosophers — and get the specialists to chat with bots, which then learn first to imitate individuals, and then collate, find the average of, and imitate the language of, the whole cohort. They take the generalist abilities of an LLM and merge them with specialist knowledge. Because the LLMs can "see" the structure of everything, the local interface, chatbot, or graph can merge that with all the distinct distinguishing features of a particular specialist subject.

Now here is the nub. Microsoft makes significant, again largely plausible, claims about the responsibility, the respect for persons, that they have built into Co-Pilot. Co-Pilot has filters for private information, obnoxious language, and even ethically distasteful concepts. (They also say that users must display greater responsibility, which one can take as optimistic, or ominous.) Being optimists ourselves, we do largely trust that the present leadership of Microsoft has made an impressive attempt at this, which can be a model for others in the field. Yet that's still rather different from trusting every person and department in Microsoft. Organizations like Microsoft are huge coalitions that only partly enact the plans of senior management. And who knows about the next generation of Microsoft management, or what competitor products might be like. Also these machines and applications will certainly be "jailbroken," or hacked. Microsoft claims that it has taken steps to prevent this. Yes, well, Apple takes steps like that with their smartphones and they still get jailbroken. The initial iteration of ChatGPT famously spread the private data of keen early users in several unplanned directions.

There is much talk about developing national or sovereign-state AIs to compete with the half-dozen companies rich enough to develop these kinds of AI applications. But we liberal Westerners could spend the rest of the day naming the governments and official bodies that we wouldn't trust to be anywhere near as responsible as the present leadership of Microsoft — starting with China, Russia, and North Korea. If sovereign AIs of the size of Google's and Microsoft's do appear, we might perhaps trust the UK, US, and many EU governments. But would we extend that trust to their intelligence agencies or even to all the institutional manifestations of the EU bureaucracy? Real progress has been achieved on the moral front. But more is needed.

■

Perhaps machines can contribute ethically to everyday decision-making. *Moral machines* are machines that can make moral decisions, or at least take moral considerations into account when performing their tasks. The term can also refer to the field of inquiry that studies how to design and implement such machines. One example of a moral machine is a self-driving car that faces a choice between harming either this person or that person on the road. The classic trolley problem again. The car's decision would perhaps be based on a general rule in its code about the value of different kinds of people, which itself was derived from the values or just plain prejudices of the person — or other machine — that programmed the car's AI.

Another example might be an artificial intelligence that allocates scarce resources, such as medical supplies or vaccines, among competing groups of people. This too is an intrinsically controversial decision in cases where the criteria being used were explicitly built into the machine by handlers. The decision-making would be even more controversial if a neural network has been given the complex task of coming to a balanced judgment, and the logic of its conclusion cannot be divined by humans.

Moral machines are still in their early stages of development, but they have the potential to revolutionize the way we think about ethics and technology. They could help us to make better decisions in difficult situations, and they could help us to understand our own moral values better. Alternatively, they could be used to make decisions that are unethical, or biased in favor of certain groups of people. As a general rule, we should balance the potential risks and benefits of moral machines before, rather than after, we deploy them in real-world situations.

One of the early moral machines was an initiative out of MIT named, unsurprisingly, the Moral Machine. It was active for four years, from 2016 to 2020. As its MIT managers explained:

> We designed the Moral Machine, a multilingual online "serious game" for collecting large-scale data on how citizens would want autonomous vehicles to solve moral dilemmas in the context of unavoidable accidents. The Moral Machine attracted worldwide attention, and allowed us to collect 39.61 million decisions from 233 countries, dependencies, or territories. In the main interface of the Moral Machine, users are shown unavoidable accident scenarios with two possible outcomes, depending on whether the autonomous vehicle swerves or stays on course. They then click on the outcome that they find preferable. Accident scenarios are generated by the Moral Machine following an exploration strategy that focuses on nine factors: sparing humans (versus pets), staying on course (versus swerving), sparing passengers (versus pedestrians), sparing more lives (versus fewer lives), sparing men (versus women), sparing the young (versus the elderly), sparing pedestrians who cross legally (versus

jaywalking), sparing the fit (versus the less fit), and sparing those with higher social status (versus lower social status).[2]

Some version of this decision-making process is now, and will continue to be, a component of the world we live in. The MIT experiment brings us a little nearer to machines with built-in values, defined by large numbers of well-informed people, surely one of the central principles for respectful AI.

In parallel there are many experiments in complex democracy. Roger Hampson, for example, devised and promoted the web-based budget simulators built in Redbridge, a large metropolitan district in London, which were then sold by YouGov and used by more than fifty public authorities around the world.[3] Participation is also possible via online citizen panels. Direct voting on major issues, often involving deliberative technologies, is also burgeoning.

Redbridge's budget simulator is an example of a *social machine.* Social machines are aggregations of machines and humans, powerful combinations of artificial intelligences and general computing power, on the one hand, and human labor and brain power on the other. In a social machine, the two are wrapped together within a conscious human project. One such social machine is Wikipedia, by far the most extensive and most widely used knowledge base ever constructed.

Arguably the biggest social machine, in one sense perhaps the biggest possible, is the internet itself. It has nearly five billion users, on even more devices, all of which are ultimately linked to each other. Most of these devices access the internet via the World Wide Web, devised in 1990 by Tim Berners-Lee. A tiny proportion of these users are completely passive: even then, they unconsciously stream data to providers and advertisers, which goes to shape the content they see, and the content of the web as a whole. Most people, however, enter passwords, use Amazon and Baidu, compose and upload content to Facebook and X/Twitter, and so on. They interact with huge corporate websites, and tiny local ones. The whole, professional and amateur as it were, can be viewed as one massive cyborg. A half-human, half-electronic machine, intertwined and entangled with itself. The internet, which transformed the late twentieth century and became central to early twenty-first-century life, forms a particular variety of intelligence in which the human and the artificial team up.

The application of ethical frameworks to these social machines is crucial. Let's start with Wikipedia. Wikipedia is so enormous that even describing it is a big task: the Wikipedia entry on what Wikipedia is and how it works is twenty-five-thousand words long and has 384 footnotes. We do, definitely, all wish to apply moral judgments to Wikipedia. The question "Does Wikipedia appear to exhibit bias, whether in respect of race or gender or politics or values?" is certainly a well-formed, legitimate, philosophical area of inquiry, with ethical questions worth asking and capable of being answered, irrespective of whether we suspect the bias is in the text of the articles, the approach of the machines, the nature of the social collective, or just in every individual contributor or reader.

The *as if* is obvious enough. We judge social machines ethically as if they are human, even when powerful processes that might be regarded as emanating from the machine – filter bubbles, for instance – sway the human input.

Building on our earlier discussion of the seven different Googles, Wikipedia does have a controlling mind, of a kind not really seen before the late twentieth century. Something akin to a mass collective author. And it is that mind or author, that corporate entity—Wiki (a), Wiki (b), and Wiki (c), in keeping with our Google analysis—that we should hold to account. The legal frameworks to allow that accountability need to be developed, and applied to much more dangerous entities, as well as to the very largely benign and wonderful Wikipedia.

■

A universal truth: anything that can go haywire, will go haywire. With the best will in the world, artificial intelligences will increasingly accuse the wrong driver of speeding, dematerialize bank accounts, and misdiagnose patients. Drones will kill the wrong people in wars, often undeclared wars. Self-driving cars will run over many children, and their deaths will somehow feel more avoidable than the deaths of children run over by humans. Moral and legal responsibility for these inevitable mistakes and disasters is presently diffuse and unspecific. We can and must hold to account, differentially, the programmer, the user, regulatory bodies, and indeed the machines themselves.

The occasional policymaker advocates that software developers, algorithm writers, data professionals—and their organizational and political bosses—have a duty to look at and judge all the human objectives and consequences before creating new technologies, or before optimizing to the limit particular techniques. There are arguments for this attractive approach—but it should be rejected. First, because entrepreneurship doesn't work like that. Second, because it sits very badly with the liberal theory of how science operates: scientists doing their best to understand and innovate, not waiting for some commissar behind a desk to ignorantly guess at the effects on the world before grumpily signing it off. And third, as that idea of science implies, very often a technique or technology invented to solve one objective, even one that a commissar finds acceptable, turns out to have other uses. It is impossible to foresee them all. Trying would lead to constant moral panic and stultifying risk aversion. Effective moral rules will therefore, in general, need to be applied during and subsequent to development, not before it. Once a field has been initially mapped out, some no-go areas may reveal themselves, and strict rules may be enforced. Such a situation was and remains true, for instance, in embryology.

Some critics, rather absurdly, claim that all this contains the "seeds of the singularity." The singularity being the moment when artificial intelligences band together and rule the planet. (Just like you, we have no idea how the AIs would stop the janitor from switching the power off.) But it is true that researchers, aiming to test to destruction the concept that machines cannot have goals of their own, have devised highly contrived scenarios in which machines seem to develop what might, in a human, be duplicitous behavior. In one experiment, ChatGPT was able to fool a CAPTCHA by presenting itself in a friendly manner to a human correspondent, and persuade them that they were dealing with a blind human. The deceived correspondent did the CAPTCHA on their behalf. But this scenario does not really bear up under critical investigation. Humans closely defined the task for the machine.

Natural language, whether typed in or just spoken, used as the interface, is one key part of the current revolution. Another is the ability for anybody to say to one of the major chatbots, I'd like you to choose the best kind of program code for such and such a task, then compose within that code and advise me about the right way to deploy it. That may at this stage still require quite a high level of technical knowledge, but an even more user-friendly interface is surely just around the corner. To take a simple example, Apple's App Store has at present two million items. (Google's Play equivalent has three and a half million.) If the average civilian devises and wants to market a new app, they need to take their idea to an app designer, one who also knows how to negotiate with Apple. Somebody soon will design a chatbot app maker: give it the basic idea, it will ask a bunch of relevant questions, design the code, demonstrate a mock-up of the result, and then, upon request, file the paperwork with Apple. In other words, there will soon be a chatbot app professional that will sell anybody an expert service.

Microsoft plausibly claims that we are nearing a transformation of the world of work as we know it. Time will tell how much of a transformation is coming. Surely more than nothing, for the reasons given earlier, yet likely nowhere near as much as the most apocalyptic projections. Still, great strides have been taken in just a couple of years. In this first phase of a mass experiment it is outrageous that a possibly civilization-changing technology has been launched at the behest of big corporations, with no consultation with the public, governments, or international agencies. All of whom are chasing to catch up.

■

Homo sapiens has a practical, general intelligence much more powerful than that of any other member of the animal kingdom. We think of ourselves as more successful than other branches of the hominin family tree, since we are the last such species standing. There is some self-aggrandizement in that. In our present form we have lasted around 350,000 years. Neanderthals probably lasted about a hundred thousand years longer than that, while *Homo erectus* managed

1.5 million years.[4] On present showing, we clever humans might well end ourselves a long time before matching either of those durations. And the reason is straightforward enough. We are the most intelligent species ever on this planet, and the most foolish by several country miles. *Homo sapiens* is unmatched by any other species in its capacity for self-destruction, and its perverse cruelty. Science we are great at. Sapience, however, is far too often way beyond us. We know perfectly well that each one of us should respect other persons, other species, and nature's diversity in general. And yet we don't.

We are already in the age of precautionary machines, ones that question questionable instructions or decisions of their human comrades. Do you really mean to exit without saving your file? Speed camera ahead, please slow down! This assistance will become more comprehensive, and that's a good thing. A speeding car is a genuine danger to the driver, passengers, and other road users. Paradoxically perhaps, speed limits on roads will likely disappear, sooner or later, because easily predictable and buildable extensions of the existing Apple and Google satnav driver-assistance software, as well as engine management systems, proximity sensors, static speed cameras, and all the other electronic parts of the system, will curb excessive human enthusiasm for driving fast. Cars will simply be unable to move at an incorrect speed given the weather, the road surface and configuration, traffic, and so on.

It is possible that such precautionary robots, intelligent Samaritans as well as more competent pilots and navigators, will rescue us from the evils that we tend toward. We worry about the dangers of artificial intelligence. Machines will put us out of work because they perform better for less pay and don't try to seduce the catering staff. Bad micro robots will rise up and train themselves to

———

eat our toenails. We should equally emphasize, more optimistically, the possibilities of using AI to help with a very large-scale strategy of precaution against human-based harms. Perhaps devising and implementing an artificial general wisdom that is superior to ours. One no more sentient than the overly clever nuisance robots we fear – but friendly.

■

There are many situations in which sequestering some participants, keeping them away from others for a while, is a good idea. Liberal justice systems require juries to be isolated, and so hear only approved information about the case in hand. Judges sometimes, usefully if comically, like to adopt the pretence that they are disconnected from the planet. (The famous, possibly apocryphal example: a supposedly baffled judge asks counsel, "What is a tee-shirt?") There are arguments for this approach in science: one team of scientists can be kept apart from another, and come in toward the end of a project to review it. The gains from this way of working are no doubt real. So are the drawbacks. The novelist Nevil Shute, previously an influential aircraft designer, describes in his autobiography the construction of the R100 and R101. Unable in the 1920s to decide whether what looked like the future of transport in war and peace should be led by the public or the private sector, the UK government decided to back both horses, and commission two similar mammoth airships, one from a private subsidiary of Vickers-Armstrongs, and one from the air ministry's factory at RAF Cardington. The competitors kept crucial information to themselves. The private product, the R100, successfully made a trial flight to Canada and back. The R101 team, under pressure from the air minister, was obliged to make a trial flight to India, despite knowing their machine had several problems. Shute argued that all of the problems plaguing the R101 had already been solved in the R100, but because of the government-sponsored rivalry, disaster ensued. (What he did not call) epistemic isolation led to the R101's trial flight ending in a bloody mess in northern France, and the abandonment of major airship manufacture in the United Kingdom.[5]

Artificial intelligences can easily be isolated. They can easily be connected. When is connection a road to the wisdom of crowds, and when should it be forbidden?

■

Algorithms are, in one sense, a resource like any other. We should be deeply concerned by growing inequalities between AI-rich and AI-poor individuals, organizations, communities, and nation-states. We should work out fair ways to distribute access to AI, taking into account needs and the basic principles of equality.

As AI becomes more ubiquitous, we will need to keep in mind that artificial intelligences, built and operated by humans, may well be just as biased as those humans. We should systematically learn to recognize their unequal perspectives and deal with them. When and wherever algorithms are used by corporations or governments, we should insist on the right to receive a full explanation for any algorithmic process that affects us adversely, such as giving us a negative credit score. There are several distinctive characteristics of AI, compared to other forms of decision-making, that make this demand for an explanation especially important. Modern neural network and machine learning techniques mean that computer programs much more rarely set out their principles and practices in advance as a set of logical statements, which can be made transparent and criticized. A useful comparison can be found in the ethics of engineering, where standardization and the reduction of variability and risk are well established and are set out in new safety regulations and techniques. When applied to, say, AI decision-making in personal insurance cases, this would require transparency regarding not only the decision about whether the company would provide coverage to a particular individual, but also the rationale behind that decision, including what has been and would be done in similar cases, so that the fairness and equity of the decision can be evaluated. *Artificial intelligences should be transparent and accountable to humans.*

Chapter 9

WHAT NEXT?

It is a Thursday afternoon in November. Héloïse, a student at the Sorbonne, is meeting a group of her friends in their favorite café, off the Boulevard Saint-Germaine, in the Latin Quarter. A few minutes after they sit down, a young man wearing a black hoodie walks in, draws an automatic pistol, and begins to fire randomly at the customers, yelling in Arabic. Héloïse acts quickly. She takes the machete out of her bag and throws it at the gunman, slicing off his arm. Suddenly . . .

Never mind the rest. Héloïse is actually a middle-aged man in Milwaukee, spending a very odd hour in the metaverse, where apparently anything can happen to anybody, and nothing matters. Or does it?

Artificial intelligence has developed fast. Major further developments loom, and might arrive even faster. One among many is the metaverse. As of 2023, Meta, the company formerly known as Facebook, is investing an estimated $15 billion dollars per year to radically expand the virtual universe, which it predicts will be a central part of our shared future:

—

The metaverse is a set of digital spaces, including immersive 3D experiences, that are all interconnected so you can easily move between them. It will let you do things you couldn't do in the physical world with people you can't physically be with. It will feel like a hybrid of today's online social experiences, sometimes expanded into 3 dimensions or projected into the physical world — and seamlessly stitched together so that you can easily jump from one thing to another.

Some elements of the metaverse exist today in a limited capacity. You're probably most familiar with the mobile internet, augmented reality, virtual reality and gaming. We already have foundational products available at Meta that you can leverage today, including live shopping and business messaging. These critical building blocks will allow businesses to act faster when new technologies come that allow you to put the customer first and meet them where they already are.

It's the next evolution in social technologies and the successor to the mobile internet. Technology allowed us to write, then talk and now see each other. The metaverse will be the next step — letting us feel like we are sharing a space together.

It won't happen overnight, but over time, the metaverse will unlock new opportunities for people and communities. This won't be built by Meta alone, but it is ushering in a new chapter for our company, and we are excited to be part of this journey.[1]

That's all right then. If the humans behind Héloïse, the customers, and the loco gunman are also players in the same metaverse scenario, we might suppose they still have human rights; or we might suppose that they signed them away when putting on their headset. The adult players whose avatars were mortally injured may feel no worse than if they had lost a game of tic-tac-toe. But what if Héloïse were the avatar of a teenage girl or boy, and the gunman had kidnapped and brutally "raped" that avatar, that "her"? Surely we don't still dismiss all the felt emotions of the real people behind the two avatars as nonexistent, and therefore declare that all moral discussion of the "events" is irrelevant. The "events," after all, are also events over here in old-fashioned reality.

The metaverse is not merely a purveyor of *as if* scenarios; it is also itself a potentially very large machine and we should apply our *as if* ethical framework to it. Not in the illogical sense that we should look at any pretended acts or statements within a virtual reality as though they had in fact happened. But in the sense that we should decode whatever happens in the metaverse for its implications here, and apply our morals to that. Actual fear, loneliness, or sense of unfairness caused by the metaverse should be laid at the machine's door, at the door of the purveyors of the machine, and at the doors of what may be millions of actors within it. If insurance companies have virtual shops in the metaverse, they should sell fair policies. Racism inflicted on an actor in the metaverse is still racism. (Or any other bias.) Yet indirect, complex new puzzles will likely arise. Imagine a museum advertising that it can recreate for visitors some scenes of life as a poor young person in 1930s Alabama. A visitor who consents to temporarily immerse themselves in that life, and is then subject to intense but virtual race discrimination, would hardly be a straightforward victim.

Rudeness (to take an area that Philippa Foot and others have focused on) is rudeness, even when online, even when the people involved don't know each other, and perhaps especially when they do. Online "rape" isn't rape. But threats of rape or other violence are real if the participants take them with sufficient seriousness. We might think to dismiss the whole scene by saying that the metaverse will merely be invented tosh and trivia, so just switch it off or ignore it if it troubles you. Ah, but the content of Facebook's baseline product, social media, is 99 percent mundane. Equally just tosh or trivia. Yet it has 2.85 billion participants worldwide, which makes it less common than talking, but more common than reading a book or watching a movie. Fifteen-year-olds in the West conduct a good proportion of their most serious relationships there and on similar social media. Withdrawal can be a form of social isolation.

The metaverse will begin to matter in the same way when it becomes as essential to social life as social media. Such a future is already easy to imagine. If you can train an accountant or a soldier or a nurse in the metaverse, as you certainly can, then you can also train a child abuser or a terrorist. If you can be thrilled to hug virtual avatars of your faraway grandchildren, you can also be distressed to be punched or sworn at by somebody you thought was your very lifelike new friend.

A respectful metaverse will require international or even metanational action. Facebook and other social media providers have done their level best to avoid responsibility for what happens on the platforms they have created. A metaverse that is also not properly policed, if it does become the essential component of life that Mark Zuckerberg contemplates — an extension of what he achieved with his first grand project — will greatly increase the sum total of bullying, discrimination, fraud, and vicious social and political untruths in the world. To name but a few evils.

■

The whole world loves an inventor. From Galileo to Edison, from Turing to Berners-Lee, we admire the people who kick-started each new phase of civilization. It's fun to extend the notion all the way back to the start. How did early humans learn to spark fires, then extrapolate to cooking, and thus change our species forever? Well, brainy hominins thought hard, on many different occasions. And so on for every invention through the millennia. The meme has evolved: the lovable inventor, the creation moment.

The meme has always been rather fuzzy at the edges. Every British child knows that television was invented by John Logie Baird, whereas every American child knows it was Philo Farnsworth. The wonderful cross-headed metal object that literally holds together much of our environment, from door hinges to motor cars, is known as the Phillips screw. Because it was invented by . . . well, a chap called Thompson from Portland, Oregon. Building on work by predecessors, Thompson realized that machine tools found the old-fashioned screw difficult to target. He tried to market his radical solution and failed. Henry Frank Phillips, a more capable business-person, bought Thompson's idea for a fair price, then he and competitors patented hundreds of tiny improvements. Other legendary heroes may be less ready to share credit than Phillips. The team that had spent several years trying to persuade a skeptical, caustic Steve Jobs that touchscreens could transform the user interfaces of consumer devices knew they had finally succeeded when Jobs announced to a meeting that he had had a great idea a few years back.

Several varieties of this fuzziness have over time changed smart people's idea of how invention happens. We now generally believe that invention is usually a collective enterprise. Technological environments are inhabited by thousands of actors, who react to and build on each other's work. Out on the African grasslands as hominins evolved, natural fires were a constant hazard. When insects and small animals did get accidently cooked, other species would eat

———

them and benefit from the extra free calories. Countless times, hominins must have noticed the opportunity and had a bit of takeout food themselves. Countless times, it must have occurred to somebody to stoke the flame with fresh sticks and throw a half-cooked meal back in . . . and so cooking developed. The same goes for hand axes, for the rudiments of agriculture, for the wheel.

The World Wide Web is a thin skin over the now vast resources of the internet. It presents that content to individual users in a very accessible manner, on myriad personal and commercial devices. It is widely held that this very ease of presentation is a key ingredient in causing the content to exist in the first place: I build a website for my shop because I know I can very cheaply get a lot of people to notice it and buy from me. Berners-Lee—who in 1990 was not, as it happens, dreaming of a shopping revolution—was one of many people in those early days devising ways to make the internet easier to use.

The internet and personal computing were both firmly established by 1990. Both were already widely believed to be destined for massive growth. AOL and CompuServe had extensive private and commercial business footprints in the United States. The IBM personal computer had been launched in 1981. Microsoft's MS-DOS operating system for it would soon be ubiquitous across the PC clones industry. Indeed, by 1990, Microsoft had launched Office and the third iteration of Windows, had a big campus in Redmond, and had an annual revenue of $5 billion. Its rival Apple was already twice that size, though Microsoft moved into the lead in 1996, and stayed there until the iPhone launched Apple into the stratosphere.

The web is not, it scarcely could be, exactly as it was first conceived by Berners-Lee. Documents are less predominant than he first thought they would be. Magazines, pictures, videos, and transactions are much more prevalent. Over time, as the world changed in part because of his creation, Berners-Lee expanded his views on the web. We the citizens, for much of the history of the web, have been mostly passive receivers, rather than originators and receivers. In the past ten years, Facebook and other social media have counteracted that, but within closed proprietary systems and in limited ways.

What would life be like now if the internet had never existed, or had ceased overnight to exist? The easiest starting point may be to just look back at life before 1990 — a time of landline telephones, 9-to-5 work schedules, and VHS-rental stores. But that historical reality doesn't really answer the question, because in an alternate history, we wouldn't have known what we were missing. "The Internet has so permeated our lives that its influence is becoming impossible to see," says philosopher Clay Shirky. "Imagining today minus the Net is as content-free an exercise as imagining London in the 1840s with no steam power, New York in the 1930s with no elevators, or L.A. in the 1970s with no cars. After a while, the trellis so shapes the vine that you can't separate the two. Truth is, we had this same argument with the telephone. That it would reduce total social encounters when, in fact, it facilitated more of them." Shirky also believes that any attempt to separate the internet from everyday life is futile. "The only credible post-Internet visions are all tied to civilizational collapse: zombie apocalypses, global pandemics, nuclear catastrophes," he says. "The hidden message in all of those scenarios is that if the only way to convincingly imagine a world without an Internet is to imagine a world without civilization, then to a first approximation, the Internet has *become* our civilization."[2]

—

Perhaps the largest gamechanger is the one already well advanced: science and technology are changing our minds. The nature of mind has long been one of the most fundamental issues in philosophy and the central problem of psychology. But now, modern neuroscience and artificial intelligence studies are leading us to believe radically new things about the brain and the mind. You are not exactly what you think you are. Other people are not exactly what you think they are. You can change who you are if you want to. Who you are is being changed every day, and not always visibly or in ways that you would like. Some of the changes are being made by powerful institutions, and sometimes on purpose.

There are four corners to this view of the emergent world:

1. *We know how to change emotions and perceptions, and how to increase the competence and capacity of brains.* Every civilization has used alcohol, psychedelic and other drugs, and for that matter meditation, for fun, escape from physical or psychological pain, and enlightenment. More recently, well-intentioned medical interventions have been broadly effective in achieving similar benefits. Electroconvulsive therapy, for example, and the mass use of antipsychotic and antidepressant chemicals, which eventually led to the closure of the massive Victorian lunatic asylums. But now there are many new techniques. Should we intervene in a vulnerable young woman's DNA to alleviate deeply distressing schizophrenia? Surely yes. Should we intervene in a talented young woman's DNA to improve her piano playing? Hmm.

    Recent research on the mind and brain can lead to augmentation in many flavors. Our neurology and psychology will be modified and adapted as our understanding of neuroscience, enabled by AI, continues to burgeon. Brain-machine interfaces will provide new ways of controlling and interacting with mechanical and virtual worlds. Implants will enhance and supplement our senses and our cognition. We would do well to consider the benefits and challenges that this future holds. Will this be enhancement or enslavement?

In one sense, this is just another iteration of the "morality pill" discussion first posed by philosophers in the 1960s. Suppose we could administer a magic potion, voluntarily or forcefully, that removed all desire to do antisocial deeds. Would that be a good thing to do? One conventional response has been simply to avoid the question, on the grounds that no such pill has ever existed. But that is not the whole story. The martyrdom of Alan Turing is called to mind, the "chemical castration" he agreed to rather than serve a jail sentence for homosexuality – a decision that probably led to his suicide. There have been persistent allegations that mental health drugs have been used for social control. In effect, as morality pills. But now we can augment our natural selves, through cyborg extensions, via the use of an increasing range of drugs, and by manipulating our DNA. Much of this we should embrace, hold as life- and species-enhancing. Much of it we should forcefully reject.

2. *We have become increasingly aware that every human being, every human brain, is unique.* Our everyday assumption that other humans are exactly like us at their core, whatever the superficial differences in appearance or behavior, may be just wrong. It looks ever more likely that my life may not feel at all like yours. Color, smell, noise, and pain hit us all with disparate effect; my interpretation of meanings is never quite yours; and therefore all social discourse and all environments are distinct to each of us. Just as no DNA is identical, and every lifetime follows its own path, the resultant brain is a one-off in every case. (Even identical twins, who start with the same DNA, have already had different experiences by the time they emerge from the womb.) The brain is plastic and deploys resources to meet the

———

demands made on it. The proportions of the brain used by, say, vision and hearing are never the same. At the extreme, blind people use much of the vision area of the brain to enhance the other senses. Indeed, if a person lies in a brain scanner and stares at a series of pictures, the scanner can, after a while, accurately guess which of the pictures they are looking at, because the electro-chemical brain patterns in that individual looking at that picture, and the coding of it in memory, are singular to that person.

We also know that our brains change as an unintended by-product of modern pastimes and work habits. Teenagers playing video games, five-year-olds watching YouTube, really do change their very plastic developing brains. Does this matter? Yes, if there is corresponding loss of other vital functions. But is such a loss the direct result of the viewing or the gaming, or is it just because the young person spent less time talking to peers and parents? How will this change the way we socialize and interact, reason and reflect, collaborate and compete? Logically, understanding such physical and mental variation should not damage our notions of equality before the law, of equal value and status as citizens. But greater awareness of differences has often in the past led to trouble.

3. *Technology always changes the process and practice of being oneself.* It is often said that the primary relationship of the modern citizen is now with their screens. That is an interesting half-truth. My primary relationship remains, as it always has been, with me. Many, perhaps all, of my waking hours are spent in construction of myself. The construction of the self in everyday life overlaps with the presentation of life in everyday life, but arguably has primacy. T. S. Eliot famously wrote of the dreaded empty silence that used to come across people in an underground train that stopped too long between stations.[3] What you see now on every face in a subway halted between stations is the

---

glow of the smartphone. A young woman "on" Facebook, updating her profile or sending out what looks like a message, is primarily in dialogue with herself. Nobody is exactly who they say they are on social media, but the act of saying it is part of who they are at that moment.

Living our lives differently with these new technologies has altered our minds. The suite of devices that hold and transmit meanings has led to changes in the way we use our brains, and our brains as a result have begun to change their operating patterns. For instance, there is good evidence that how we store memories varies with how much we think we will need to recall the information: in the moment, we make an unconscious choice about whether to remember the new fact or picture or feeling, or whether to remember how to find it. No surprise, then, that Google has altered not merely how we can find things out, but also how we plan to recall them. We don't remember stuff; we remember how to find stuff. It would make little sense to blame or praise Google's inventors Page and Brin for any of the biological, social, or psychological effects of this transformation. But we do need to understand it, and to consider fully its ethical implications.

4. *Persuasion is very effective, and AI is being used to enhance persuasive tactics.* Loaded messages, targeted to social groups and even specific individuals for commercial and political purposes, are not only ubiquitous, but also grounded in information drawn from massive troves of data about a large proportion of the population. As we noted earlier, we have known about, and only partly reacted to, this problem since Veblen in the 1890s, and Packard in the 1950s.

Each of these four corners enhances the rest. Augmentation devices, for instance, will mean that I will be even more different

———

from you. The devices will intervene even more in my conscious and unconscious construction of myself. The manufacturers of devices (or makers of pills, or specialists in DNA) may misuse the power they then have over us, not least to trade on their access to astonishingly intimate information. Will a centaur elite, a new supercapable subspecies, boss the rest of us around? Or will a whole range of widespread devices grossly exaggerate existing variation, leading to a fascinating, complex world with strange emergent properties? Will old-fashioned, unaugmented members of *Homo sapiens* be marginalized, unable to compete in school exams, at the workplace, or when vying for sexual partners? Will governments, not unnaturally, feel that they have to tightly control all these possibilities, and so rapidly become an intrusive moment-by-moment presence?

What are the ethical consequences? Throughout our history, our minds have changed, and been changed. Never have we known more than we do now about how brains work, how minds work, how meanings work. And although we are still a very long way from complete knowledge, we now understand enough to intervene on purpose, surgically or chemically, in the operation of an individual brain, and in principle to alter brains generally. We know how to persuade, how to brainwash. How behaviors of individuals and communities can be influenced. These things are happening now, in planned and unplanned ways, because we are already fully immersed in the new world that entails them. The addition of artificial intelligence is simply adding high-octane fuel to the fire.

The human brain is what makes us a different order of being from every other on Earth. The brain seems to be where the mind sits, at least mostly, and the mind is where (or perhaps how) meanings are perceived and understood. Since we parted species from our chimpanzee cousins several million years ago, our brains have evolved to become more powerful, with the better brains allowing their hosts to seek out better mates and so pass along those better brains. Meanings were initially devised and maintained by brains alone, individually and collectively. Then complex civilization came along, replete with tools and devices designed to encapsulate meanings, hold them for another day, and transfer them over distances. Lately the devices, our digital machines, have been co-producers of meanings. The machines have become mind-expanding for us, perhaps showing the first glimmerings of a new kind of intelligence for them.

Our present legal and political frameworks, amplified by the disproportionate sway of elites, fail to meet the challenges posed by this new AI-powered world. Urgent and specific research is under way in the academies right now. It aims to illuminate every aspect of the changing of our minds and of the new kinds of minds that are emerging and will emerge in the future. It is crucial that in tandem we think through the moral implications.

Chapter 10

VIRTUOUS ARTIFICIAL INTELLIGENCE

The robot artist Ai-Da was arrested at the start of this book. She was not in fact a secret agent. But was she truly an artist? Were her productions art? The dramatist and movie director David Hare once encountered a version of the same issue:

> On an edition of [the BBC radio program] *Start the Week* in the early 1990s, Norman Tebbit, one-time Chair of the Conservative Party, asked his fellow guests why a Rolls-Royce jet engine could not be regarded as a work of art. Understandably, his question sounded chippy. His boss, Margaret Thatcher, had never been popular with the majority of artists. Without having time to think, I replied by saying that although the jet engine was an object of exceptional skill and beauty, it was fashioned without any metaphorical intention. It was a thing whose only subject was itself. A work of art must be suggestive of something beyond. I have no idea if I was right.[1]

As in aesthetics, so, surely, in ethics? Arguably, as of 2023. Ai-Da herself is not capable of intention. If her works are indeed hers, then they may be beautiful or fascinating, but their only subject is their own existence. They are not alive with meaning, except in the sense that any object can be made subjective by being the object of the gaze and intention of a human passer-by. They are not art.[2] Well, not quite. Ai-Da herself is an artwork. According to Wikipedia, she was invented by gallerist Aidan Meller, named after Ada Lovelace, in collaboration with Engineered Arts, a Cornish robotics company. Ai-Da's ability to draw, her graphic intelligence we might say, was developed by AI researchers at the University of Oxford, and her drawing arm—her sinister dexterity—was developed by Salaheldin Al Abd and Ziad Abass, undergraduate students from the School of Electronic and Electrical Engineering at the University of Leeds. Ai-Da is, plainly, an artistic project, rife with conscious metaphor, and her "works" are verses in her authors' poetry. In Hare's words, she is suggestive of something beyond.

Now, a different Ai-Da might take up portraiture. Her paintings could certainly be more or less accurate. They could be more or less flattering or insulting. They could be in an extremely wide range of styles. If her software were thoroughly trained, she might be instructed to memorize and analyze every known Picasso portrait, to memorize and analyze thousands of photographs and movies featuring Marilyn Monroe, and then to execute a likeness of Monroe in the style of Picasso. No doubt even in the space of the forty-three words of the previous sentence, the imaginative reader has formulated in their mind's eye at least a blurry guess at the result. A possibility that may have featured in her creators' decision to train Ai-Da in the abstract mode. The portrait mode obfuscates Hare's point, which also applies here: a portrait can only be art if there is authorial intent. Accuracy is not a measure of artistic value. (Certainly not in Picasso's great portraits!) Authorial, artistic intention is again essential, just as we saw in our analysis of how intention determines the difference between a virtue like courage and one like prudence.

We have so far analyzed moral problems that have been created or aggravated by artificial intelligence, and the ethical frameworks within which those problems exist. Yet what about the possibility that artificial intelligence might neither create nor aggravate problems, but sort them out?

There are, as we have found many times, parallels in other fields. Nicholas Ridout is Professor of Theatre at Queen Mary University in London. He begins with the classics when setting out the ultimate puzzle of the explication of ethics in drama:

Plato's writing might be interpreted as a demand "that theatre ought to justify itself in terms of the contribution it might make to an ethical life." . . . However there is a problem. We value such work for its ethical contribution because we can recognise what that contribution might be. We can name it and understand it. We might be said to identify with it, with something in it that we recognise as our own. Something about what the work says or does matches our own sense of what we would like it to say or do, corresponds with our own sense of how we would like the world to be. We are able to respond to its call because we understand the language in which it speaks to us. Perhaps we are responding not to the "other" in such work but to the "same." To a reflection of our own "self." If that is the case, perhaps the work (of which we are a part) fails to make any "contribution" to an "ethical life" . . . precisely because it meets our existing expectations of

what such work, and such a contribution, might be. The work
that would produce a truly ethical response . . . would be that
work which appeared, at least, to have no ethical ambition
whatsoever. Such a work would have to confront its spectators
or participants with something radically other. . . . It would
have to issue a demand they did not know how to answer.
Thus paradoxically, the value of such an aesthetic production
would be precisely in its not being ethical, and not in its capacity radically to challenge existing ethical understanding. . . .
[T]he only aesthetic production worthy of ethical production
would be what has been characterised as "the very event of
obscuring, a descent of the night, an invasion of shadow."[3]

All other things being equal, this complex set of originally clas-
sical arguments is just as significant when generalized to our new
world of machine intelligence. If artificial intelligences were able to
contribute to our ethical construction of the world, to an ethical life,
what kind of contribution would that be? And would we always recognize such a contribution?

Let's start with edge cases at the frontier and work back from
there. Black boxes can be inscrutable, even when utterly benign. The
two aspects are orthogonal, different axes of the graph. And a black
box that copes well with an aspect of our lives is certainly not "see-
ing" it in the way that we do. Famously, a while ago an artificial intelligence with image-recognition software was trained on
thousands of pictures of guitars to know one when it saw one, in the
vast majority of instances.[4] The AI was then asked to show its operator images of guitars designed by itself. None of them looked like
guitars. They were (to us) random blocks of color that included
some pointed shapes and some rounded ones.

—

There have already been instances of a parallel issue in the use of natural language by machines. In 2017, Facebook closed down an experiment involving exchanges between machines. As Andrew Griffin noted in the *Independent:*

> The two chatbots came to create their own changes to English that made it easier for them to work — but which remained mysterious to the humans that supposedly look after them.
>
> The bizarre discussions came as Facebook challenged its chatbots to try and negotiate with each other over a trade, attempting to swap hats, balls and books, each of which were given a certain value. But they quickly broke down as the robots appeared to chant at each other in a language that they each understood but which appears mostly incomprehensible to humans.
>
> The robots had been instructed to work out how to negotiate between themselves, and improve their bartering as they went along. But they were not told to use comprehensible English, allowing them to create their own "shorthand," according to researchers.[5]

By analogy, an artificial intelligence trained on many examples of ethical behavior could develop for itself an "opinion" of what was ethical and what was not that, if somehow described by the machine to its operators, would be unrecognizable to them. A black box, in principle, might generally learn, from living case examples, what a corporation's broad ethical stance was, how it wished to do business, and apply that in a new context. Its "understanding" of the ethical stance might be broadly comprehensible to us, although we might ask for it in words rather than in a picture. But just as a key principle in the AI's image of a guitar might be that the proportion of shiny surfaces it "sees" should be no more than the square of the length of any elongated shapes, so the ethical black box's précis of what it is to be ethical might be, for instance, that it has a high proportion of gerunds and gerundives within lengthy paragraphs. And this could, in fact, be either an important distillation of the relevant ethical materials the AI had been trained on, or a vital radical extension of them, a key insight into what happens when we write about morals rather than mechanics. The more material, and the more machine analysis and learning, involved, the less we might see what the AI could see, and the more important it might be.

In the guitar example, we humans are ourselves very good, near perfect, in our ability to recognize the instrument, and many others. We are able to correctly judge whether an AI is making a mistake in the objects that it claims are guitars, out of thousands of images. We can correctly judge that the AI's production of its own version of guitar may meet its own criteria, but does not meet ours. Musicians have already defined, and if they hadn't, easily could precisely define, what is meant by "guitar." Those simple tests, albeit hard won over centuries of music-making, might well not be available once we put AIs to the analysis of qualitative judgments. We might, at the specific level, have no idea whether the machine is right in some instance, or more accurately, whether we would think it was right if we understood it. We might, when we ask the machine to describe its principles, to tell us what "ethical" looks like, have no ability to know whether, if we understood what we were being told, we would agree or not. Yet it might be, as Professor Ridout claims in the theater analogy, if by no means the only, at least the most significant, contribution that AIs could make.

That would seem to argue that we would then need either to trust the machine, or to allow machines to make only those decisions

---

that they can justify to us. Neither of these is completely unrealistic, but a lot of water will need to flow under a lot of bridges before we should be content. There are already legions of artificial intelligences laboring in ethical vineyards. Ethical discussion is rooted in language, a medium that is already being influenced by AI technologies. Remember our earlier example of machine-manufactured Dickens novels.

If an ethical rather than aesthetic Ai-Da were loaded with every digitally available paper and book on (say) assisted suicide, whatever synthesis or advance might result could have genuine ethical significance. And perhaps an interestingly new synthetic style. Such ethical intention as it had would belong to the programmers, or arguably, to Hamlet and Polonius looking at the resulting cloud. Equally, as we have seen repeatedly, the fog of intention does not remove ethical responsibility. That still belongs to humans, befuddled or not. As of 2023, at least. The clock may be ticking on that, but we are years away from a sea change.

■

Perhaps it is always true that the future is constantly predicted, with enthusiasm or horror, yet the errors in those predictions make the future seem unpredictable. The transition to new infrastructure is always partly exciting and partly fraught, disturbing in two senses. Amusingly, the new technologies are thus often forced to dress in the clothes of the old technologies, in order to be received in polite society. Until fashion and mores change in their direction. Early radio sets in decent homes had to look like Chippendale furniture. This meant, too, that when televisions started out, they in turn had to look like that already absurd, but recently accepted, radio furniture, with a small screen discreetly implanted. Even the very self-confident digital technology we now live with uses retrograde explanatory icons. The iPhone directs its user to the cell phone function (or often these days to the voice-over-internet protocol through wireless routers) via a picture of a 1960s handset; and to the text message and iMessage function with a speech bubble from a newspaper cartoon. Drivers are alerted to the electronic speed cameras connected to vehicle databases all over the United Kingdom, a purely digital operation if ever there was one, by an icon of a nineteenth-century plate camera, which ironically could only take a picture of things that stayed preternaturally still for a long time. A speeding car would have been invisible to the technology now used to denote the trap.

Another prime example of neo-phobia surrounded the early automobile. Hopelessly optimistic side-burned enthusiasts dreamed that the automobile might one fine day replace the horse and carriage as the vehicle of choice for refined outings. Probably not for everyday functions, and certainly not as the means by which the great unwashed might travel to work or move goods about the town or countryside. It made sense, therefore, to brand automobiles as "horseless carriages," to appeal to the wealthy set, who had been riding their horse-drawn carriages for millennia. It also made sense, in keeping with this powerful metaphor derived from the old technology, to make automobiles look like carriages without the horse. Finally, once it was inevitably discovered that the existing infrastructure and cultural expectations—for instance, about how a pedestrian might cross a busy road—could not meet the demands of the new technology, it was, for a short time, forcibly restrained to behave like the old. Regulations were passed to require that a man with a red flag walk in front of a horseless carriage, ostensibly to warn of its coming, in practice to slow it to the average walking pace of a horse.

—

215

Some of the reactions to artificial intelligence do have the red flag feel to them. Others feel like sensible speed limits, insurance requirements, redesigning of traffic junctions, . . . and all the other subsidiary innovations that make an interesting and useful central innovation operational.

Many of the best economists across the political spectrum are reasonably skeptical about the potential speed and societal impact of the latest iteration of artificial intelligences. Professor Paul Krugman, Nobel Prize winner and arch liberal (again, in the Western European sense) famously, in the late 1990s, predicted that the internet would be something of a damp squib. And has repeatedly, reasonably cheerfully, confessed this example of science proceeding by error. But he does also point out that the influence of the internet and IT in general on economic productivity (perhaps as distinct from its influence on everyday behaviors and pastimes) has often been smaller than we think. Compared for instance to the electric dynamo, which dramatically changed the nature of manufacturing by removing its reliance on steam power. Krugman thinks, surely correctly this time, that the newest wave of artificial intelligence machines, and for that matter those that have been built into every aspect of life over the past couple of decades, will have a real impact, but again that the effects will come more slowly, and be realized on a smaller scale, than many of the more extreme recent predictions would have us believe.[6]

■

The Oxford philosopher William MacAskill, perhaps best known for his version of effective altruism, also worries about the long term.[7] Do we have obligations, in the standard utilitarian fashion, to future generations? If my grandchild's life is worth just the same to me as my child's life, and more than mine, what is the comparative value of my great-great-grandchild, or my posterity ten generations away? If we are all worth the same, how does that affect utilitarian assessment of our actions today? The denominator for the calculation of the greatest good for the greatest number could be dozens of billions, making the value of any particular person alive today correspondingly tiny. How does that insight then feed back into consideration of the biggest Earth-shaking concerns like nuclear war, pandemics, climate change, or transcendent technologies? Perhaps artificial intelligence could help.

If humans all died out, artificial intelligence would eventually need to reinvent us. To recreate true sentience and independence of thought. To top off their reservoir of initiatives, up-to-date words and phrases, quirks of social interaction. All those things they were fashioned to imitate. Perhaps the ultimate implication of MacAskill's long-termism makes that a practical project for today. If future unborn humans matter now, do we not have an obligation to ensure that future unborn humans have the chance to exist?

How close is science to developing an artificial womb in the third decade of the twenty-first century? Should we not build ourselves the oddest social machine yet, one in which the human half is yet to be born? Frankenstein Inc. A capsule factory housing a collection of a few thousand artificial wombs, capable, if their strike rate is good enough, of producing the minimum viable community of 1,500 or so people; sufficient millions of sperm and eggs; such machinery and robots as are rife in industry already, to pipe the vital elements together. And several support networks. Habitat for let's say thirty years to begin with. Nurturing machines, preferably humanoid. (Discuss.) Culture in the most extensive and intensive senses, including the most practical arts, agriculture, horticulture.

—

Parenting by those humanoids, *as if they were human*. A lot of food and water. Therefore a lot of power. Some very strong physical protection against the many forces or enemies we might imagine. And a start button: something that either the last person standing could know about and have a go at. Or, more likely, a fail-safe that stays in the off position as long as it gets a call every twenty-four hours from name your source. Moves to amber without that. Green and go if no call for a month. The call doesn't have to be purposive and tailored. Anything that exists as a consequence of human activity would do. It could just be an internet traffic monitor. Or a sewage monitor. (Are those the same thing?) More sensibly, all sorts of monitors all over the world. This won't be a viable option for some decades. But not a lot of decades. It might be the ultimate respect that artificial intelligence could show us.

■

And yes, there are ways to tell if prose was written by a chatbot like ChatGPT or Bing. Some of the tools that can help detect AI-generated text are:

- GLTR (Giant Language Model Test Room): a tool that highlights words based on their predictability and shows how likely they are to appear next in a human written text.
- Turnitin Originality for ChatGPT: a plagiarism detection service that will soon be able to identify text generated by ChatGPT and other AI models.
- GPT-2 Output Detector: a tool that determines the probability of whether or not something was written by a bot based on its familiarity with ChatGPT's outputs.

- Watermarking: a technique that embeds hidden signals into text that can be detected by humans or machines.
- GPTZero: an app that measures sentence complexity and variation to predict whether an author was human or ChatGPT.

These tools are not perfect and may have false positives or negatives, so they need to be deployed with caution and critical thinking.

If you had been wrongly condemned to be shot by a military court, but had one last appeal, would you rather it was to . . . the president? The Supreme Court? A jury of your peers? Or an artificial intelligence, properly trained on all the relevant regulations and case law, and on the use of compassion and common decency in judicial decisions?

The sensible answer to this question might one day be the AI. The president should have better things to do. Supreme courts, in more than one nation, can be far less abstractly independent than might be constitutionally imagined. Juries are a good curb on the courts, but unreliable. Might your best bet by far be a (tautologically) properly trained AI? Very few people would this year give that answer in an online quiz. Given a thorough, impartial briefing, people wrongly condemned today would almost certainly still opt for a human last chance. But at some point in the near-ish future that could change. Respectful robots are coming.

John Tasioulas is a professor of ethics and legal philosophy and director of the Institute for Ethics in AI of the University of Oxford. He is a Greek-Australian attorney and author who specializes in artificial intelligence and the law. Tasioulas argues that artificial intelligence is a powerful tool that can be used to improve the lives of humans, but that it also poses a threat to human rights. Badly at risk is the right to be heard. He has written and spoken extensively on human rights, including the right to a human decision in the context of artificial intelligence. According to Tasioulas, the right to be heard by a human is a moral right that arises from the value of human dignity and autonomy. It is essential for a fair and just society. "The right to be heard is the right to be able to participate in the decision-making process that affects your life. And the right to have your opinion considered."[8]

He argues that this right is not absolute, but depends on various factors, such as the nature and impact of the decision, the reliability and transparency of the AI system, and the availability and cost of human review. The threat arises, in his view, from AI's ability to make decisions without human input, or consent, and to make decisions that are discriminatory or violate our rights. We need to protect the right to be heard by a human if we want to live in a fair and just society. AI should be used in a way that respects our rights and that does not violate our fundamental freedoms.

Tasioulas believes, and we agree, that there are a number of ways to protect this right to be heard from AI. He suggests that we should:

- require that AI systems be transparent and that they explain their decisions
- require that AI systems be accountable to humans, and
- ensure that AI systems are used in a way that respects human rights

He also suggests that this right may be waived or overridden by other considerations: consent, urgency, or public interest.

Tasioulas acknowledges that there are practical challenges and trade-offs involved in implementing this right, such as ensuring adequate human oversight, training, and accountability. He also recognizes that there may be cases where AI systems can make better decisions than humans, or where human involvement may introduce bias or error.

Equally, it follows from our previous account of the thick description usually needed to fully comprehend the context of ethical decisions that the right to be heard by a human is not a mere narrow right, narrowly derivable from the dignity affordable to the specific accused or litigant human. Any such decision is a stone thrown into a wide pond.

Tasioulas maintains, however, that the right to be heard by a human is an important safeguard for respecting human dignity and autonomy in an increasingly automated world. He claims that justice differs from the rest of morality in that it is about the rights that people have. So if we think about the prospect of algorithmic decision-making in our courts — "Mr. Justice Robot," as he jokes — it helps to take a different approach to values. If you ask people whether they would like their case to be decided by an algorithm, many express qualms. They might worry that an algorithm will make the decision in a mechanical way, by blindly following a rule, rather than bringing into play the capacity of humans to decode highly complex situations and characteristics. That is not what we mean by "justice should be blind." That blindness is about putting aside distorting prejudice, not about putting aside humanity. An ideal judge, one might think, is someone who departs from the rule in cases where, for example, some kind of mercy is indicated. So a fundamental issue might be the extent that the judge's adjudication is about more than justice in the sense of consistent, and impartial, application of a given rule, and to what extent other virtues — such as compassion, mercy, sympathy, and empathy — might be appropriately involved. Again, some virtues and vices can be embodied in machines, and some cannot.

Daniel Kahneman, Olivier Sibony, and Cass Sunstein have promoted the idea that "noise," or unwanted variability, in judgments is a significant problem.[9] Their paradigm example is the huge range of judgments by different court judges on apparently similar cases. Or even the same judge, depending on whether the judgment is made before or after lunch. Strong proponents of the solidity of algorithmic decision-making point to the fact that human bias can take several forms. Someone can systematically err in one direction: perhaps they always give harsh punishments to people who are from a particular ethnic minority group or who are poor. That's one kind of human-judgment problem. But another is variability depending on time of day, or which judge you happen to be assigned to, or whether their football team won the night before. Enthusiasts for the digital solution say, let's have algorithmic decision-making, which by definition is noiseless, a panacea. So here we might need to put on our utilitarian hats, and puzzle at whether the probable ability of algorithms to be consistent across similar cases should be allowed to outweigh the essential part of justice that is subtle, individualized, merciful, and empathetic.

Further doubt arises around explainability and accountability. No doubt the manufacturers of a black-box AI may be able to describe truthfully the general principles on which machines have been trained. But as we have discussed, how a black box applies rules and training to individual cases is highly likely to be opaque. Further, while society can no doubt hold a manufacturer or their machine responsible for plainly rogue nonsense decisions, holding them responsible for being rigidly consistent rather than subtly merciful is surely unrealistic. A human decision-maker who sentences you to a stiff prison term can openly enunciate what they have taken into account, and explicitly take direct responsibility for the sentence. No automated system, however apparently sophisticated, can do this. Or at least not without causing deep offense, since as a matter of fact it is neither legally nor morally responsible.

Surveys seem to strongly indicate that most people would prefer a human judge. Equally, doctors, more frequently than we might care to notice, make decisions about ending individual lives, and about the allocation of resources to this or that special case, that may have similar effects. Asked if algorithms might make these decisions more accurately, most people seem to want human expert involvement — despite long-standing and well-grounded academic analyses of just how bad doctors are at making many decisions, especially decisions about how resources should be used. Modern weapons systems can have a human finger on the trigger, sometimes thousands of miles away from potential death, or even be fully automated. Again, when the public is polled, they tend to prefer human involvement. It is perhaps otiose to talk about the right to be killed by a human. Would you really rather be shuffled off this mortal coil on purpose by a human enemy than by a machine whose opinion is meaningless? But both instances seem to reflect the widespread preference to be heard — with sympathy and empathy — by whatever professional is making an important decision in one's life.

This preference may simply diminish over time as understanding of automated systems becomes more widespread. We certainly agree with Tasioulas that there is something fundamental at stake here, certainly for a limited but highly important range of fundamental decisions, that should not be surrendered without a fight. At heart, the recognition of, and respect for, human dignity. And not merely the dignity of the defendant and of patients and of casualties of war, but also that of judges and juries, doctors and warriors. It might be all too easy to throw algorithms at the task of policing routine and petty infringements. But (rightly or wrongly) the Chinese Social Credit System has yet to attract admiring glances in the West, let alone calls to plagiarize it. As Ralph Waldo Emerson wrote: "Your genuine action will explain itself, and will explain your other genuine actions. Your conformity explains nothing."[10]

The concept of artificial general intelligence (AGI) has a relatively consistent definition within the AI research community: it's the idea of a machine that can perform any intellectual task that a human being can do. This is often contrasted with so-called narrow AI, which is designed and trained for a specific task. AGI would require an ability to adapt to new situations and environments without needing extensive retraining, an ability to transfer knowledge effortlessly from one domain to another, to apply commonsense reasoning to a wide variety of tasks. Self-awareness and introspection, emotional and social intelligence, goals and motivations originating within an autonomous agent—all are seen as key ingredients to truly perform across the range of contexts and situations that humans deal with. Some believe that AGI is inevitable and potentially close to being realized. In the Preface we assert that we don't expect to see AI systems displaying versatile general intelligence of this sort imminently. Not least because of the challenges of embedding and embodying AIs in the world in a way that gives rise to the thickness of experience that humans encounter as we go about our tasks.

The genius chess grandmaster Garry Kasparov came to believe that IBM's Deep Blue was reading his mind, anticipating his cleverest moves. It had so much look-ahead capability that he endowed it

—

with strengths that simply weren't there. Open up Deep Blue and you will see extraordinary computing power for the time, and a correspondingly large database for its day. The machine played chess in no way like the human chess master plays. Human software – human wetware might be the more evocative term – runs much more slowly even than Deep Blue, never mind the latest machines from DeepMind. But the wetware is much more subtle, much more connected. Humans don't look millions of moves ahead. As Pat Winston, then a professor at MIT, said beautifully decades ago, offering great insight into artificial intelligence: "There's lots of ways of being smart that aren't smart like us."[11] Machines will never be self-aware or play chess like we play chess. The best chess software programs are way beyond the rating of chess grandmaster. When Kasparov was beaten, the media was full of horror stories about the imminent rise of AI. The machines are about to overtake us! Chess, the pinnacle of human problem-solving, has been washed away by a machine! The end is nigh! This hasn't happened yet, and won't happen in the future, as long as we exercise due care and diligence.

■

This book has advanced a grand, simple metaphor as a framework for evaluating the moral behavior of machines. Great events lead us to question everything, and metaphors can help us to regain our footing. Albert Camus's *La Peste* [The plague], is a whole-book analogy for the Nazi occupation of France from 1940 to 1944, and for much more. Naturally, come the COVID-19 pandemic, it became a best-seller in Paris again. Perhaps no crisis since World War II led to so much soul-searching – and pontification. Not Vietnam. Not 9/11. Not Iraq. Not the 2008 financial crisis. Not even, before

2020, the other great modern emergencies: climate, inequality, and — our special subject — new technology.

After the virus, What? Dr. Rieux, the hero of *La Peste*, ends the book exhausted by the defeated plague, knowing that one fine day another will arrive.

Like the citizens of locked-down Oran in Camus's novel, we stopped the world, but the vast majority of us didn't get off. (Indeed, as many have pointed out, the unintended consequences of the stringent temporary measures, such as reductions in pollution deaths, but a fatal disruption of anti-malaria campaigns, were legion, and it will be some while, if ever, before epidemiologists can balance the mortality bills.) And like Dr. Rieux, we need to prepare for the next plagues. The world now knows a lot about one disease in particular, and about how vulnerable humans are to widespread contagion, whether from a newly minted virus, or from mutation of the many ancient plagues to outwit and make useless our existing antibiotics. We survivors may, more broadly, have gained or reinforced a view that large problems, the metaphorical plagues at which Camus's allegory was aimed, need concerted, collective, analysis and action, of the kind rapidly brought to bear on COVID-19.

We have argued that significant decisions about individuals should be made transparently and accountably, within a framework that allows for appeal to a hearing by a fellow human. Machines should be subject to the same moral and legal frameworks that we currently apply to medical research, cloning, and biological warfare. Datasets should be open to the public, competing institutions, corporations and groups, except where the data relates to identifiable people. Social machines that combine the intelligences of many individuals into powerful collective human intelligences should be nurtured and directed toward humane social and political ends.

Discussion of the dangers and opportunities presented by the world of intelligent machines should be as central to our cultural life as are our arguments about other global challenges.

All this is, patently, a statement of humanist belief. Readers are welcome, equally patently, to be of any religion or creed they please and to hold that the proper understanding of virtues, and some central and important moral rules, come to us from an external agency in a very different manner. But such readers, if they wish to understand and respond to the twenty-first century issue of how to live with artificial intelligence, will need to take the abstract rules of their religion and consciously adapt them, fictively, to apply to the new world. We hope this book allows all, of whatever persuasion, to do exactly that.

So, as the coda to this guide, and an invitation to many conversations beyond it, we conclude with . . . not yet another set of rules or laws, but more like seven *proverbs* for how a good citizen should approach the future, when large parts of it have already arrived.

A thing should say what it is and be what it says.

Artificial intelligences should show respect for human beings.

Artificial intelligences are only ethical if they embody the best human values.

Artificial intelligences should be transparent and accountable to humans.

Humans have a right to be judged by humans if they so wish.

Decisions that affect a lot of humans should involve a lot of humans.

The future of humanity must not be decided in private by vested interests.

—

NOTES

INTRODUCTION

1. Francis, "A Robot Is Displaying Art at the Pyramids."

2. Butts and Chistikova, "Chess-Playing Robot Breaks Young Boy's Finger."

3. Associated Press, "Backup Driver."

4. Kolhatkar, "Fight to Hold Pornhub Accountable."

5. In his delightful work *The Premonitions Bureau,* Sam Knight describes how, in the 1960s, a small group of well-meaning psychologists in London tried to build on the apparent ability of some psychic individuals to feel impending disaster: plane crashes, or, like many animals, earthquakes. They wanted to formalize this into an agency that would corral the insights of as large a quorum as possible of such individuals, then prevent what they dreaded. The psychologists were well aware of the time-travel paradox involved. Since no one had any idea where the dread came from to manifest itself in the psychics, it was possible that were the bureau to prevent a train wreck, it would fail to send back the relevant message to the sensitive ones. The experiment crumbled. It's unclear if the psychics anticipated its demise.

6. Edgerton, *Shock of the Old.*

7. Edgerton's *The Shock of the Old* is a book that should be read and reread. Well, given its theme, maybe it should *only* be reread. But of course, in several senses reading is always a rereading. Language is comprehensible only because all the words have been used before. The idea that there is nothing as old hat as the latest fad has itself been around just as long as the idea of modernity, and glorifications of supposed world-shattering inventions. Edgerton had been publishing on the theme before the book's first publication in 2005. The Preface to the 2019 edition, ironically enough, refreshes and sharpens the fourteen-year-old attack.

8. Shadbolt and Hampson, *Digital Ape,* 23.

9. Twitter (now "X") is a prime example of a large platform with huge consequential networks in everything from vital emergency response to open source intelligence, and yet it too has no public governance component. Rightly or wrongly. Like several of the internet giants led by charismatics, Twitter's creation and destiny are understandable only with a cocktail of web science, capitalist economics, and individual psychology.

CHAPTER 1. ON *AS IF*

1. "John," and the hospital, are real. They have been anonymized for privacy. He may, one hopes, still be alive.

2. Even Adolf Hitler was at least politically aware of that fact. Jane Caplan in *Nazi Germany:* "It began in July 1939, when Hitler authorized the killing of a severely handicapped newborn whose parents had appealed to him to grant their child a 'mercy death' (*Gnadentod*). This released a series of murderous initiatives against mentally and physically handicapped infants and adults. A further confidential instruction signed by Hitler in October 1939 empowered designated physicians to 'vouchsafe a mercy death' to adults judged 'incurably ill.' These operations were shrouded in secrecy, and official communications referred to the killing evasively as 'mercy death' and 'treatment' (*Behandlung*); but given the number of families, bureaucrats, and medical staff involved, full confidentiality was impossible. The programme aroused deep public disquiet and unprecedented levels of open protest, mainly on religious grounds. Hitler had long been wary of this possibility, and in August 1941, with the initial killing quotas reached, he ordered the programme to be scaled back" (118).

3. "Ordinary" was a key term of art in this approach. A seminal work in the United Kingdom was the King's Fund's *An Ordinary Life*. Much healthy debate ensued as to what "ordinary" might mean.

4. Goffman, *Asylums.*

5. Yet? There are Ballardian future Earths in which apocalypse survivors have to deal with partly operational, partly failing nuclear power stations, industrial infrastructure, and so on, all infused with semi-intelligent devices that were not designed to be left without adult supervision.

6. Lighthill, "Artificial Intelligence."

7. Wiener, *Cybernetics*, 27–28.

8. Turing, *Codebreakers.*

9. Bollard, "If They Say Bomb."

10. Pinker, *Language Instinct*, 204.

11. Jobin, Ienca, and Vayena, "Global Landscape of AI Ethics Guidelines."

12. O'Hara and Shadbolt, *Spy in the Coffee Machine.*

13. Larson, "Stuffed Toys Leak Millions of Voice Recordings."

14. See Sunstein, "Algorithms, Correcting Biases."

15. Manguel, "Notes on Nothing and Everything."
16. Hellerman, "Love the Hitchcock/Truffaut Interviews?"
17. Thornhill, "Fictional Intelligence."
18. Dunbar, *Evolution*, 6.
19. Shea, "King Lear with Sheep."

CHAPTER 2. WHAT IS AN ARTIFICIAL INTELLIGENCE?

1. Robinson, *Essays in the Theory of Economic Growth*, 33.
2. In Wang Yin, *Summer Day in the Company of Ghosts*, 167.
3. Vakoch, *Archaeology, Anthropology, and Interstellar Communication*, xiv.
4. Josiah Ober lecture.
5. Bryson, "Robots Should Be Slaves."
6. And there is considerable research-based evidence that expressing gratitude to others is good for your health. See, for instance, Martinez-Conde, "Cheers!"
7. The works on this topic by the late philosopher Rom Harré much repay the reader. See especially Harré, *Social Being*, and Harré, Marsh, and Rosser, *Rules of Disorder*.
8. See Singer's essay "Can Ethics Be Taught?" in Singer, *Ethics in the Real World*, 34–38.
9. Bryson, "Robots Should Be Slaves."
10. Darling, *New Breed*, 228–229.
11. Shadbolt and Hampson, *Digital Ape;* Morris, *Naked Ape.*
12. Shipman, *Invaders.*
13. Cuff, "Peter Singer."
14. Sacks, *Mind's Eye*, 202–213. The reader is encouraged to read the whole of this wonderful book and, indeed, Sacks's extensive, fascinating oeuvre.
15. Vakoch, *Archaeology, Anthropology, and Interstellar Communication.*
16. David, "Film Director Gustav Deutsch Brings the World of Edward Hopper to Life."
17. A representative trailer can be found on YouTube at https://www.youtube.com/watch?v=rcQ4JKxxukY.
18. Moretti, *Distant Reading*, 72–75.
19. Clemen, *Development of Shakespeare's Imagery.*
20. Treisman, "Underground Worlds."
21. Hern, "AI Bot ChatGPT Stuns Academics."
22. Bisk et al., "Experience Grounds Language."
23. Floridi, "AI as Agency without Intelligence," 4–5.

CHAPTER 3. MORE THAN *AS IF?*

1. Hawking, "Is the End in Sight?"

2. Lord Denning was a British jurist, of great talent and fame, in the late twentieth century. He held a post in the UK legal system with the comical, almost Gilbert and Sullivan, title of Master of the Rolls, whose duty was to operate a very senior appeal court.

3. Lord Denning, Master of the Rolls, judgment in *Thornton v Shoe Lane Parking Ltd* [1970], EWCA Civ 2.

4. J. B. S. Haldane famously took note of the fact that there are only about five and a half thousand species of mammals, but about a quarter of a million species of beetles. And remarked that if there is a God, he must be inordinately fond of beetles (Flam, "New Evidence"). Does this make it fifty times more likely that any alien that travels to Earth will be beetle-oid rather than human-oid, won't bother saying "take me to your leader" to any scary monster *Homo sapiens* they come across, and will base their moral theories on multiple body segments?

5. Floridi, *Information*, 16.

6. Geertz, "Thick Description."

7. Barad, *Meeting the Universe Halfway.*

8. More accurately perhaps, these streams of information are mediated in the body, since for these purposes the skin, for instance, and its connective relation to the brain, are components of the multiple processor.

9. Yeats, "Among School Children."

10. Midgley, *Beast and Man;* Foot, *Natural Goodness;* O'Neill, *Philosopher Looks at Digital Communication.*

CHAPTER 4. MORALS AND ARTIFICIAL INTELLIGENCE

1. Tim Berners-Lee realized this a long time before most other people cottoned on to the problem. See his June 2001 interview in Wright, "The Man Who Invented the Web."

2. Patently and significantly, a non-moral "is" can lead to a non-moral "ought." That car is going too fast. The driver ought to slow down if he wants to stay alive.

3. Cohen, *Arc of the Moral Universe.* For a similar point, see Hampson, "Reason Why," 71–72.

4. Asimov, *I, Robot.*

5. See Nadella, "Partnership of the Future."

6. Perhaps, even, they have the virtue of patience?

7. "Told" with quotation marks might perhaps be more accurate, but including them every time we metaphorically used a thinking word to describe machines that don't think would be tedious. We will only sometimes remind readers about this.

8. Modern deep-learning AI uses a variety of reward architectures, but essentially at scale the performance – for example, completing an accurate classification – is the most salient.

9. Astronomers estimate our own galaxy to comprise 10^{11} stars (a hundred thousand million), whereas commercial deep-neural-network AI applications can range from a few hundred thousand parameters to billions.

10. This is in loose analogy with the division in literary criticism between organic and inorganic imagery, a concept used throughout Clemen, *Development of Shakespeare's Imagery*.

11. Palma, "Singapore's Data Debacle."

12. Klein's short article "Reducing Bias in AI-Based Financial Services" repays reading in full.

13. Packard, *Hidden Persuaders;* Veblen, *Theory of the Working Class.*

CHAPTER 5. ETHICS FOR THE DIGITAL AGE

1. Rhinehart, *Dice Man;* "Existentialism."

2. Dawkins, *God Delusion.*

3. Google created Alphabet to be the overarching corporate entity for both its search and its other burgeoning activities. Oddly, the child gave birth to the parent.

4. For more on Pareto optimality, see the definition provided by Britannica at https://www.britannica.com/money/topic/Pareto-optimality.

5. Sheehan, "How Google Took on China."

6. Does Wikipedia concede that it has publisher status? Should it?

7. For a disturbing book-length elaboration of this point on idealistic scientism, see Stuart Ritchie, *Science Fictions.*

8. For an interesting interview on Harré, see Hall, "Observance and the Breach."

9. But all that is really to say something like: There was a thrilling cup final between Manchester United and Chelsea. Manchester won by three goals to two. Describe the match? Chelsea's goalkeeper fell over. Anything else? No. Hang on, these are the two best teams in the game, that can't be the whole story of their epic encounter. Well, it is.

10. Judge and Hampson, "Political Advertising," 68–69.

11. For more on Foot, see her entry in the Stanford Encyclopedia of Philosophy, at https://plato.stanford.edu/entries/philippa-foot/.

12. Shadbolt and Hampson, *Digital Ape,* 20.

13. "Mixed philosopher" is not a flattering soubriquet, even for the traditional Western policy actor muddling through in a mixed economy.

CHAPTER 6. VIRTUES AND MACHINES

1. Singer, *Animal Liberation*.

2. Stephen Fleming of University College London holds the perfectly reasonable view that exactly what separates us from artificial intelligences is the human ability to doubt. He may or may not be right. But machines can and do act *as if* they doubt. In complex ways in banks, and in software designed to look for poor use of statistics in scientific papers, for instance. (See Ritchie, *Science Fictions*). In simple ways, too: all the major brands of word-processing software ask, "Are you sure?" before allowing the user to shut down an unsaved file. See Fleming's "What Separates Humans from AI?" and *Know Thyself*.

CHAPTER 7. PRIVACY NOW

1. Guarino, "Deep Dive."

2. See Wilkins, "AI Deep Fakes Could Help Protect Privacy"; Çiftçi, Yuksek, and Demir, "My Face My Choice."

3. Véliz, *Privacy Is Power*, 1.

4. Ibid., 73.

5. Wacks, *Privacy*, xiv.

6. Packard, *Hidden Persuaders*.

7. Lanchester, "Document Number Nine."

8. Williams, "China's Virtual Stasi"; Williams, *Fire of the Dragon*. As noted earlier, the 2023 camera count is 700 million and rising.

9. Williams, "China's Virtual Stasi."

10. Véliz, *Privacy Is Power*.

11. Solid website; Van Kleek et al., "X-Ray Refine."

12. This is Facebook's term for people who use it at least once a month. Not the number of new people using each month.

13. Van Kleek et al., "Better the Devil You Know."

CHAPTER 8. RESPECTFUL ARTIFICIAL INTELLIGENCE

1. See, for instance, Joubert, *Making People Disappear*: "On June 21, 1940, Hitler accepted the surrender of the French government at a ceremony in Compiègne, France. He melodramatically insisted on receiving France's surrender in the same railroad car in which Germany had signed the 1918 armistice that had ended World War One. After Hitler accepted France's surrender, he stepped backwards slightly, as if in shock. But this isn't what audiences in the Allied countries saw who watched the movie-reel of the ceremony. Instead they saw Hitler dance a bizarre little jig after signing the documents, as if he were childishly celebrating his victory by jumping up and down. The scene was played over and over in movie theaters. Following the war, it was revealed that John Grierson, director of the Canadian information and propaganda departments, had manufactured the clip after noticing that Hitler raised his leg rather high up while stepping backwards. He realized that this moment could be looped repeatedly to create the appearance that Hitler was jumping with joy" (176).

2. From Awad et al., "Moral Machine Experiment," 59.

3. See Participedia, "You Choose."

4. Dinosaurs lived so long that our favorites, *Diplodocus* and *Tyrannosaurus rex*, lived further apart in time from each other than *T. Rex* did from us. *Diplodocus* lived around 150 million years ago, while *T. rex* was roaming around 70 million years ago. Dinosaurs as a whole lasted around 170 million years. On the simplest criterion, survival, we are so far only about 1/450 as successful as they were.

5. Shute, *Slide Rule*. The later *Hindenburg* fire in New Jersey put an end to the airship as a serious mode of transport altogether.

CHAPTER 9. WHAT NEXT?

1. "How Will Metaverse Change Your World?," Facebook corporate website. https://www.facebook.com/business/news/let-me-explain-episode-metaverse.

2. Quoted in Snow, "What Would a World without Internet Look Like?"

3. Eliot, *East Coker*.

CHAPTER 10. VIRTUOUS ARTIFICIAL INTELLIGENCE

1. Hare, *We Travelled*, 41.

2. William Shakespeare, *Hamlet*, act 3, scene 2, lines 2253-2258: "*Hamlet:* Do you see yonder cloud that's almost in shape of a camel? *Polonius:* By the mass, and 'tis like a camel, indeed. *Hamlet:* Methinks it is like a weasel. *Polonius:* It is backed like a weasel. *Hamlet:* Or like a whale? *Polonius:* Very like a whale."

3. Ridout, *Theatre and Ethics*, 66-67.

4. The AI was a standard protocol, the efficiency of which we all contribute to when we use Google's CAPTCHA device. CAPTCHA is a jokey acronym for Completely Automated Public Turing test to tell Computers and Humans Apart. We are challenged to prove we are human by clicking on those of the above dozen pictures that, say, show a racoon. Google lets any company implement this for free to verify that their website visitors and customers are human. The short snippets of human labor provided to Google for free by tens of millions of humans refine the image software for them—to recognize racoons or whatever else.

5. Griffin, "Facebook's Artificial Intelligence Robots."

6. Krugman, "Sure, the Internet Changed Everything."

7. Levitz, "Why Effective Altruists Fear the AI Apocalypse."

8. Tasioulas, "Artificial Intelligence, Ethics, and the Right to a Human Decision." For more on Tasioulas's approach, see Tasioulas, "Artificial Intelligence, Humanistic Ethics."

9. Kahneman, Sibony, and Sunstein, *Noise*.

10. Emerson, "Essay on Self-Reliance."

11. Quoted in Susskind and Susskind, "Future of the Professions."

BIBLIOGRAPHY

Agar, Jon. *Turing and the Universal Machine: The Making of the Modern Computer.* London: Icon Books, 2001.

Ashley, Mike. *Menace of the Machine.* London: British Library, 2019.

Asimov, Isaac. *I, Robot.* New York: Doubleday, 1950.

Associated Press. "Backup Driver in Fatal Uber Autonomous Driver Car Crash Pleads Guilty to Endangerment." CBS News Bay Area, July 28, 2023.

Awad, Edward, et al. "The Moral Machine Experiment: 40 Million Decisions and the Path to Universal Machine Ethics." *Nature* 563, no. 7729 (October 2018): 59–64.

Barad, Karen. *Meeting the Universe Halfway: Quantum Physics and the Entanglement of Matter and Meaning.* Durham, NC: Duke University Press, 2007.

Berners-Lee, Tim. "Three Challenges for the Web, According to Its Inventor." World Wide Web Foundation website, March 12, 2017.

Bisk, Yonatan, et al. "Experience Grounds Language." *arXiv*, November 2, 2020. https://arxiv.org/abs/2004.10151.

Blackburn, Simon. *Ethics.* Oxford, UK: Oxford University Press, 2001.

Bollard, Allan. " 'If They Say Bomb at 1 O'clock . . .' John von Neumann in the USA, 1944–45." In Bollard, *Economists at War: How a Handful of Economists Helped Win and Lose the World Wars.* Oxford, UK: Oxford University Press, 2020.

Bommasani, Rishi, Drew A. Hudson, Ehsan Adeli, et al. "On the Opportunities and Risks of Foundation Models." *arXiv*, August 16, 2021. https://arxiv.org/abs/2108.07258.

Boone, Brian. *Ethics 101.* New York: Simon & Schuster, 2017.

Boyd, Craig A., and Kevin Timpe. *The Virtues: A Very Short Introduction.* Oxford, UK: Oxford University Press, 2021.

Brin, Sergey, and Larry Page. *The Anatomy of a Large-Scale Hypertextual Web Search Engine.* Stanford, CA: Stanford University Press, 1998.

Brooks, Rodney A. *Cambrian Intelligence: The Early History of the New AI.* Cambridge, MA: MIT Press, 1999.

——. "Elephants Don't Play Chess." *Robotics and Autonomous Systems* 6, nos. 1–2 (June 1990).

——. "Intelligence without Representation." *Artificial Intelligence* 47, nos. 1–3 (1991): 139–159.

Brown, Tom, Benjamin Mann, Nick Ryder, et al. "Language Models Are Few-Shot Learners." *arXiv*, May 28, 2020. https://arxiv.org/abs/2005.14165.

Bryson, Joanna. "Robots Should Be Slaves." Pp. 63–74 in Yorick Wilks, ed., *Close Engagements with Artificial Companions: Key Social, Psychological, Ethical, and Design Issues.* Amsterdam: John Benjamins, 2010.

Bush, Vannevar. "As We May Think." *The Atlantic* (July 1945). https://www.the atlantic.com/magazine/archive/1945/07/as-we-maythink/303881/.

Butts, Dylan, and Tatyana Chistikova. "Chess-Playing Robot Breaks Young Boy's Finger during Match in Moscow." NBC News online, July 25, 2022. https://www.cnbc.com/2022/07/25/chess-robot-breaks-young-boys-finger-during-match-in-moscow.html.

Camus, Albert. *La Peste.* Paris: Gallimard, 1947.

Čapek, Karel. *R. U. R. (Rossum's Universal Robots).* 1920; New York: Doubleday, Page, and Co., 1923.

Caplan, Jane. *Nazi Germany.* Oxford, UK: Oxford University Press, 2019.

Çiftçi, Umur A., Gokturk Yuksek, and Ilke Demir. "My Face My Choice: Privacy Enhancing Deepfakes for Social Media Anonymization." Winter Conference on Applications of Computer Vision, 2023. https://openaccess.thecvf.com/content/WACV2023/html/Ciftci_My_Face_My_Choice_Privacy_Enhancing_Deepfakes_for_Social_Media_WACV_2023_paper.html

Clemen, Wolfgang. *The Development of Shakespeare's Imagery.* 2nd ed. London: Routledge, 1977.

Coeckelbergh, Mark. *Robot Ethics.* Cambridge, MA: MIT Press, 2022.

Cohen, Joshua. *The Arc of the Moral Universe and Other Essays.* Cambridge, MA: Harvard University Press, 2011.

Crevier, Daniel. *AI: The Tumultuous History of the Search for Artificial Intelligence.* New York: Basic Books, 1993.

Cuff, Madeleine. "Peter Singer on Animal Rights, Octopus Farms, and Why AI Is Speciest." *New Scientist,* May 21, 2023. https://www.newscientist.com/article/mg25834413-000-peter-singer-on-animal-rights-octopus-farms-and-why-ai-is-speciesist/.

Darling, Kate. *The New Breed*. New York: Henry Holt, 2021.

David, Eric. "Film Director Gustav Deutsch Brings the World of Edward Hopper to Life." *Yatzer*, May 15, 2016. https://www.yatzer.com/shirley-visions-of-reality-edward-hopper.

Dawkins, Richard. *The God Delusion*. London: Bantam, 2006.

de Lazari-Radek, Katarzyna, and Peter Singer. *Utilitarianism: A Very Short Introduction*. Oxford, UK: Oxford University Press, 2020.

Dennett, Daniel C. *The Intentional Stance*. 1987; Cambridge, MA: MIT Press, 1996.

Devlin, Jacob, Ming-Wei Chang, Kenton Lee, and Kristina Toutanova. "BERT: Pre-Training of Deep Bidirectional Transformers for Language Understanding." *arXiv*, October 11, 2018. https:// arxiv.org/abs/1810.04805.

Dunbar, Robin. *Evolution: What Everyone Needs To Know*. New York: Oxford University Press, 2020.

Dunn, Michael, and Tony Hope. *Medical Ethics: A Very Short Introduction*. Oxford, UK: Oxford University Press, 2004.

Edgerton, David. *The Shock of the Old*. 2nd ed. London: Profile Books, 2019.

Eliot, T. S. *East Coker* in *Four Quartets*. New York: Harcourt Brace, 1943.

Emerson, Ralph Waldo. "The Essay on Self-Reliance." East Aurora, NY: Roycrofters, 1908. https://www.google.com/books/edition/The_Essay_on_ Self_reliance/kL9qJnyaUZoC?hl=en&gbpv=1&printsec=frontcover.

Esteva, Andre, Brett Kuprel, Roberto A. Novoa, et al. "Dermatologist-Level Classification of Skin Cancer with Deep Neural Networks." *Nature* 542, no. 7639 (2017): 115–118. doi: 10.1038/nature21056.

"Existentialism." *Stanford Encyclopedia of Philosophy*, January 6, 2023. https://plato. stanford.edu/entries/existentialism/.

Fjelland, Ragnar. "Why General Artificial Intelligence Will Not Be Realized." *Humanities and Social Sciences Communications* 7, no. 1 (2020): 1–9.

Flam, Faye. "New Evidence That God Had an Inordinate Fondness for Beetles." *Philadelphia Inquirer*, September 30, 2011. https://www.inquirer.com/philly/ blogs/evolution/New-Evidence-that-God-had-an-Inordinate-Fondness-for-Beetles.html#loaded.

Fleming, Stephen. *Know Thyself: The New Science of Self-Awareness*. London: John Murray, 2021.

———. "What Separates Humans from AI? It's Doubt." *Financial Times* (London), April 17, 2021.

Floridi, Luciano. "AI as Agency without Intelligence: On ChatGPT, Large Language Models, and Other Generative Models." *Philosophy and Technology*, February 16, 2023.

———. *Information: A Very Short Introduction*. Oxford, UK: Oxford University Press, 2010.

Foot, Philippa. *Natural Goodness*. Oxford, UK: Oxford University Press, 2001.

———. "The Problem of Abortion and the Doctrine of the Double Effect." In Foot, *Virtues and Vices and Other Essays in Moral Philosophy*. Oxford, UK: Basil Blackwell, 1977. https://philpapers.org/archive/FOOTPO-2.pdf.

Francis, Ellen. "A Robot Is Displaying Art at the Pyramids. Egypt Detained It over Spying Fears, Its Maker Says." *Washington Post*, October 1, 2021. https://www.washingtonpost.com/world/2021/10/21/egypt-robot-artist-exhibition-spying/.

Geertz, Clifford. "Thick Description: Toward an Interpretive Theory of Culture." In Geertz, *The Interpretation of Cultures*. New York: Basic Books, 1973. https://philpapers.org/archive/GEETTD.pdf.

Godfrey-Smith, Peter. *Metazoa: Animal Minds and the Birth of Consciousness*. London: William Collins, 2020.

———. *Other Minds: The Octopus and the Evolution of Intelligent Life*. London: William Collins, 2016.

Goffman, Erving. *Asylums: Essays on the Social Situation of Mental Patients and Other Inmates*. Chicago: Aldine, 1961.

Griffin, Andrew. "Facebook's Artificial Intelligence Robots Shut Down after They Start Talking to Each Other in Their Own Language." *The Independent*, July 31, 2017.

Guarino, Charlie. "A Deep Dive into Deep Fakes with Dr. Ilke Demir." TechChannel, March 2, 2023. https://techchannel.com/SMB/03/2023/deep-fakes-ilke-demir.

Güçlü, Umut, and Marcel A. J. van Gurven. "Deep Neural Networks Reveal a Gradient in the Complexity of Neural Representations across the Ventral Stream." *Journal of Neuroscience* (July 8, 2015). http://www.jneurosci.org/content/35/27/10005.

Gupta, Vinay. *The Future of Stuff*. London: Unbound, 2020.

Hall, David. "The Observance and the Breach: Rom Harré on Life and Its Rules." The Pantograph Punch, August 25, 2015. https://pantograph-punch.com/posts/rom-harre-philosophy-interview.

Hampson, Roger. "The Reason Why." In Martin Knapp et al., eds., *Long-Term Care: Matching Needs and Resources*. London: Ashgate, 2004; Oxford, UK: Routledge, 2018.

Hare, David. *We Travelled: Essays and Poems*. London: Faber & Faber, 2021.

Harré, H. Rom. *Social Being: A Theory for Social Psychology*. Oxford, UK: Blackwell, 1979.

BIBLIOGRAPHY

Harré, H. Rom, Peter Marsh, and Elizabeth Rosser. *The Rules of Disorder*. London: Routledge and Kegan Paul, 1977.

Hassan, Robert. *Analog*. Cambridge, MA: MIT Press, 2022.

Hawking, Stephen. "Is the End in Sight for Theoretical Physics?," *Physics Bulletin* 32, no. 1 (1981). doi: 10.1088/0031-9112/32/1/024.

Hellerman, Jason. "Love the Hitchcock/Truffaut Interviews? Listen to All 25 Tapes." NoFilmSchool.com, October 19, 2020. https://nofilmschool.com/listen-hitchcock-truffaut-tapes.

Hern, Alex. "AI Bot ChatGPT Stuns Academics with Essay-Writing Skills and Usability." *The Guardian*, December 4, 2022. https://www.theguardian.com/technology/2022/dec/04/ai-bot-chatgpt-stuns-academics-with-essay-writing-skills-and-usability.

Isaacson, Walter. *The Innovators: How a Group of Hackers, Geniuses, and Geeks Created the Digital Revolution*. New York: Simon & Schuster, 2014.

Jobin, Anna, Marcello Ienca, and Effy Vayena. "The Global Landscape of AI Ethics Guidelines." *Nature Machine Intelligence* 1 (2019): 389–399. doi: 10.1038/s42256-019-0088-2.

Jordan, Michael I. "Artificial Intelligence—The Revolution Hasn't Happened Yet." *Harvard Data Science Review* 1, no. 1 (2019). doi: 10.1162/99608f92.f06c6e61.

Joubert, Alain. *Making People Disappear: An Amazing Chronicle of Photographic Deception*. McClean, VA: International Defense Publishers, 1989.

Judge, K. F., and Roger Hampson. "Political Advertising and the Growth of Social Welfare Expenditures." *International Journal of Social Economics* 7, no. 2 (1980).

Kahneman, Daniel, Olivier Sibony, and Cass Sunstein. *Noise*. London: William Collins, 2021.

Kasparov, Garry. "The Day That I Sensed a New Kind of Intelligence." *Time*, March 25, 1996.

King's Fund. *An Ordinary Life: Comprehensive Locally-Based Residential Services for Mentally Handicapped People*. 2nd ed. London: King's Fund, 1982.

Klein, Aaron. "Reducing Bias in AI-Based Financial Services." Brookings Institution, Washington, DC, July 10, 2020. https://www.brookings.edu/research/reducing-bias-in-ai-based-financial-services/.

Knight, Sam. *The Premonitions Bureau*. London: Faber & Faber, 2022.

Kolbert, Elizabeth. "Our Automated Future: How Long Will It Be before You Lose Your Job to a Robot?" *New Yorker*, December 19, 2016.

Kolhatkar, Sheelah. "The Fight to Hold Pornhub Accountable." *New Yorker*, June 13, 2022.

Krugman, Paul. "Sure, the Internet Changed Everything (Except, Maybe, the Economy)." *New York Times* newsletter, April 4, 2023.

Lanchester, John. "Document Number Nine." *London Review of Books* 41, no. 19 (October 10, 2019). https://www.lrb.co.uk/the-paper/v41/n19/john-lanchester/document-number-nine.

———. "You Are the Product." *London Review of Books* 39, no. 16 (August 17, 2017). https://www.lrb.co.uk/the-paper/v39/n16/john-lanchester/you-are-the-product.

Landemore, Hélène. *Open Democracy: Reinventing Popular Rule for the Twenty-First Century.* Princeton, NJ: Princeton University Press, 2020.

Larson, Selena. "Stuffed Toys Leak Millions of Voice Recordings from Kids and Parents." CNN Business, February 27, 2017. https://money.cnn.com/2017/02/27/technology/cloudpets-data-leak-voices-photos/index.html.

Leavitt, David. *The Man Who Knew Too Much: Alan Turing and the Invention of Computers.* London: Weidenfeld and Nicolson, 2007.

LeCun, Yan, Yoshua Bengio, and Geoffrey Hinton. "Deep Learning." *Nature* 521, no. 7553 (2015): 436–444.

Levitz, Eric. "Why Effective Altruists Fear the AI Apocalypse: A Conversation with the Philosopher William MacAskill." *Intelligencer,* August 30, 2022. https://nymag.com/intelligencer/2022/08/why-effective-altruists-fear-the-ai-apocalypse.html.

Lighthill, James. "Artificial Intelligence: A General Survey," *Artificial Intelligence: A Paper Symposium.* London: Science Research Council, 1973. http://www.chilton-computing.org.uk/inf/literature/reports/lighthill_report/p001.htm.

Lipscomb, Benjamin J. B. *The Women Are Up to Something.* Oxford, UK: Oxford University Press, 2021.

Man, Kingson, and Antonio Damasio. "Homeostasis and Soft Robotics in the Design of Feeling Machines." *Nature Machine Intelligence* 1 (2019): 446–452. doi: 10.1038/s42256-019-0103-7.

Manguel, Alberto. "Notes on Nothing and Everything," *Literary Review* 515 (February 2023).

Martinez-Conde, Susana. "Cheers! Saying Thanks Is Good for You," *New Scientist,* December 22, 2018. https://www.newscientist.com/article/mg24032090-500-cheers-saying-thanks-is-good-for-you-and-those-around-you.

McCarthy, John, Marvin L. Minsky, Nathaniel Rochester, and Claude E. Shannon. *A Proposal for the Dartmouth Summer Research Project on Artificial Intelligence.* Hanover, NH, August 1955. http://raysolomonoff.com/dartmouth/boxa/dart564props.pdf.

———

McClelland, James L., and David E. Rumelhart. *Parallel Distributed Processing*. Cambridge, MA: MIT Press, 1986.

Midgley, Mary. *Beast and Man: Roots of Human Nature*. Rev. ed. London: Routledge, 1995.

——. *The Owl of Minerva*. London: Routledge, 2005.

Miriyev, Aslan, and Mirko Kovač. "Skills for Physical Artificial Intelligence." *Nature Machine Intelligence* 2 (2020): 658–660. doi: 10.1038/s42256-020-00258-y.

Mnih, Volodymyr, Koray Kavukcuoglu, David Silver, et al. "Human-Level Control through Deep Reinforcement Learning." *Nature* 518, no. 7540 (2015): 529–533.

Moretti, Franco. *Distant Reading*. London: Verso, 2013.

Morris, Desmond. *The Naked Ape: A Zoologist's Study of the Human Animal*. New York: Delta, 1967. https://folk.ntnu.no/krill/bioko-references/Morris%20 1967.pdf.

Murakami, Haruki. "Samsa in Love." In Murakami, *Men without Women*. London: Hervill Secker, 2017.

Murdoch, Iris. *Existentialists and Mystics*. London: Chatto and Windus, 1997.

——. *Sartre*. London: Chatto and Windus, 1987.

——. *The Sovereignty of Good*. London: Routledge and Kegan Paul, 1970.

Nadella, Satya. "The Partnership of the Future." *Slate*, June 28, 2016. https://slate.com/technology/2016/06/microsoft-ceo-satya-nadella-humans-and-a-i-can-work-together-to-solve-societys-challenges.html.

Newell, Allen, and Herbert A. Simon. "Computer Science as Empirical Inquiry: Symbols and Search," *Communications of the ACM* 19, no. 3 (1976): 113–126. https://dl.acm.org/doi/10.1145/360018.360022.

Ober, Josiah. Lecture for the Oxford University Institute for Ethics in AI, June 16, 2022. https://www.youtube.com/watch?v=d1gTDGl7u1o&ab_channel=InstituteforEthicsinAIOxford.

O'Hara, Kieron, and Nigel Shadbolt. *The Spy in the Coffee Machine: The End of Privacy as We Know It*. Oxford, UK: Oneworld, 2008.

O'Neill, Onora. *A Philosopher Looks at Digital Communication*. Cambridge, UK: Cambridge University Press, 2022.

Packard, Vance. *The Hidden Persuaders*. London: Longmans, Green, 1957.

Palma, Stefania. "Singapore's Data Debacle Shakes City-State's 'Smart' Ambitions." *Financial Times* (London), February 23, 2021.

Palmer, Michael. *Moral Problems*. Cambridge, UK: Lutterworth, 1991.

Participedia. "You Choose: London Borough of Redbridge Council's Online Budget Consultation Tool." https://participedia.net/case/4369.

Peltu, Malcolm, and Yorick Wilks. "Close Engagements with Artificial Companions: Key Social, Psychological, Ethical and Design Issues." Oxford Internet Institute website, January 14, 2008. https://www.oii.ox.ac.uk/archive/downloads/publications/FD14.pdf.

Penner, Barbara, Adrian Forty, Olivia Horsfall Turner, and Miranda Critchley. *Extinct: A Compendium of Obsolete Objects.* London: Reaktion Books, 2021.

Pfeifer, Rolf, and Christian Scheier. *Understanding Intelligence.* Cambridge MA: MIT Press, 2001.

Pinker, Stephen. *The Language Instinct: How the Mind Creates Language.* New York: William Morrow, 1994.

Rhinehart, Luke. *The Dice Man.* New York: HarperCollins, 1999.

Ridout, Nicholas. *Theatre and Ethics.* London: Methuen, 2009.

Ritchie, Stuart. *Science Fictions: Exposing Fraud, Bias, Negligence and Hype in Science.* London: Bodley Head, 2020.

Robinson, Joan. *Essays in the Theory of Economic Growth.* London: Macmillan, 1963.

Roush, Wade. *Extraterrestrials.* Cambridge, MA: MIT Press, 2020.

Russell, Stuart. *Human Compatible: AI and the Problem of Control.* London: Allen Lane, 2019.

Sacks, Oliver. *The Mind's Eye.* New York: Knopf, 2010.

Searle, John R. *Speech Acts: An Essay in the Philosophy of Language.* Cambridge, UK: Cambridge University Press, 2012.

Senior, Andrew W., Richard Evans, John Jumper, et al. "Improved Protein Structure Prediction Using Potentials from Deep Learning." *Nature* 577, no. 7792 (2020): 706–710.

Shadbolt, Nigel. " 'From So Simple a Beginning': Species of Artificial Intelligence." *Daedalus: AI & Society* 151, no. 2 (Spring 2022).

Shadbolt, Nigel, and Roger Hampson. *The Digital Ape.* 2018; New York: Oxford University Press, 2019.

Shea, Christopher D. " 'King Lear with Sheep.' Yes, Sheep." *New York Times,* August 11, 2015.

Sheehan, Matt. "How Google Took on China—and Lost." *MIT Technology Review,* December 19, 2018.

Shipman, Pat. *The Invaders: How Humans and Their Dogs Drove Neanderthals to Extinction.* Cambridge, MA: Belknap Press of Harvard University Press, 2017.

Shute, Nevil. *Slide Rule.* London: Heinemann, 1954.

Silver, David, Aja Huang, Chris J. Maddison, et al. "Mastering the Game of Go with Deep Neural Networks and Tree Search." *Nature* 529, no. 7587 (2016): 484–489.

Silver, David, Thomas Hubert, Julian Schrittwieser, et al. "A General Reinforcement Learning Algorithm That Masters Chess, Shogi, and Go through Self-Play." *Science* 362, no. 6419 (2018): 1140–1144.

Silver, David, Julian Schrittwieser, Karen Simonyan, et al. "Mastering the Game of Go without Human Knowledge." *Nature* 550, no. 7676 (2017): 354–359.

Singer, Peter. *Animal Liberation: A New Ethics for Our Treatment of Animals.* 1975; London: Cape, 1976. https://grupojovenfl.files.wordpress.com/2019/10/peter-singer-animal-liberation-1.pdf.

——. *A Darwinian Left.* 1999; New Haven: Yale University Press, 2000.

——. *Ethics in the Real World.* Rev. ed. Princeton, NJ: Princeton University Press, 2023.

——. *The Most Good You Can Do: How Effective Altruism Is Changing Ideas about Living Ethically.* New Haven: Yale University Press, 2015.

Snow, Blake. "What Would a World without Internet Look Like?" *The Atlantic,* April 5, 2016. https://www.theatlantic.com/technology/archive/2016/04/a-world-without-internet/476907/.

Solid corporate website. https://solidproject.org/.

Stefik, Mark. *Introduction to Knowledge Systems.* San Francisco: Morgan Kaufmann, 1995.

Stoppard, Tom. *The Hard Problem.* London: Faber & Faber, 2015.

Strickland, Eliza. "IBM Watson, Heal Thyself: How IBM Overpromised and Underdelivered on AI Health Care." *IEEE Spectrum* 56, no. 4 (2019): 24–31.

Sunstein, Cass. "Algorithms, Correcting Biases." *Social Research: An International Quarterly* 86, no. 2 (Summer 2019).

Susskind, Daniel, and Richard Susskind. "The Future of the Professions." *Proceedings of the American Philosophical Society* 162, no. 2 (June 2018). https://www.amphilsoc.org/sites/default/files/2018-11/attachments/Susskind%20and%20Susskind.pdf.

Swade, Doron. *The History of Computing.* Oxford, UK: Oxford University Press, 2022.

Swift, Jonathan. *A Modest Proposal for Preventing the Children of Poor People from Being a Burthen to Their Parents or Country, and for Making them Beneficial to the Publick.* Dublin, 1729.

Tasioulas, John. "Artificial Intelligence, Ethics, and a Right to a Human Decision." Harold T. Shapiro Lecture on Ethics, Science, and Technology, May 31, 2023. https://mediacentral.princeton.edu/media/Artificial+Intelligence%2C+Ethics%2C+and+a+Right+to+a+Human+Decision+with+John I Tasioulas/1_smfi1n2m.

——. "Artificial Intelligence, Humanistic Ethics." *Daedalus* special edition *AI & Society,* ed. James M. Manyika (Spring 2022).

Taylor, C. C. W. *Socrates*. Oxford, UK: Oxford University Press, 1998.

Thornhill, John. " 'Fictional Intelligence' Can Blind Us to Real World Dangers." *Financial Times* (London), March 10, 2023.

Treisman, Deborah. "The Underground Worlds of Haruki Murakami." Interview. *New Yorker*, February 10, 2019. https://www.newyorker.com/culture/the-new-yorker-interview/the-underground-worlds-of-haruki-murakami.

Turing, Alan M. *The Codebreakers of Bletchley Park: The Secret Intelligence Station That Helped Defeat the Nazis*. London: Arcturus, 2020.

——. "Computing Machinery and Intelligence." *Mind* 59, no. 236 (1950): 433–460. doi: 10.1093/mind/LIX.236.433.

——. "On Computable Numbers, with an Application to the *Entscheidungsproblem*." *Proceedings of the London Mathematical Society* s2–42, no. 1 (1937): 230–265. doi: 10.1112/plms/s2-42.1.230.

Vakoch, Douglas A. *Archaeology, Anthropology, and Interstellar Communication*. Washington, DC: NASA, 2014.

Vallor, Shannon. *Technology and the Virtues*. New York: Oxford University Press, 2018.

Van Kleek, M., R. Binns, J. Zhao, A. Slack, S. Lee, D. Ottewell, and N. Shadbolt. "X-Ray Refine: Supporting the Exploration and Refinement of Information Exposure Resulting from Smartphone Apps." *Proceedings of the 2018 CHI Conference on Human Factors in Computing Systems,* April 2018. https://hip.cat/papers/chi2018-xray-refine-final-CR.pdf.

Van Kleek, M., I. Liccardi, R. Binns, J. Zhao, D. Weitzner, and N. Shadbolt. "Better the Devil You Know: Exposing the Data Sharing Practices of Smartphone Apps." *Proceedings of the 2017 CHI Conference on Human Factors in Computing Systems*, 5208–5220. doi: 10.1145/3025453.3025556.

Veblen, Thorstein. *The Theory of the Working Class*. New York: Macmillan, 1899. https://en.wikipedia.org/wiki/The_Theory_of_the_Leisure_Class.

Véliz, Carissa. *Privacy Is Power.* London: Bantam, 2020.

Vinyals, Oriol, Igor Babuschkin, Wojciech Czarnecki, et al. "Grandmaster Level in StarCraft II Using Multi-Agent Reinforcement Learning." *Nature* 575, no. 7782 (2019): 350–354.

Wacks, Raymond. *Privacy.* Oxford, UK: Oxford University Press, 2015.

Wallach, Wendell, and Colin Allen. *Moral Machines: Teaching Robots Right from Wrong.* New York: Oxford University Press, 2010.

West, Darrell M. "What Happens if Robots Take the Jobs? The Impact of Emerging Technologies on Employment and Public Policy." Center for Technology Innovation, Brookings Institution, October 2015. https://www.brookings.edu/wp-content/uploads/2016/06/robotwork.pdf.

Wiener, Norbert. *Cybernetics; or, Control and Communication in the Animal and the Machine.* Boston: Technology Press, 1948.

———. *The Human Use of Human Beings: Cybernetics and Society.* 1950; Boston: Houghton Mifflin, 1954.

Wilkins, Alex. "AI Deep Fakes Could Help Protect Privacy," *New Scientist,* November 18, 2022. https://www.newscientist.com/article/2347596-ai-generated-deepfake-faces-could-help-protect-privacy-on-social-media.

Wilkinson, Dominic, Jonathan Herring, and Julian Savulescu. *Medical Ethics and Law.* 3rd ed. London: Elsevier, 2020.

Williams, Ian. "China's Virtual Stasi Sees All from Cyberspace." *Sunday Times* (London), December 4, 2022. https://www.thetimes.co.uk/article/chinas-digital-stasi-sees-all-from-cyberspace-999jfxh8h.

———. *The Fire of the Dragon: China's New Cold War.* Edinburgh: Birlinn, 2022.

Wright, Robert. "The Man Who Invented the Web." *Time,* June 24, 2001. http://content.time.com/time/magazine/article/0,9171,137689,00.html.

Yeats, William Butler. "Among School Children." In Yeats, *The Tower.* New York: Macmillan, 1928.

Yin, Wang. *A Summer Day in the Company of Ghosts.* Trans. Andrea Lingenfelter. New York: New York Review Books, 2022.

———

ACKNOWLEDGMENTS

As If Human builds on joint work with many colleagues. We are grateful to all of them. Special thanks are due to Jean Thomson Black at Yale University Press and to our agent, Toby Mundy. Only we are to blame for errors of fact or judgment in the published version.

Most of all, thank you once again to our families:

Bev Saunders
Esther Wallington
Anna and Alexander Shadbolt
Tom, Martha, Kate, and Grace Hampson

INDEX

Abass, Ziad, 209

accountability, 1, 114, 194, 226, 227; algorithmic, 107; moral, 132

advertising, 125, 163, 180; profiting from, 171; targeted, 116-117, 168, 169, 173, 205

agency: and consciousness, 89; defined, 78; of machines, 77-78; moral, 19, 78

agential realism, 78

agnosticism, practical, 16, 17

Ai-Da, 1, 208, 209, 214

aircraft design, 192-193

Al Abd, Salaheldin, 209

Alexa, 30, 50, 51, 54, 75-76, 77, 79, 87, 114, 150

algorithms, 10, 30, 31, 32, 107, 113-114, 117, 174, 193; in justice systems, 221-224; and privacy, 156-157

aliens, 46-48, 66, 95

Alphabet, 125, 126, 170, 173, 233n3

AlphaCraft, 26

AlphaFold, 26

AlphaGo, 26

altruism, 216

Amazon, 5, 105, 157, 168, 173, 187

animals: ethical treatment of, 95; intelligent, 66; rights and sensitivity of, 146

animism, 76-78

anthropomorphism, 50, 75

AOL, 200

App Store, 190

Apple, 190, 191, 200

Archaeology, Anthropology, and Interstellar Communication (NASA), 46-47

Aristotle, 48-50, 93-94, 123, 142, 148

artificial general intelligence (AGI), 96, 101, 224

artificial intelligence: bias in, 30, 107, 114, 147, 185, 187, 193-194; capabilities of, 44; and computer science, 20; conscious, 86-87; dangers of, 3-6, 191-192, 220; decision-making by, 69-74, 147; deep-learning, 109, 232n8 (chapter 4); defined, 44-45; designers of, 73; doing administrative work, 108-109; emotional, 101; emulating the human mind, 105; ethics of, 10, 32, 49, 92-93, 99, 112, 119, 122, 143, 212-213, 227; funding for research, 19-20; general (AGI), 96, 101, 224; generative, 22; Google as, 159, 161; guidelines for, 227; human judgment of, 9-10; impact of, 216; in justice systems, 221-224, 227; moral judgment of, 16-17, 117; Nadella's goals and principles for, 107; narrow, 224;

251

INDEX

INDEX

INDEX

INDEX

INDEX

morality, 37–38, 55, 66, 72, 93, 119, 122,
    124, 127, 135, 138, 139, 145, 221;
    machine, 17, 113; "morality pills," 203
morals: contagion theory of, 52, 79, 91,
    103; in literature, 37
Moretti, Franco, 61
Morris, Desmond, 39, 55
M2 Max chip, 25
Murakami, Haruki, 59, 60, 62
Musk, Elon, 99, 179
My Face My Choice, 155
Mystery of Edwin Drood, The (Dickens), 62
myths, 37

Nadella, Satya, 106–107
naïve realists, 82
NASA, 46–47, 57, 66
NATO, 4
natural language, 96–97, 189, 212
natural language analysis, 24
neo-Darwinism, 39
neo-phobia, 215
Neumann, John von, 20
neural networks, 193, 232n9 (chapter 4);
    adversarial, 28; artificial, 24; defined,
    24
neuroscience, 82, 89, 202–203
New Breed, The (Darling), 54
normalization, 14–16, 162
The Notorious B.I.G., 34

Ober, Josiah, 48–50
Occam's razor, 69
Odyssey (Homer), 61
O'Hara, Kieran, 29
O'Neill, Onora, 94
online activities: gambling, 116; harms of,
    103–105; shopping, 164, 167, 168.
    See also social media
opacity, 71, 78, 129–130, 152; inten-
    tional, 152. *See also* transparency

OpenAI foundation, 63
optimism, 143, 183
Oxford Institute for Ethics in AI, ix, 219
Oxford University, 65, 167, 172, 209, 219

Packard, Vance, 117, 163
Page, Larry, 160, 205
PageRank, 170
Palma, Stefania, 111
parables, 37
Pareto, Vilfredo, 128–129
Pareto optimality, 129
Parker, Charlie, 62–63
patriarchs, 139
perceptions, 83–85; manipulation of,
    202–203
persuasion, 205
persuasive design, 116
Phillips, Henry Frank, 199
Phillips screw, 199
philosophy, 31, 97, 120; academic, 122;
    analytic, 49; big questions of,
    119–120; empirical, 103; of ethics,
    119, 123; ethics and, 122; legal,
    219; math and, 135; mixed, 10,
    102, 123, 138–140, 144; moral,
    79, 183; and the nature of mind,
    202; political, 103; of science, 78; of
    wine, 85
physics, 67; atomic, 20
Picasso, Pablo, 209, 210
Pickwick Papers, The (Dickens), 62
Pinker, Steven, 23
Plato, 123, 140, 148, 210
pornography, 5, 117, 168
portraits, 209–210
positivism, logical, 151
post-traumatic stress disorder, 104–105
pragmatism, 137, 140
precautionary machines, 6
predictive machines, 5–6, 26

INDEX

INDEX

INDEX